THE MORAL PARAMETERS *of*

GOOD TALK

a feminist analysis

MARYANN NEELY AYIM

Wilfrid Laurier University Press

This book has been published with the help of a grant from the Humanities and Social Sciences Federation of Canada, using funds provided by the Social Sciences and Humanities Research Council of Canada.

Canadian Cataloguing in Publication Data

Ayim, Maryann
  The moral parameters of good talk : a feminist analysis

Includes bibliographical references and index.
ISBN 0-88920-282-6

1. Sociolinguistics.   2. Language and languages – Sex differences.   3. Feminist theory.   I. Title.

P40.A94 1997   306.4′4   C96-931453-1

Copyright © 1997
WILFRID LAURIER UNIVERSITY PRESS
Waterloo, Ontario, Canada   N2L 3C5

Cover design by Leslie Macredie and George Kirkpatrick
Cover illustration: *Trio*, from the series "Songs of the Sea" (1991),
            by Ruth Thorne-Thomsen

∞

Printed in Canada

With more love than I can express on paper, I dedicate this book to the memory of my late uncle, Cliff Cassidy, whose language was a model of what I've called "good talk" in these pages. I never knew him to hog a conversation or interrupt another speaker. In his language, as in his other behaviour, he contributed his share with joy and welcomed the contributions of others with enthusiasm. It therefore feels especially appropriate that I dedicate this work to him. Throughout my life, he has been a model of decency, fairness, honesty, and compassion; his premature death is one of the saddest events I have ever had to face.

Contents

Acknowledgments

This book has been published with the help of a grant from the Humanities and Social Sciences Federation of Canada, using funds provided by the Social Sciences and Humanities Research Council of Canada. I am grateful not only for this financial support, which made publication possible, but also for the advice of their two anonymous referees, from which the work benefited significantly. I extend my thanks to the referees themselves; I hope they read this book and see the improvements that came about as a direct result of their detailed and insightful feedback.

Special schedule arrangements for teaching and research endorsed by my former deans Harry Fisher and Kym Kymlicka as well as my former divisional chairperson, Bob Gidney, and current divisional chairperson Greg Dickinson made it possible for me to isolate blocks of time for writing, which is for me the optimal setup for both writing and teaching. I am very grateful that they were willing to tailor my schedule to my particular needs. I also wish to thank Bob Gidney for his general enthusiastic support of my research over the years, in his roles both as divisional chairperson and graduate chairperson.

There are four people to whom I owe a different and very special sort of thanks—people who read drafts of various parts of this manuscript, who listened patiently to many telephone and person-to-person conversations about it, and who managed always to convey the impression that they never tired of the topic! For their loving encouragement, constant support, passionate feedback, and dependable honesty, I owe an enormous debt to my friend Barbara Houston, my daughter Martha Ayim, my friend Leslie Thielen-Wilson, and my husband Jim Mullin. Without them, I don't think this book would have made it through to completion.

For my general love of delving into arguments and assessing people's positions on issues, I thank my father, Walter I. Neely. I learned from him at an early age that even authorities are fallible, and that one must make one's own decisions, as best one can, about what is true and what is right. From my mother, Anne M. Cassidy Neely, I learned as a young child the importance of applying feminist analyses to the everyday and to the personal aspects of life. Although not academics themselves, my parents created for me conditions that were conducive to passionate engagement in scholarship.

For their competent and cheerful work revising the text of this manuscript on the computer, I am deeply grateful to Stephanie Macleod and Linda Colvin, members of the Division of Educational Policy Studies, Faculty of Education, The University of Western Ontario.

Finally, I wish to thank two members of Wilfrid Laurier University Press for their invaluable help: first, Sandra Woolfrey, director of the Press, for her support of the idea of this manuscript since my earliest communication to her about it, as well as for her help and encouragement in making improvements in the original version; second, Carroll Klein, for her general enthusiasm about the manuscript as well as her exceptional copy editing.

Chapter One

Introduction

A world in which vital resources are fairly shared, in which people treat one another with consideration, respect, and kindness, is surely a world to which we morally aspire in principle, even if we fall short in practice. By contrast, practices and institutions in which the already privileged garner ever increasing levels of social goods at the expense of those who can least afford to lose what little they have could not be sanctioned by any defensible moral theory. While we recognize the temptations individuals may feel who are in a position to take unfair advantage of others, we also recognize that it would be wrong, even if understandable, for them to give way to such temptation.

Simple as it is, this moral claim, extended to language, is the underlying thesis of this book. Thus I urge that we should treat other people with consideration and respect in our linguistic, as in other, interactions with them. This may entail soliciting their point of view in conversation and listening carefully as opposed to interrupting and overriding them. It may entail making an extra effort to ensure that

---

The notes to this chapter are on p. 23.

those who are shy and reticent feel comfortable enough to contribute to the conversation. When they do speak, it may entail avoiding a stony silence and responding to what they say in a manner that demonstrates interest and support, even where there is disagreement.

None of this is profound. Most of us were taught the merits of general fairness at kindergarten. We learned to take one cookie rather than a handful when the plate was passed around, so that everyone else could have a cookie too, just as we learned to say "please" and "thank you," and to take turns with favourite toys. Most of us have no difficulty in applying this kindergarten lesson, at least in principle, to behaviour generally. The hesitancy occurs when the notion of behaviour is extended to specifically include language. Thus most people would agree that our behaviour should be governed by basic codes of fairness, and that we shouldn't take unfair advantage of others, even if those others would permit and endorse the unfairness, having been brought up, perhaps, to believe themselves less worthy. We don't think bigger kids should push smaller kids off the swings simply because they are physically able to do so. Nor do we think they should grab all the cookies because the plate got to them first. Yet when individuals grab all the talking time and push others out of the conversation, this is seldom seen as problematic in the same sort of way. There has been little, if any, working out of what it would mean to apply general moral standards of fairness to how we talk to one another. That is the central task that I have undertaken in this book. Since gender is connected in important and well-established ways to who grabs the handful of linguistic cookies and who isn't passed the plate, it is not possible to provide any sort of discussion of the moral aspects of talking without, on some level, taking gender into account.

Those who take a perspective different than my own on this issue may wonder: Why should language be judged by moral criteria? This basic question is raised by the title of the book. Why does it make any sense to even think about language as behaviour that occurs within a moral context? Wouldn't it be more sensible and convenient to hold us all accountable to moral standards for our "real" behaviour, while exempting "mere talk" from such accountability? My response to this query has two facets.[1] First, to minimize the impact of talk by referring to it as "mere talk" in a discussion of accountability is a serious error; second, exempting talk from the moral standards expected and exacted of other forms of behaviour is convenient and sensible only for *some* people, not for *all*. In my view, these claims apply to both the content and the dynamics of talk. I shall discuss each of these facets in some detail.

First, the characterization of talk as "mere talk" is problematic and erroneous: I shall develop this claim by initially pointing out the amenability of talk to control, then discussing the context from which the minimization of the importance of talk emerges, and next examining what I call "the evidence to the contrary." I turn now, briefly, to the issue of control. I would argue here for the pragmatic position that it makes no sense at all to morally censure that which is not amenable to control.[2] But how we talk is, within limits, of course, very much subject to our control. It is possible to alter such linguistic styles as persistently interrupting other speakers, controlling the topic of conversation, and monopolizing the discussion. In terms of linguistic content, the impediments in the way of combatting institutional racism, for example, are much more overwhelming than the impediments to combatting the racism in our own discourse. This is not to say that changing our language will be straightforward or easy. Language patterns, like any form of habitual behaviour, will resist change. But there are enough instances of people who have succeeded in carrying out such reforms in their own speech and writing to make it clear that such changes are at least *possible*. Furthermore, language reform on an individual level will be instrumental to achieving language reform on an institutional level, and this will in turn be instrumental to achieving more widely sweeping institutional reforms critical to eliminating the "chilly climate" frequently experienced by women, Native people, Black people, and people living with disabilities.

If, as I believe, it is *possible* to control and reform our language, we are now left with the question as to whether we *ought* to engage in such control and reform. Let me initiate my response to this question by filling in some of the context of the analysis that is used to exempt speech from ethical considerations. The constitutional protection of *many* (I shall discuss this notion more fully under the second facet) forms of expression, including, for example, hate talk (at least in the university context), has a peculiarly American flavour, with freedom of expression in the U.S. receiving special constitutional protection under the first amendment. It is important to note that this legislation, originally instituted to protect people who criticized the government against reprisals, is now being used to protect sexist and racist discourse. This point will be further elaborated below. There are few other nations, and *no* socialist nations, where expression or speech is accorded this kind of special treatment. Even Canada, the country most similar to the U.S. in this regard, does not accord such sweeping exemption from legal censure to speech. This (largely) American notion that expression should be free and untrammelled by fear of any kind of censure has been highly influential in academic circles, however, because of the enormous volume of U.S. academic writing dealing with this issue. Although I am less interested in legal sanctions than moral sanctions, this brief discussion of speech and U.S. constitutional law nevertheless provides a clear indication of the context out of which my discussion emerges. Those who believe that speech, unlike more overt forms of behaviour, should be exempt from legal or moral censure, will disagree with one of the most basic premises of my argument. I ask this reader to be patient and to withhold judgment until the end of the book, by which time I hope the arguments and illustrations therein will have eroded at least the sharp edge of initial disagreement. It is not my purpose to write a critique of constitutional law; that would require a book of its own, and a very different book from this one. However, I do want to address the widely held view that "mere talk" should not be held accountable to moral (or legal) standards in the same way as "real" behaviour should be. If, as I have claimed, the context out of which it is typically argued that "mere" talk should not be evaluated morally in anything like the same way as "real" behaviour, if this context describes people's views concerning the *content* of talk, then it is even more descriptive of people's views concerning the *dynamics* of talk. As I shall demonstrate, particularly in the next five chapters of this book, the literature focusing on the dynamics of talk is almost exclusively a *descriptive, empirical* literature, with essentially no *moral* analysis whatsoever of the dynamics of talk.

This brings me to what I have referred to earlier as "the evidence to the contrary." In two very important respects—namely, the potential of talk to harm or benefit others and the amenability of talk to control—talk is in fact a paradigm case of behaviour that should be held accountable to moral standards. Having already discussed the issue of control, I turn now to the potential of talk to harm or benefit others. As it may be argued that morality does not strictly require us to benefit other people, whereas it does require us not to positively harm them, I shall restrict my account to that of harm. In terms of the dynamics of discourse, I shall use the feature of *amount of talking done* to illustrate my claim about harm. If the time available for discourse and the energy level and attention span of all the participants were infinite, then everyone could talk as much as they wanted, with no negative implications for eroding the time available to others. Conversational time, like other social goods, is finite, however, and it is this limitation that imposes the necessity of rules ensuring a fair apportioning of the time that is available. If in classrooms, male students who make up about half the class, do approximately three-quarters of the talking and take approximately three-quarters of the teacher's time and attention, the harm to female students and the need for rules to offset such harm are clear. In terms of the *content* of talk, the new genre of literature referred to as "critical race theory" provides a careful and detailed account of the ways in which racist hate talk create harm. Matsuda writes:

> The negative effects of hate messages are real and immediate for the victims. Victims of vicious hate propaganda experience physiological symptoms and emotional distress ranging from fear in the gut to rapid pulse rate and difficulty in breathing, nightmares, post-traumatic stress disorder, hypertension, psychosis, and suicide. (1993, 24)

Delgado claims that victims of racist hate talk suffer "higher blood pressure levels and higher morbidity and mortality rates from hypertension, hypertensive disease, and stroke" (1993, 92). Aside from these direct physiological harms, obvious psychological harms result from the lowered self-esteem, financial harms result from having to sell one's home to move away from a neighbourhood in which one is being bombarded with hate messages (Matsuda 1993, 14), and harm to one's career may result from the psychological frame of mind that results from exposure to hate messages (Delgado 1993, 92). There are dozens of other scenarios in which it is all too easy to see clearly the harm that racist hate speech does to its victims. Such talk harms the perpetrators as well, according to Delgado, "by reinforcing rigid thinking, thereby dulling their moral and social senses" (ibid.). This is reminiscent of Peirce's view regarding the very real impact of signs. Peirce writes, "It [the sign] produces this effect, not in this or that metaphysical sense, but in an indisputable sense" (1931-1958, 8.191). This "indisputable sense" is somewhat clarified by the following passage from Peirce: "The meaning of any sign for anybody consists in the way he reacts to the sign" (1931-1958, 8.315). When we encounter signs that affect us, we react to them, sometimes in a direct physical way, sometimes in a more symbolic way by creating new signs. Our beliefs are affected by the signs we encounter, and our habits are in turn affected by our beliefs. The indisputable sense in which signs produce effects is through their capacity to alter beliefs and habits; far from being "metaphysical," such effects are anchored in the down-to-earth reality of lived experience.

Racist expression, like sexist expression, entails harm to people. Furthermore, the harm is in most cases foreseeable. I realize that censoring expression entails harm as well, and that in particular instances it may be an open question as to whether more harm emanates from allowing or forbidding the expression. My position, the central tenet of this book, should be much less controversial, however, for even though there *may* be reasons for not *legally outlawing* certain forms of racist hate speech, it nevertheless seems clear that racist hate speech is *morally problematic*, and that we should therefore do our best to stop ourselves and to discourage others from speaking in such ways. Hare, in what I believe is a very important and much neglected paper, urges that one of the consequences of the features of moral language is the importance of people's developing "the ability to discern the feelings of others and how our actions will impinge upon them" (1973, 161). Such discernment should prove a helpful guide for getting clearer about the impact of our talk on others. I have argued that the characterization of talk as "mere talk" is problematic and erroneous. Talk has real and often far-reaching consequences on people's lives. Racist hate talk and sexist hate talk take their toll mainly on victims but also on perpetrators. Thus owing to both the amenability of talk to control and the capacity of talk to engender real and foreseeable harm, I would urge that any attempt to minimize moral responsibility for our talk, and to construe talk as some lesser form of behaviour (or *Only Words*, to borrow MacKinnon's title [1993]) is seriously erroneous.

I based my decision to apply moral criteria to talk on two facets, the first of which, the mistaken minimization of talk, I have just dealt with. I turn now to the second facet, that exempting talk from the moral standards expected and exacted of other forms of behaviour is convenient and sensible only for *some* people, not for *all*. In the classroom example, it is clear that exempting such classroom dynamics from moral judgments is convenient to the male students, who dominate class discussion and receive far more than their fair share of the teacher's time and attention. Thus to the male students, it might seem quite sensible to place such classroom dynamics well outside the parameters of moral relevance; one would expect the perspective of the female students, who are being cheated in an obvious way by the current arrangements, to be quite different in terms of what is convenient and what is sensible. I alluded to this point earlier when I claimed that *many*, but not *all* forms of expression receive constitutional protection in the U.S. In other words, U.S. constitutional law alone accords to speech sweeping exemptions from the legal requirements exacted of other forms of behaviour, but even in the U.S., not *all* expression fits into this privileged category. It is of course true that freedom of expression, on some level and in some ways, benefits us all. Executions and other human rights atrocities committed against individuals who, in repressive societies, speak out against powerful officials and (usually military) governments give us just cause to celebrate the relative freedom available to many of us who live in societies that endorse our right to speak in such critical ways. But to see this as a justification for exempting verbal expression from any form of sanction or control would be naive for two reasons. First, expression that criticizes government policy (which is what freedom of expression legislation was designed to protect) is in a very different category from expression that promotes racial or sexual hatred through portraying members of certain groups (Black people and women, for example), as disgusting, stupid, and generally less than human. The importance of protecting critical political commentary is evident, but this in no way entails a justification for protecting bigoted racist and sexist speech. To think that it does seems to me bizarre. MacKinnon captures this perfectly when she says, "The operative definition of censorship accordingly shifts from government silencing what powerless people say, to powerful people violating powerless people into silence and hiding behind state power to do it" (1993, 10).

There is a second difficulty with exempting verbal expression from any form of sanction or control. This second difficulty emanates from the very uneven benefits and penalties ensuing from such exemption. I shall use sexist and racist discourse to illustrate the discussion that follows, although the same analysis could as readily be applied to classist or homophobic discourse. The force of this example depends upon our acknowledging that the current context—political, social, economic, and personal—is based upon oppression of women and Black people. As illustrations of such oppression, I would include employment statistics on who holds the high-status and well-paid posts, who earns the higher income for doing work of equal value, who is victimized by crimes of rape and domestic violence, who has in the past been denied admission to institutions of higher education, who is likely to be subject to poverty following marriage break-up and in one's "golden years," and so on. These empirically documented facts seem to me to demand an acknowledgment of sexist and racist oppression. If we begin with this acknowledgment, then it is no great revelation that many of our current norms, including our linguistic norms, springing from this self-same context, endorse and promote the very oppression just discussed. But if this is so, then exempting sexist and racist discourse from censure and sanction disproportionately harms those who are victimized by such language. The toll of racist language on people of Colour has been referred to earlier; it is clear that even the most anti-racist of white people does not pay this sort of price, and that many of us not targeted by such hate language would experience little, if any, anguish of any form. As Delgado (and Mill before him) pointed out, however, those not targeted by racist and sexist language, indeed even the perpetrators of such language, are harmed insofar as they experience a "dulling [of] their moral and social senses" (Delgado 1993, 92) and the false "notion of . . . [their] inherent superiority" (Mill 1970, 218). Further elaboration of MacKinnon's work will be useful in expanding this discussion, as she very clearly illustrates the unevenness with which expression is protected. "Libel law . . . has become a tool for justifying refusals to publish attacks on those with power, even as it targets the powerless for liability" (1993, 78). Focusing specifically on pornography, she adds, "Protecting pornography means protecting sexual abuse *as* speech, at the same time that both pornography and its protection have deprived women *of* speech, especially speech against sexual abuse" (ibid., 9, author's emphasis).

I have argued that it is to a large extent possible for us to control the ways in which we talk, and that, because our talk has the capacity to harm other people, we ought to do our best to bring our talk into conformity with moral norms. How we talk is a matter for moral concern. To deny this seems to me to be ludicrous. Language is behaviour. When we talk, we behave or act in ways that have implications for other people. In this regard, language is no different from any other sort of behaviour. Bigoted sexist or racist talk hurts people and we should thus strive not to talk in these ways. To shift the discussion from the *content* to the *dynamics* of talk, if people talk too much, if they take more than their fair share of the conversational time available, this is directly analogous to taking more than their fair share of the apple pie or the blueberry cheesecake. By the same token, not contributing to the conversational exchange at all is like going to a potluck and not contributing a dish. Sattel provides an informative account of how men use inexpressiveness to achieve their own ends and to maintain power (1983, 118-124).

This is a feminist book written within a feminist context. In calling myself a feminist I mean to point out, among other things, that the sexual stratification of society is a matter for moral concern. The fact that women are paid less than men for doing essentially the same work, that they are valued negatively compared to men when they behave in precisely the same ways, that they have fewer opportunities which are reflected in diminished aspirations, these are not *simply* factual matters but travesties of social justice. How justice gets defined is obviously a crucial element in this discussion, as well as a very complex one, which I cannot even begin to spell out in any detail at this point. I do wish to point out that sexual justice has often been identified with equal access by the sexes to social goods; unless both females and males participate in identifying, defining, and administering the social goods, however, equal access comes nowhere close to achieving justice. Consider as an example access to a professional education, such as engineering. Even if women were admitted to engineering faculties in roughly equal numbers with men (subject only to their meeting the admission criteria), this would be only a minimal step towards gender equity; gender equity would require in addition a non-sexist curriculum, a pedagogy that takes female learning patterns into account, female professors to serve as role models, and so on. Equal access to male-defined "goods" does not constitute gender equity.

I am dismayed and saddened that many of my students disclaim the label of feminist, not wanting to be associated with the notion, as though being a feminist somehow tainted them. Many women students have little sense that they are where they are, for example, enrolled in degree-granting programs in a university, because of feminist battles to allow them a modicum of financial control over their own lives, access to birth control measures, admission to university, and admission to the professions. There are some exceptions, of course, and a few students are very knowledgable about these issues and deeply committed to furthering equity along lines of gender, race, class, state of ablebodiedness, and sexual preference. One cannot count on a person's sense of justice on one category extending to other categories, unfortunately. For example, even a person with an impressive understanding of, sensitivity towards, and commitment to reform along lines of classism may harbour deeply homophobic and heterosexist ideas.

In many people's minds, including some of my students', feminism is inextricably linked to man-hating and male-bashing. I believe this link accounts for many young women's disavowal of feminism. Yet the link made between feminism and man-hating is both false and unfortunate. The feminists whom I know (and this includes virtually all of my friends, many of my more casual acquaintances, and some of my family members) are *not* man-haters. They do not adore, worship, or specially *prefer* males, however, and this accounts for their frequently being perceived as man-haters. In other words, the norm (what many see as a *neutral* stance) involves a strong preference for male over female, in some instances amounting to an adoration or worship of the male; anything less than a strong preference for the male, such as *equal* valuing and treatment of male and female, is perceived, against this norm, as man-hating and male-bashing.

On these standards, this book may appear to many to be antimale. It is not; rather, it makes a strong argument against any preferential valuing and treatment of males. I am reminded here of a class in which one of my students referred to an article that I would classify as a luke-warm liberal feminist critique of education, which simply called attention to some historically sexist aspects of education, as "male-bashing." Another student in the same class clarified the issue with the response, "This article is not male-bashing—it's just telling it like it is!" Notice that for the first student, simply calling attention to sexist practices which have penalized *females* constituted *male*-bashing! This exemplifies my claim that what is not strongly *pro*-male is frequently perceived as being *anti-male*. For this reason, my book is likely to be perceived, mistakenly so, as anti-male. Neither is it pro-female, although it may appear to many readers to be that as well.

The book may appear pro-female and anti-male for another reason as well. It is unashamedly anti-dominance and pro-supportiveness; one of the obvious consequences of this is that there is a great deal in the male lifestyle that will fall under criticism in this work, and a great deal in the female lifestyle that will garner praise. Hence

my position does favour many of the actual characteristics traditionally attributed to females as opposed to those traditionally attributed
to males. There is no *necessary* sex link here, however; there are
many supportive males in the world, and many dominant females. In
other words, nothing follows from the claims made in this book
regarding the *innate* superiority of any one sex. In fact, there is not
even a necessary link to species. There are some lessons about curbing violent and aggressive tendencies that we could learn from non-
human animals, beavers providing us with one good example. According to Hope Ryden, what survival of the fittest is all about is the preservation of "characteristics that favor successful production" as
opposed to the preservation "of belligerent *individuals*" (1989, 225,
author's emphasis).

Any changes we make in the ways in which we socialize boys and
girls will be of critical importance; our current socialization practices
exacerbate the problem in the worst possible way. As Dale Spender
says, "The false logic of dominance demands too high a price and can
no longer be afforded" (1982, 96). We persist in teaching violent
aggressive norms to little boys while we heap on them a level of valuing never accorded to little girls (Hoffman 1988, 305-306, 310-311).
Indeed, the character traits inculcated and valued in little girls further
aggravate the problem; for little girls are taught to condone, even
applaud, both the unfair distribution of valuing, as well as to clean up
after and cover up for male aggression. The more capably females do
this work, the less able we will all be to achieve any understanding of
the damage wreaked by aggression.

A passage in an account of sex differences in human communication by Eakins and Eakins illustrates this clearly. The authors, discussing the different value systems of men and women, draw a parallel between humans and the cichlid fish. This point is so important
to my thesis that I quote at considerable length.

> Sexual behavior is coupled with aggressive behavior in the male; in the
> female, sexual behavior is related to fear. The strange phenomenon
> manifests itself in this way: fear and sexuality cannot exist in the male
> at the same time. If the male has the slightest fear of his partner, his
> sexuality is curbed. Conversely, if the female has so little *fear or awe* of
> her partner that her aggression is not suppressed, she does not react
> sexually to him. The result is that a male can mate only with an *awe-
> inspired and therefore submissive* female, and a female can mate only
> with an *awe-inspiring and therefore dominant* male. The sexuality of
> the male cichlid depends on the female's *awe*. She must defer to him,

or his masculinity is extinguished. He must be dominant, or he literally ceases to be a male, and the female will not conceive. (1978, 20, my emphasis)

The slip from frightening to awe-inspiring and from frightened or terrified to awe-inspired is instructive. Ordinary use of the language tells us that not everything that is frightening is awe-inspiring. A lightning storm on a mountain pass inspires both awe and fear, but an abusive husband and a rapist inspire no awe when they terrorize their victims. Yet the authors write as though the man's capacity to induce fear in a woman when relating to her sexually makes him somehow deserving of reverence; the woman, if she refuses to revere the man who is the occasion of terror for her, is accused of extinguishing his sexuality. It does not occur to Eakins and Eakins that a sexuality predicated on the creation of fear in a partner is better extinguished. The authors continue to draw an explicit human parallel:

> One can draw a parallel between human beings and cichlids. Human male sexuality, like the cichlid's, may be vulnerable to female aggression and diminished by lack of female subservience or awe. It is often dependent on deference. Even though male sexuality can endure cultural restraints and physical mistreatment, it may not be able to withstand the cichlid effect. This vulnerability of male sexuality is apparently social and based on relationships with women. (Ibid.)

Without having intended to, the authors thus illustrate dramatically the sense in which our society prizes and rewards male aggression, while ensuring that the rest of the population, the females, behave and act in ways that legitimate the intolerable.

This book is both a theoretical and an applied work; it both embraces a philosophical perspective and ignores traditional philosophy; at one and the same time, it pays attention to an enormous body of empirical literature and shrugs off with impatience the endlessly contradictory messages generated by empirical research; the message is both rational and highly emotional; it addresses itself to particular, specific individuals, yet it dares to believe that it deals in universals.

I shall look at language itself—what we as researchers say about it and what it says about us as human beings—as the starting place for reform. Although I limit myself to vocal and written language in this account, language itself knows no such limits. Sign language, for example, although it falls outside the limits of my competence to assess, is subject to sexist abuses similar to those characteristic of vocal and written languages. While speaking of linguistic reform, it is relevant to point out that the public's attitude towards sign languages could itself benefit from reform. Sign languages are often mistakenly dismissed as simple collections of gestures, with no understanding of their complex grammar and symbolic underpinnings. Where there has been acceptance of sign languages, this has often been limited to the signed equivalents of spoken languages (such as Signing Essential English or Comprehensive Signed English) and has specifically excluded those signed languages (such as American Sign Language) which have a unique grammatical structure and are not merely signed translations of spoken languages. Even educational policy reveals irrational devaluing of signed languages. For a long period of time, for example, the policy of the Ontario Department of Education exclusively promoted aural communication in classrooms for children who were deaf or hearing impaired. Hard as it is to believe, no form of signing was permitted in such classrooms. When the Ministry of Education did introduce signed communication into the classrooms of students who were hearing impaired or deaf, it was strictly the signed equivalents of English that were permitted, and teachers who communicated in American Sign Language were subject to censure. The students were not allowed to converse in American Sign Language in the classroom, even though, for most of them, American Sign Language was their native language. There are important parallels to be drawn between this "educational" policy implemented for those who are deaf and hearing impaired and for Native students in the Canadian school system. Fortunately, today there are few if any schools in the province that outrightly disallow classroom communication in American Sign Language, although there is still limited understanding of the innovative and complex grammatical structure and highly symbolic nature of this language. While my analyses are limited largely to spoken and written English, the concerns raised in this account extend to all languages, including sign languages.

This is a work that is both fearful and hopeful. Its optimism is based in the strength of language itself, the power of language to shape our perceptions and our attitudes, the scope of language within the educational process, the centrality of our own individual language use to a definition of who we are, and most important of all, the universality of language. Not everyone in the world enjoys wealth, formal education, authority, or respect. Virtually all of us have language, however. Language reforms or even linguistic revolutions could theoretically be performed by any or all of us. The potential for language-generated social change is thus enormous.

Language is not only at the very least quasi-universal; it is also the heart of who we are and where we are—a sign in every sense, at once iconic, indexical, and symbolic.[3] We have progressed far beyond the days when language was perceived as a mere vehicle for our thoughts, a kind of garment in which our thoughts could be clothed so as to be displayed to others and hence ushered into the public arena where exchange and interaction could occur. Benjamin Whorf's radical hypothesis of linguistic determinism, according to which we are incapable of thinking thoughts that we cannot formulate in our language (Whorf 1956, 252), although probably rejected in its extreme formulation by most, nevertheless approaches closer to our sense of the significance of language than does the traditional conservative view. It is important to be clear that in claiming that language is quasi-universal, I am *not* claiming that the English language, or the Indo-European family of languages, or the "dominant system of meaning"[4] in North America is quasi-universal, although many linguists and scholars in general have written as though this were precisely the case.[5] What I *am* claiming, rather, is that with only minimal exceptions, every human being has a language that is of critical importance in shaping and constructing that person's world view, sense of self, and ways of relating to others.

If we subscribe to even relatively weak views of just how much impact our language has on our manner of thinking and our way of perceiving the world, it becomes clear that there are important moral parameters surrounding our use of language. In other words, the more central language is to how we perceive, categorize, and reason, the more important it will be that our language not be unjust, or that it not discriminate unfairly against certain classes of people, for example. Yet surprisingly, there has been but little exploration of these moral parameters. I must clarify this claim. Certain aspects of language have in fact been subjected to intense scrutiny vis-à-vis their moral character. I refer here to promise keeping, lying, breach of contract, defamation, and misleading advertising, for example. The philosophical as well as the legal literature provides us with an abundant discussion of the moral issues that surround these particular forms of language.

There has, however, been little sustained discussion of the moral parameters of *ordinary conversational exchanges*, and I hope to initiate just such a discussion in this book. Andersson and Trudgill's *Bad Language* (1990) would appear, from its title alone, not to mention a chapter specifically entitled "Moral" (ibid., 181-195), to deal with precisely this topic. What the authors attempt to do throughout the book, however, is to divest the word "bad" of any moral import, suggesting instead that bad language is merely what people regard as bad and hence not necessarily bad at all (ibid., 6-7). Thus it is not surprising that slang, swearing, double negatives, and words like "ain't" are prominent among their examples of bad language (ibid., 8). They do give three examples of what they call "truly bad language" (ibid., 29), namely, verbosity, racist language, and sexist language (ibid., 29-31), but then state immediately that they will not be discussing the issues of racist and sexist language any further (ibid., 31). Perhaps it is because they leave aside important linguistic issues like racism and sexism that they are able to confidently claim in the conclusion to their book that "[b]ad language is no threat to our civilization" (ibid., 194).

Paul Grice's work on conversational implicature (1975, 1981) does provide an extensive discussion of the logic of ordinary discourse. His focus is on a *logical* rather than a *moral* analysis; nevertheless, there is some overlap between these two focuses, and his analysis is too important to be overlooked. I shall discuss Grice's analysis in some detail in Chapter Five. Habermas' discussion of communicative competence (1970) comes the closest to providing a moral analysis of the interactive realm in ordinary conversational exchanges; Habermas' work will also be discussed in considerable detail in Chapter Five.

My emphasis in this book will be specifically on the realm of interaction, and I shall argue (in Chapter Five) for a set of moral criteria not totally unlike Grice's maxims and a closer approximation yet to Habermas' conditions of communicative competence. Interestingly, Pamela Fishman mentions that women's interactional linguistic support is often perceived as a moral requirement (*for women*), but she does not develop this idea any further (1983, 99). The closest we have come to developing a moral analysis of conversational styles is to be found in the literature on gossip; unlike making a promise or telling a lie, for example, the notion of a conversational exchange is at least part of the meaning of gossip. Although promise making or lie telling could occur in the context of a conversation, they could just as well occur outside such a context. Not so for gossip, which ceases to exist the moment the conversation shuts down. One can promise or lie while hogging the conversation so thoroughly that no one else has a chance to speak, but one can gossip only in conversation. Part of the reason for this would seem to be that one can promise, lie, or write a letter of reference "from the top down," from authority to underling, whereas one gossips with one's peers. At its heart, gossip is a peer-based activity.

In light of the fact that gossip is the only form of *conversational language* that has received serious investigation as a moral phenomenon, it is particularly interesting that gossip has largely been associated with women's speech in the literature and that it has been soundly condemned from a moral perspective (Spacks 1985, 24-30, 38-41). (See, however, Goodman and Ben Ze'ev [1994] for some refreshingly different characterizations of gossip!) It is not surprising that the moral criticism heaped on gossip relates to the content rather than the interactive features. Thus gossipers have been charged with making false claims, making claims based on insufficient evidence, making claims that could not be rebutted by their subject (as gossip is conducted in the absence of the subject), or making public claims about people's private lives. Yet it is not self-evident that gossip is immoral; in this regard, it differs from lie telling and breach of promise, for example, which *by definition* involve a violation of moral principles. (This does not commit us to the view that lie telling or promise breaking need always be, on balance, immoral. It is to claim that, other things being equal, telling lies or breaking promises is immoral, and will be judged immoral unless offset by other, overriding circumstances.) There does not appear to be any moral principle that is automatically violated by gossip, however.

It seems odd, at least on the surface, that anything as pervasive within and vital to social functioning as conversational styles and patterns should have managed to evade the scrutiny of our moral theory-making apparatus. On the other hand, our resistance to interpreting and evaluating conversational exchanges along moral lines makes perfect sense. We are naturally reluctant to open ourselves up to the possibility of guilt in areas of behaviour that have traditionally spared us such unpleasantness. If our conversational patterns are simply a result of upbringing, or habit, or etiquette, or sex-role socialization, then it feels as though we can sit back and relax, for forces over and above those governed by personal responsibility would appear to be at work. While I disagree with this in the sense that *even* if our conversational patterns *did* result from habit, sex-role socialization, upbringing, or etiquette—and I do agree that these are all powerful factors—it doesn't follow that moral judgments are without relevance. We may be brought up, for example, to hold classist attitudes, yet acting upon these attitudes will likely constitute a violation of moral principles. Nor does this mean that upbringing and socialization are irrelevant to the ascription of praise and blame; white racist bigots are often themselves victims of poverty and class stereotypes. We have the right to expect more of those with more privileged backgrounds, which often permit entry to higher levels of formal education and expanded opportunities for travel, for example. (It has not, however, been my experience that working-class people harbour greater levels of race bias than middle-class people.)

So even if we can *explain* much of our language by virtue of such factors as habit, sex-role socialization, upbringing, or etiquette, it still does not follow that we are never required to *justify* our language by appealing to moral features. I realize, of course, that this distinction is not quite as straightforward as I have suggested, for even the identification of "relevant facts" in an explanation presupposes value judgments which are the hallmarks of justifications.[6] The point I wish to make here, however, is that we may understand why some people speak in certain ways (racist ways, for example) in terms of their own upbringing, victimization, and relative powerlessness, without thereby exonerating them from responsibility for such behaviour.

Even having said this, however, I do understand our reluctance to extend the sweep of moral judgments. For in so doing, we broaden the range of possible guilt, and who needs more guilt? The discussion following the presentation of a paper I attended at the 1991 meetings of CRIAW (Canadian Research Institute for the Advancement of Women) illustrates this resistance. A paper defending vegetarianism as an ecofeminist position was presented. The paper was excellent in my opinion, containing what I considered to be a lot of interesting and important facts about the harmful effects of farm animal (particularly beef cattle) excrement on the environment. I did not find the paper offensive in any way. Yet many of those who were present did. One woman, obviously angry, asked for a show of hands of those who were vegetarians. Most people complied, some explaining that they were vegetarians on religious grounds or for reasons of health. The woman who had asked for the show of hands responded that she didn't mind if people were vegetarians because of their health or their religion, but that she couldn't stand people who chose vegetarianism as a lifestyle for other reasons. I think that what she said was highly relevant to what I am trying to explain now. The "other" vegetarians, those who chose vegetarianism not out of a religious faith, nor out of medical necessity, chose it presumably for moral reasons, thus suggesting strongly that the choice to be a carnivore was immoral. While the speaker had in fact been extremely careful to make no such *explicit* claim, I thought, with the commenter, that such a claim had to be implicit. And the commenter resented it! Her anger, I felt, was a direct expression of her resistance to being made to feel guilty for not being a vegetarian herself.

Extending the sweep of moral judgments not only causes us to broaden the range of guilt we feel over areas of our lives that we would rather not have to think about in this way but also causes us to broaden the range of blame we attribute to others, and this may be even more distasteful than harbouring ever-increasing layers of guilt. Tannen claims that her sociolinguistic "approach to relationships makes it possible to explain these dissatisfactions without accusing anyone of being crazy or *wrong*, and without *blaming*—or discarding—the relationship" (1990, my emphasis). Like Tannen, I too want to understand the sociolinguistic issues involved; but in a moral context, part of what understanding means is assigning responsibility and acknowledging that those who shirk their responsibilities are wrong in doing so. In other words, the refusal to lay blame in a moral context is indicative of a failure in understanding. Furthermore, I have very little confidence that understanding will be sufficient to rectify the problem, whether it resides in a speech pattern, a relationship, or a social institution. Such understanding will be a necessary first step to any long-term solution, but unless it is accompanied by action and reform, the consequences of such understanding will extend no further than linguistics publications. If a relationship is based on immoral premises, then blaming someone, distasteful as it may be, is exactly what is required. Of course, it will not be as simple a matter as merely assigning individual blame, for the problems in the relationship, for example, may emanate not only from the individuals involved, but also from broader social structures and traditions—in other words, the problem may have systemic as well as individual roots. Nevertheless, when people behave in immoral ways, it is important to be clear to ourselves, to them, and to others that they are wrong. Simply understanding that they are different from us is not sufficient.

There is a trend in the literature on gender and language that displays a reluctance, like Tannen's, to blame anyone for anything, but in particular, a reluctance to blame men for their linguistic behaviour. Much of the impetus behind the rejection of the male dominance theory of gender and language springs, I believe, from this reluctance. This point will be developed in more detail in the chapters that follow.

I shall also directly address the criticism that the extension of the moral realm to our ordinary language involves overmoralizing at a later point in the book—Chapter Five. Now, however, I want to come to terms with the apparent oddity of our *not* analyzing conversational styles and patterns within a moral framework. As I suggested earlier, something as vital to our social functioning as conversational styles seems precisely the sort of thing that should naturally receive a moral analysis. Our reluctance to broaden the range of things over which we feel guilt gives us part of the explanation.

But there is more, and to understand this we must understand some of the many assumptions that have traditionally governed the public/private dualism. First assumption: The public realm represents the place where real work is performed, for when men enter their private domiciles, the respite which they expect to find there from the harsher public realm is one of the major reasons for the existence of the private realm. Second assumption: The public realm is complex and opaque, the private realm simple and transparent; hence only the public realm is in need of or worthy of intellectual analysis and investigation. Third assumption: The public realm is task-oriented, unlike the private realm, the orientation of which is more accurately perceived as one of nurturing or sustaining. Fourth assumption: Education and high-level training are required to prepare one to perform in the public realm, but instinct and maturation are quite sufficient to ensure competence in the private realm. Further, education and high-level training may be positive liabilities in the private realm, actually interfering with the performance of the roles properly relegated to this realm. Fifth assumption: Argument, debate, rhetoric, and public speaking are the sorts of language styles most appropriate to the public realm, whereas conversation is the style most suited to the private realm. Sixth assumption: Men rightly occupy the public realm and women the private; those women who do enter the public arena must learn to think, act, and speak like men if they expect to succeed.

The tallying of these assumptions makes it evident, I believe, why conversational styles have until recently escaped any form of intellectual analysis whatsoever, and explains in part why they continue to evade detailed moral analysis. It is only recently that we have begun to assess the familial context against the same sorts of standards that have traditionally been applied in the public context. Rape was once, and not too long ago, perceived as violent sexual assault that happened between strangers. Rape of friends or dates was an uneasy fit for our sense of the crime, and rape of one's wife failed to match at all, thus rendering inconceivable or nonsensical the notion of marital rape. So the familial remained insulated from or immune to many of the concerns, including moral ones, applied to the public realm.

It is in just this sense, I believe, that ordinary conversational exchanges and interactions have failed to be perceived as appropriate moral phenomena. Conversations, because they represented the communication style of the private rather than the public realm, were historically never subjected to the kind of rigorous intellectual scrutiny of arguments, debates, rhetoric, or public speaking. And even now, in the wake of the dramatic impact that feminism has had in focusing the intellectual spotlight on the private realm, ordinary parlance still remains in most people's minds outside the boundaries of moral discourse.

In the chapters that follow, I shall attempt to fill in this lacuna to some extent. There are two levels of theory relating to gender and language that roughly reflect the distinction between fact and value which is frequently made in philosophy. First, there is a set of theories that purports to explain the "facts" of gender difference (or gender similarity, for which some linguists argue); second, there are theories that interpret or evaluate these gender differences (or similarities). There is, of course, significant overlap between these two, and the work of any researcher writing on this topic is likely to contain both levels of theory, either explicitly or implicitly. Many writers on gender and language, particularly prior to the 1980s, wrote as though their accounts dealt only with explanations of the facts about gender and language, but in reality their accounts were riddled with implicit evaluations, many of which entailed highly negative evaluations of language identified with women; this is dramatically true of Lakoff's early work (1975), although many other accounts of gender and language contained some such presuppositions (Ayim 1983; Dubois and

Crouch 1975; Eakins and Eakins 1978; Erickson et al. 1978, 267-268; Pearson 1985). Such accounts, where they posited sex differences in language, frequently interpreted male language patterns as normal, strong, direct, honest, in a word, exemplary, while female language patterns were interpreted as deviant, weak, indirect, devious, and overall, deficient. As the interpretive or evaluative aspects of researchers' work became more explicit, it also became less obviously sexist (Spender 1980). While most of the evaluative aspects of researchers' work was strongly anti-female, some, particularly that which analyzed parental language interactions with children, urged a complementary position (Gleason 1987; Greif 1980; Key 1975; Tannen 1990); other researchers, although these were in the minority, argued for the superiority of female language patterns (Ayim 1987b; Shakeshaft 1987).

It is important for me to acknowledge from the outset some limitations of the research dealing with gender and language. First, most of this research is based on white middle-class populations, rendering generalizations beyond this group problematic. Some of the research examined has explicitly addressed this limitation, however; see, for example, Abrahams 1972, 1975; Augustine 1990; Martha Ayim 1992; Maryann Ayim 1990, 1992b; Delgado 1993; Delpit 1988; Doughty 1980; Giele and Gilfus 1990; Goodwin and Goodwin 1987; Ihle 1990; Lightfoot 1980; Matsuda 1993; McKellar 1989; Phoenix 1987; Pollard 1990; Smitherman-Donaldson and van Dijk 1988; Walker 1982. Nevertheless, we must be wary of assuming a homogeneity that often does not exist and hence careful not to assume that a study of a particular population sample applies equally as well to different population samples. Furthermore, even if we are satisfied that a researcher has revealed some significant characteristics of a particular population, not *all* members of even that limited population will share the characteristic. In other words, many of the researchers make claims about gender trends, to which there will be exceptions. Not all men and not all women, even within the particular sample in question, will speak in the ways portrayed by the research.

I shall examine the three overarching theories that purport to explain the interface of gender and language—namely, the male dominance theory, the sex roles socialization theory, and the appropriate registers theory. The male dominance theory and the sex roles socialization theory alike presuppose *that there are* female/male differences in speech, although their accounts of the reasons for these differences are often highly dissimilar; the appropriate registers theory, however, frequently rejects this presupposition, urging us to examine the research on gender differences in language with a more critical eye than we have done in the past. The appropriate registers theory focuses on the speaker's use of the appropriate style within the context—for example—a male *or* female employee may opt for a conciliatory tone when being addressed by their boss. Hence, according to this theory, other aspects of one's situation, such as an employee-boss context, are as likely as gender to account for language styles.

By and large, proponents of the male dominance theory of gender and language, the sex roles socialization theory, and the appropriate registers theory, purport to explain the "facts" of gender and language, but they contain as well many evaluative judgments regarding this data. I shall argue that none of these three theories can sensibly be held up as any kind of guide to our linguistic behaviour without being supplemented by a moral framework. This claim is tautological in an obvious sense, but that has, unfortunately, not prevented people, many of them linguistics scholars, from missing it. Because there is a huge kernel of truth in each of these theories, they are very persuasive and have many followers. There is a temptation for those who hold these theories to perceive whatever has been identified as the "facts" of gender and language as fully accounted for and not requiring further analysis. It is of critical importance that a *moral* analysis be performed in the context of each of these three theories, however; otherwise we may fall into the trap of believing that what has been explained has automatically been justified as well.

Having discussed these three major theories of gender and language, I will formulate my list of moral criteria and employ those criteria as a vehicle for discussing gender and language. The research discussed in this context illustrates in a particularly strong way the prevalence of sexist interpretations and presuppositions even in the writing of those who have believed that they restricted themselves to an objective description of the data, as well as those who have explicitly undertaken to eschew sexism in their work.

I shall devote some time to an analysis of vocabulary choices explicitly, particularly substitute terms for the term "woman" in the English language. The topic of violent metaphors in academic and ordinary discourse will be addressed, as will the popular contemporary topic of political correctness, focusing on the race and gender dimensions of this literature. The book will end with a discussion of impediments to and expectations for educational reform, examining in particular some of the current literature on women in educational administration.

Notes

1 There is a third facet as well, that the difficulties associated with characterizing talk as behaviour and judging it appropriately are in fact not overwhelming. I will broach this discussion at the end of the chapter, but postpone a more detailed discussion until Chapter Five.

2 Like Peirce, I think that "moral judgment . . . is inapplicable to what we cannot help" (1931-1958, 8.191). I refer to the *Collected Papers of Charles Sanders Peirce* in the conventional way; i.e., 8.191 indicates volume 8, paragraph 191.

3 I use these terms in the sense in which Charles Sanders Peirce used them in one of his many classifications of signs (1931-1958, 8.119). According to Peirce's usage, an icon is a sign that represents something because it really resembles that thing; for example, a highway sign depicting a curve in the road actually replicates the curve. An index is a sign that represents something because it is actually affected by that thing; for example, the rising mercury column of a thermometer represents a fever because the mercury expands under heat. A symbol is a sign of something because of a convention linking it to that thing; for example, a green traffic light is a sign to proceed whereas a red traffic light is a sign to stop.

4 I wish to thank Leslie Thielen-Wilson for reading an earlier version of this manuscript and providing me with a great deal of helpful and insightful feedback. The phrase "dominant system of meaning" is hers.

5 Habermas (1970) takes the disclaimer I am making here one step further, by challenging Chomsky's claim to a universal grammar embedded within the deep structure of human languages.

6 The importance of this clarification was also made clear to me by Leslie Thielen-Wilson's comments on my manuscript.

Chapter Two

The Male Dominance Theory of Gender and Language

This theory suggests that male/female speech patterns are a clear reflection of a patriarchal universe. Dale Spender's analysis of education, as well as language, is clearly based on a theory of male dominance. She says,

> I am not advocating a conspiracy theory—that is, that men have deliberatively [sic] constructed a theory and practice designed to support and sustain male dominance—but that one outcome of taking *exclusively* for themselves the power to determine the parameters of education, has been to *exclude* women and thereby to perpetuate male dominance. (1981, 161, author's emphasis)

While Spender disclaims attributing intentionality to the patriarchy, it is clear that intentionality is a vital part of her perception of the feminist redress to patriarchy. She says, "Feminism is a social and political movement, a revolutionary movement, *aimed at the redistribution of power*. It has developed its own form of organization and dissemination of knowledge which reflects its political nature and aspirations" (ibid., 170, my emphasis).

According to proponents of the male dominance theory, the general dominance of men and boys over women and girls will be reflected in their language patterns. The underlying spirit of this theory is captured clearly by these words of Cheris Kramarae:

> Action on the part of members of the socially inferior group—women—to change the relationship between the two groups will be met with strong action from members of the dominant group, [i.e., men] who will attempt to maintain their distinctiveness, superiority, and control. (1980, 84)

In the words of Sheila Ruth, "Since culture governs the internalization of values, and our culture is masculinist, it is not surprising that both women and men value men and maleness over women and femaleness" (1981, 46, n. 4).

Sankoff, in her discussion of the social aspects of language, claims that what makes a language dominant is the political dominance of its speakers (1980, 13-14). She suggests that the placement of any group in an inferior political position will result in a devaluing of that group's language (ibid., 15). In her study of language and political power in Papua New Guinea, Sankoff claims that Tok Pisin, the pidgin German acquired by some of the native speakers during the period of German colonialization, eventually became the language of power in the country, and that those who spoke it enjoyed more political power and privilege than those who spoke only the native languages (ibid., 21). Eventually Tok Pisin became the language deemed appropriate for such local level political functions as "village meetings . . . particularly the . . . morning meetings where people (particularly women) are supposed to line up and receive orders about the work they are to do later in the day" (ibid., 22). Hence the language of colonial domination became the language of sexual domination.

Although Sankoff is not particularly interested in sex as a determinant of political or linguistic dominance, it is nevertheless interesting to examine her comments from this perspective. Does the political dominance of males result in male speech patterns that are more forceful and dominant? Or are male speech patterns, whether dominant or not, simply *evaluated* as stronger and more forceful because males occupy stronger positions in the political hierarchy? If males retained a position of political dominance but exhibited in their speech the qualities usually associated with women's speech, would their speech patterns nevertheless be perceived as superior? There is definite evidence to suggest that this second situation is indeed the case. Keenan has studied the speech of a Malagasy community in Madagascar. In this community, the men's speech is indirect and subtle—they show respect to others by avoiding confrontation in their speech, and in general "behave in public in such a way as to promote interpersonal ease . . . they avoid creating unpleasant face-to-face encounters" (1989, 137); women's speech, on the other hand, is direct and straightforward, characteristically involving the "open expression of anger towards others . . . they express feelings of anger or criticism directly to the relevant party" (ibid.). Keenan informs us that in this community, "[m]en and women alike consider indirect speech to be more difficult to produce than direct speech" (ibid., 140). It follows from this that men are considered to be the more skilful speakers (ibid., 137). "Men alone are considered to be able speechmakers" (ibid., 141). Women and men are agreed, Keenan tells us, "that women have *lavalela*, a long tongue" (ibid, 137, author's emphasis).

Some of the most commonly identified forms of linguistic domination are interrupting other speakers, pausing for inordinately long periods of time before responding to a speaker, hogging the conversation, insisting on the selection of the topic of conversation, refusing to cooperate in developing the conversational topics introduced by other speakers, non-reciprocal hierarchical behaviour, such as calling a person by their first name while insisting on honorific titles for oneself, using terms of endearment for another in a context where these would be inappropriate for oneself, or referring to another speaker's physical appearance in either negative or positive ways in contexts in which one would not oneself expect to be thus referred to, and generally behaving in a rude, brusque fashion linguistically. Zimmerman and West, among the most prominent of those whose analyses of conversational interactions reflect the male dominance theory,

> view the production of both retarded minimal responses and interruptions by male speakers interacting with females as an assertion of the right to control the topic of conversation reminiscent of adult-child conversations where in most instances the child has restricted rights to speak and to be listened to. (1975, 124)

They continue to say,

> We are led to the conclusion that, at least in our transcripts, men deny equal status to women as conversational partners with respect to rights to the full utilization of their turns and support for the development of topics. Thus we speculate that just as male dominance is exhibited through male control of macro-institutions in society, it is also exhibited through control of at least one micro-institution. (Ibid., 125)

Eakins and Eakins, in a similar vein, describe interrupting as exercising "a form of control over another's speech" (1978, 21). They also document another feature often associated with dominance in language—hogging the conversation. Their analyses of amount of talking done at university faculty meetings indicated that male faculty members both took over twice as many turns at talking as female faculty members and spoke for almost twice as long per turn (ibid., 26). In the same spirit, Bublitz claims that if a conversation is to reflect "not a one-sided but a joint and cooperative procedure" (1988, 122), then the conversational rules must "exclude one speaker's solo acting independently of the others" (ibid.).

In the realm of "body language," such female features as taking up little space, persistent smiling, or physical touching of one's own body, together with such male features as expansive postures, moving into or encroaching upon other people's space, and physical touching of others are frequently cited as illustrations of male dominance (Hall 1987, 185-186). Cline and Spender (1987, 66-95) provide a detailed analysis of female fashion trends and body shape ideologies as reflecting and reinforcing male dominance.

Although the male dominance view is advocated by such prominent writers on the topic of gender and language as Dale Spender (1980, 76-105; 1982, 65; 1983, 371), it has fallen into disrepute in many quarters and for several reasons, three of which I shall discuss in detail here. First, it has been pointed out by researchers that the mere identification of linguistic features is too coarse a measure on which to base claims of either dominance or submissiveness. (See, for example, Aries 1987, 156.) Consider silence, as a case in point. Extended silence on the part of a conversational participant *may* indicate submissiveness and a relinquishing of conversational control to a stronger participant—this has been the standard interpretation of silence. But it *could* indicate quite the reverse—i.e., a power play whereby one "freezes out" other participants by telling them in the most eloquent way possible, utter silence, that what they are saying isn't worthy of a response. Silence may be supportive insofar as it may represent curbing one's own speech in order to pay careful attention to someone else's, or it may be the most hostile of speech acts, indicating a refusal to waste one's time engaging in a conversation. Before we can assume that silence is supportive, we must know that it is linked to listening, among other things. We can all identify occasions when, unable to physically exit, we have performed the mental equivalent by literally "tuning out" the speaker. Our silence in this context does not mean that we have respectfully relinquished the floor to someone whose opinions we are eager to hear; rather, it suggests that we are totally indifferent to the speaker's point of view. We are so sure that nothing worth listening to will be said, that we don't waste our time listening. As mentioned earlier, Zimmerman and West have argued that periods of silence before responding to a speaker (together with persistent interruption of a speaker), "function as topic control mechanisms" (1975, 124).

So silence is no guarantee that one is according the speaker the respect of listening; at the same time, one's failure to listen may not be readily apparent in certain contexts. Many people become clever at providing acceptable responses to disguise lapses of listening; many students have become very adept at this, and provide responses that satisfy the professor even when they have listened to very little of what the professor has said. In fact, "tuning out," but disguising this with an appropriate verbal response as required, may exemplify an act of rebellion of the relatively powerless.

Similarly, interruption of another speaker is not necessarily an indication of dominant behaviour; it could be a sign of highly supportive behaviour, an excitement induced by what the other speaker says that prompts one to exclaim aloud immediately. Elizabeth Aries claims that interruption might "be related to involvement and spontaneity rather than to dominance" (1987, 152-153) and that it may manifest "agreement and support" (ibid., 153). Before labelling interruption dominant, we need to know more. For example, did the interrupter endorse or augment what the speaker was saying, as opposed to contradicting the speaker? Leet-Pellegrini (1980) criticizes the earlier work of Zimmerman and West (1975), claiming that her analysis of the relationship of gender to interruption is superior, because in her research, "unlike earlier studies, several aspects of situation and context were included" (Leet-Pellegrini 1980, 103). Leet-Pellegrini provides several examples of recorded dialogue which, although they technically qualify as either overlap or interruption, are in fact instances of highly supportive verbal behaviour. In these examples, the so-called interrupters "either recycled current speakers' words exactly or they completed current speakers' apparently intended message" (ibid., 100). In this case, a simple identification of interruption as dominant behaviour would have been seriously misleading; we require a more finely tuned analysis that delves deeper into the actual content of what was said to permit the recognition of what Leet-Pellegrini calls the "as-if-one-voice phenomenon" (ibid.), a phenomenon indicative of both careful listening to the speaker as well as making a supportive contribution. In her discussion of overlapping speech, Tannen claims that such speech may be used "in a cooperative way . . . without intending to interrupt" (1982, 218); it may exemplify cooperative rather than destructive behaviour and may not involve the attempt "to exercise dominance and violate others' rights" (1990, 202).

The automatic identification of tag-questions with hesitant insecure speech provides us with yet a third example of an instrument too coarse for generating accurate insights into language. A tag question is a questioning phrase inserted at the end of a regular declarative statement, for example, "We're having a very warm January, aren't we?" Lakoff's early analysis of tag-questions (1975, 14-17) has been criticized for its claim that tag-questions characterized women's speech to a far greater extent than men's; research done by Dubois and Crouch generated findings dramatically opposite to Lakoff's claims in this regard (1975, 293). Lakoff's claim that the tag-question was an indication of uncertainty has also been subject to much criticism (Aries 1987, 156-157; French and French 1984a, 58; Spender 1980, 8-10).

In their attempt to controvert Lakoff's claim that the use of the tag-question is an indicator of uncertainty, Dubois and Crouch assert the dubiousness of this claim *on the basis of their observations that tag-questions are more likely to emanate from men's than from women's speech.* They say:

> Insofar as there is at least one genuine social context in which men did, and women did not, use tag questions, the claim that such questions signify an avoidance of commitment, and cause the speaker to 'give the impression of not being really sure of himself, of looking to the addressee for confirmation, even of having no views of his own', is open to serious doubt. (Dubois and Crouch 1975, 294)

Thus Dubois and Crouch illustrate Spender's claim that sexist biases in linguistic scholarship have led researchers to automatically interpret what they perceived as female speech patterns in a negative way, and what they perceived as male speech patterns in a positive way (Spender 1980, 8-11).

A closer look at the context in which the tag-question appears may reveal it to actually function as a very dominant action, an attempt to influence or control other people's points of view, or an "overbearing [usage], intended to forestall opposition" (Dubois and Crouch 1975, 292). The context may also reveal the tag-question to function in a quite different way, as a mechanism to get people talking, to involve them in the conversation; Aries, for example, believes that the tag-questions found in women's speech in particular often function "to express solidarity by facilitating the addressee's contribution to discourse" (Aries 1987, 156). French and French claim that "a statement of tag frequencies may mask what is happening in interactions. Speakers *might* be expressing tentativeness in using them; on the other hand, they might not" (1984a, 58, authors' emphasis). We must be wary of any account which automatically assumes that inviting the participation of others is a mark of insecurity or submissiveness. In the same vein, Kramarae suggests that "hedges are not always used to express subordination or uncertainty" (1981, 139).

A fourth example is provided by a speaker's changing the topic of conversation. As Bublitz claims,

> a topic can not only be changed or broken off or shifted or suspended for a digression because the speaker wants to enforce his topic, to impose it on the interlocutors and to substitute it for the previous unwanted topic, but also because, on the contrary, he endeavours to remove a resulting discord, an impending difference of opinion or a now apparent contrast of interests. (Bublitz 1988, 135-136)

These observations suggesting caution against automatically interpreting particular language features in a single way—for example, interpreting interruptions as bullying dominant speech and tag-questions as hesitant speech—make sense. I may interrupt another speaker because I am "on the same wave length," virtually matching their thoughts with my words; or I may interrupt because I am so enthusiastic about what the speaker is saying, that I cannot contain my excitement, and it bursts out in my words; or I may interrupt because I am too impatient to hear the speaker out, and because it is so clear to me that what I have to say is of such greater import that I do not even recognize what I am doing as overriding the other speaker or think of myself as interrupting. Interruptions may take any of these forms, and many more. To interpret an interruption intelligently, we must know something of the context in which it occurred, not merely that it was an interruption. Insofar as proponents of the male dominance theory have simply counted occurrences of interruption in male speech and tag-questions in women's speech, taking these counts to be ample evidence of male dominance, their research has been seriously lacking.

This does not establish that the male dominance theory is false, only that this one strand of evidence typically used to support it does not in fact offer support. The evidence is too crude, failing to distinguish in any meaningful way among the various sorts of contexts in which interruptions or tag-questions may occur. Where cognizance has been paid to the context, however, the research does appear to support a hypothesis of male dominance. LaFrance and Carmen distinguish between interruptive statements and questions; they claim that women use more interruptive questions than men do, but that these questions indicate greater responsiveness in their speech, not greater assertiveness (1980, 42). Similarly, research conducted by Adams and Ware, which focuses on different applications of the tag-question, indicated that while men use tag-questions to intimidate the listener into accepting their point of view and to foreclose discussion, women use tag-questions to generate discussion and involve others in the conversation (1979, 496). Aries claims that women use tag-questions in a facilitating way, encouraging others to contribute to the conversation, three times as often as men use them in this way (1987, 156). This more sophisticated research on particular speech patterns therefore appears to offer support for a male dominance theory of gender and language.

There is a second reason why the male dominance account of gender and language is frequently regarded with scepticism. Elizabeth Aries' research on gender and communication indicates that the differences between female and male speech patterns emerge most dramatically in same-sex speech groups. Aries claims that the stereotypes associated with men's language—"aggression, competition, victimization, and practical joking" (1987, 164)—are much less frequently engaged in by men in mixed-sex groups than in all-male groups. Research conducted by Crosby and Nyquist indicated that male speech to other males contained less of the traditionally identified female items than male speech to females (1977, 317). According to Judith Hall, "the finding that several nonverbal differences are more pronounced between males and females in same-gender dyads than between males and females in mixed dyads" (1987, 188), directly controverts the dominance theory. (See also Hall 1984, 152-153.) Presumably Hall believes that if gender differences in language patterns were in fact caused by male dominance, one should expect to see the most dominant of male speech patterns occurring in male interactions with females, rather than in male interactions with other males; by the same token, one should expect to see the most submissive of female language patterns emerging when females interact with males rather than when they interact with other females. However, Elizabeth Aries' research, like Hall's, demonstrates the reverse of this—namely, that the most dramatic gender differences occur in same-sex rather than mixed-sex conversations (Aries 1987, 160).

The research of Goodwin and Goodwin also supports the hypothesis that gender differences in language are more prevalent in same-sex than in mixed-sex conversations, although their work gives only weak support for the hypothesis. Studying the speech patterns of Black working class children in the Philadelphia area, the Goodwins claimed that there were far fewer differences than there were similarities in the speech of the girls and the boys whom they studied (1987, 205); nevertheless, they did claim that the girls, although they generally showed a propensity for strong, confrontational language, used more "insults, commands, or accusations . . . in their interactions with boys than when by themselves" (ibid., 230). In her discussion of the Goodwins' work, Christine Tanz suggests that if one were to examine only same-sex conversations, a very deceptive and exaggerated picture of sex differences in conversation might emerge as a consequence (1987, 171-172). The same point is made by Barrie Thorne; she claims that the sex differences research has tended to exaggerate differences, masking "the possibility that gender arrangements and patterns of similarity and difference may vary by situation, race, social class, region, or subculture" (1986, 168).

Tanz also poses the important question, "Why does the boys' style set the framework for cross-sex disputes?" (ibid., 172). In the same vein, Tannen notes that while both women and men appear to compromise in what they talk *about* in mixed-sex conversations, such conversations follow a male rather than a female *style* (1990, 236-237).

Aries' and Hall's research, as we have seen, appears to support the opposite assumption to that prompting Tanz's question; for Aries claims, as we have noted, that male speech patterns are more supportive and personal and less combatative in mixed-sex than in same-sex conversations (1987, 160). In the same vein, Judith Hall claims that "several nonverbal differences are more pronounced between males and females in same-gender dyads than between males and females in mixed dyads" (1987, 188). Jacqueline Sachs, although her study did not involve mixed-sex groups, notes that even in all-male groups, the boys showed themselves quite capable of using "mitigated utterances when the situation called for them" (1987, 186). I believe that, contrary to initial appearance, the assumption of Tanz is quite compatible with that of Aries and Hall. For male speech, although more personal and *less* combative in mixed sex than in same-sex groups, may nevertheless remain *highly combative*, especially relative to female speech in mixed-sex groups. Furthermore, I do not find these observations surprising. If, in their language, men are dominant and women are submissive, men will have no need to overtly express such dominance when conversing with women, for women's submissiveness will highlight the dominance of men without men even needing to engage in any struggle to exhibit their dominance. One could even afford a show of pomp and chivalry to those who clearly pose no threat to the established dominance hierarchy.

In fact, it is interesting to ask whether chivalrous displays are themselves the ultimate in dominant behaviour—if men resisted the display of chivalry towards themselves, but insisted on women accepting such displays graciously, this would go some distance towards establishing precisely this point. A colleague of mine once complained to me that while driving in to work his offers of help to a woman motorist had been declined. Having spotted a woman whose car obviously had a flat tire, he had pulled over and offered to change it for her. She, however, was well underway with the job herself, having already positioned the jack under the car, and had thanked him for his offer, but assured him she didn't need his help. He told me that he would have liked to have kicked the jack out from under her car. I suspect that this is not a typical reaction, and that many men are relieved that they are no longer expected to leap to the rescue of stranded women motorists. Nevertheless, my colleague's reaction illustrates in the clearest possible way that his behaviour embodied male dominance masquerading as chivalry. The fact that chivalry, unlike ordinary politeness, for example, is always *unidirectional*, male to female, is cause to suspect it; if chivalry *cannot be refused* by women, then we should be even more suspicious that is a manifestation of oppression.

Even if one agrees that gender differences in language emerge more strongly in same-sex than in mixed-sex conversations, I am less convinced than Aries and Hall that the dominance theory is contro-verted by this finding. If male dominance is being appealed to as the root cause of the language differences, then it makes sense that domi-nant people will be more dominant with others of their kind. What is the point of dominance against someone who is utterly submissive? There appears to be no obvious need for dominance in this context, except perhaps to "keep such persons in their place" if they show any signs of "uppity" behaviour.

Just as it would make sense for dominant people to display more dominant behaviour to others of their kind rather than to display such behaviour to non-dominant people, much the same point can be made about many reported female linguistic patterns, such as active soliciting of others to join in the conversation. It would be quite astonishing if this behaviour were as strongly demonstrated in mixed-sex conversations as in same-sex conversations. There seems little need to prompt, coax, or cajole those who are already dominating the conversation to join in and contribute their point of view. Yet it has been my experience that whenever men *have* appeared hesitant to speak up, as in a women's studies class, where there *may* be some men present who hang back and appear reluctant to express them-selves, the women in the class will actively press them for contribu-tions, striving to make the men feel valued and important partici-pants in the discussion. However, not all studies support the findings of the Goodwins, Aries, Crosby and Nyquist, and Hall in this regard. Leet-Pellegrini, in her study on conversational dominance and exper-tise, found that female experts engaged in more of the assenting behaviour traditionally associated with female speech when they con-versed with males than when they conversed with females (1980, 102).

The third reason advanced against the viability of the male domi-nance theory is the most interesting from my perspective. Deborah Tannen rejects the dominance theory of gender patterns in language in essence because she is not comfortable with heaping moral blame on members of ethnic minorities for what people may consider to be obnoxious moral behaviour. The juxtaposition of gender and ethnicity poses a dilemma for her, and we cannot have it both ways, she insists.

> If it is theoretically wrongheaded, empirically indefensible, and morally insidious to claim that speakers of particular ethnic groups are pushy, dominating, or inconsiderate because they appear to interrupt in con-

versations with speakers of different, more "mainstream" ethnic backgrounds, can it be valid to embrace research that "proves" that men
dominate women because they appear to interrupt them in conversation? . . . In short, such "research" would do little more than apply the
ethnocentric standards of the majority group to the culturally different
behavior of the minority group. (Tannen 1990, 207-208)

According to Tannen, since it would be wrong of us, theoretically,
empirically, and morally, to label members of various ethnic groups
domineering because they interrupt mainstream speakers, to be consistent, we must relinquish any temptation to label males as domineering on the grounds that they seem to interrupt women in conversations. This is the crux of Tannen's rejection of the male dominance
hypothesis. Some members of some ethnic minorities, she says, talk
in ways that may appear to be pushy and aggressive, whereas in fact
these forms of speaking are simply part of a cultural heritage. As a
Jewish woman she identifies herself as a member of just such an ethnic minority group; she says, "I am offended by the labelling of a feature of my conversational style as loathsome, based on the standards
of those who do not share or understand it" (1990, 209).

While I agree with some of Tannen's observations, I am unable
to accept her solution to the dilemma, which is to construe male
interruption of females as essentially a cultural phenomenon. I agree
with Tannen totally that negative stereotyping of ethnic and racial
minorities is rampant in scholarship, as in all other aspects of society.
I also agree with her that such stereotyping is both wrong and harmful. I cannot agree to any wholesale condemnation of research that
suggests that the speech patterns of any particular ethnic group are
pushy or domineering, however. Unlike Tannen, I cannot accept that
"it is theoretically wrongheaded, empirically indefensible, and morally
insidious to claim that speakers of particular ethnic groups are pushy,
domineering, or inconsiderate" (1990, 207-208). Like Tannen, I
would be inclined to be suspicious of such research as springing from
intolerance and lack of understanding of the culture in question, and
when I read the research, I would keep the possibility of such author
bias uppermost in my mind. Scholarship does not have a good track
record in this regard, so any research which makes negative claims
about members of oppressed groups must be carefully perused. In this
I agree with Tannen. Unlike Tannen, however, I would want to
peruse it *before* throwing it out. Some speakers of particular ethnic
groups *may* be domineering, pushy, and inconsiderate.

My most serious difficulty with her position is her equating claims about pushy domineering minorities with claims about pushy domineering males, and rejecting a male dominance position on that basis. For these two claims, where they have emerged in scholarship, are not identical, but are fundamentally different. Negative claims about minority group members have typically been made by mainstream "authorities" or "experts," scholars operating from positions of enormous privilege. The same cannot be said about the feminist literature, which posits the male dominance position. When these writers talk of dominance, they do so as members of a historically silenced group, not the "authorities" and "experts" who have silenced all but their own mainstream position. In other words, the problem that hounds any attribution of negative features to oppressed people by their oppressors does not necessarily hound the attribution of negative features to the oppressors by the oppressed; these two situations are not identical, as Tannen would have us believe, but are radically different. While linguistics research which claims that Black people and Jewish people are mouthy and loud is suspect as applying "the ethnocentric standards of the majority group to the . . . behavior of the minority group" (1990, 208), feminist criticisms of male language as domineering could not, under any ordinary interpretation of these terms, be taken to constitute an application of "the ethnocentric standards of the majority group to the . . . behavior of the minority group" (ibid.). This does not mean that I believe that all feminist scholarship to point an accusing finger at men is good scholarship. Some is and some isn't, and one must read it to make the distinction.

Maltz and Borker argue that their theory (to be discussed in Chapter Five) is superior to the dominance theory, among others, because it is capable of making important connections. They say:

> The power of our approach lies in its ability to suggest new explanations of previous findings on cross-sex communication while linking these findings to a wide range of other fields, including the study of language acquisition, of play, of friendship, of storytelling, of cross-cultural miscommunication, and of discourse analysis. (1982, 214)

Yet it is not clear that the male dominance theory is incapable of making such connections, for a context of sexist oppression will have obvious implications for language acquisition, play, friendship, and storytelling, for example.

Although I would agree that the male dominance theory is not capable of explaining the entire spectrum of documented gender differences in language, I am loathe to abandon it entirely; I believe there are some facets of language that cannot be accounted for by any other explanation. Furthermore, some of those aspects of our experience which can only be accounted for by a notion of outright oppression are of primary importance.

The research on classroom dynamics is one such case: French and French, for example, claim that their research on British primary school classrooms supports a description of male dominance. They describe one particular lesson, "which comprised 66 pupil turns at interactions, [and] 50 of these were produced by boys who numbered less than half the class" (1984a, 61). They add that "a good many of these turns were not 'spontaneously' allocated to boy pupils by the teacher, but achieved through interactional techniques designed to gain the teacher's attention" (ibid.). Dale Spender documented many situations in which teachers, striving to overcome traditional favouring of male students, self-consciously set out to balance the amount of time and attention they gave to the girls and the boys in their classrooms. After some time spent trying to rectify the imbalance, many of the teachers' own analyses of the situation was that they had inadvertently gone overboard, that they had given more than their fair share of attention to the girls, with the unfortunate result that they had unfairly discriminated against the boys. Spender says that when the classroom interactions of such teachers were videotaped, it was "often found that over two thirds of their time was spent with the boys who comprised less than half the class" (1982, 54). In other words, in a situation where the boys should have received somewhat less than half the teacher's attention, they were perceived as having been shortchanged when they received two-thirds of such attention.

Furthermore, when teachers cease to devote the traditional share of attention to male students, these students become obstreperous in class, requiring the teacher to devote the bulk of her attention to them in order to maintain control in the classroom (Cline and Spender 1987, 58; Spender 1982, 54, 56-58). This seems to suggest that males feel they have a right to what they have been traditionally allotted, and that they feel themselves shortchanged with anything less. This example strongly supports the male dominance theory.

It is, unfortunately, easy to list other examples explicable by the dominance theory. Consider these: (1) A school board is seeking to fill a principal's position. Because the school in question contains a number of male teachers, the board members assume that the principal should be male—it isn't right to make men work under women. (2) Medical research dollars are diverted by far greater proportions into research on traditional male diseases—such as heart ailments— than traditional female diseases—such as breast cancer. (3) Teaching hospitals perform far higher proportions of optional surgery on female than on male patients, suggesting that it is more acceptable to use women as learning tools or guinea pigs than men. (4) Foreign agricultural aid to developing nations is almost entirely directed to male agricultural workers, even though the vast bulk of the agricultural labour is in fact performed by women. (5) Women doing exactly the same work as men are paid less for doing it. (6) Readers for the primary years are selected on the basis of their containing a preponderance of main male characters, as little boys prefer these books. (7) In a classroom in which there are not enough computers for every student, males dominate at the computer terminals. (8) Software programs selected for use in classrooms feature video games that are contest-oriented and filled with mock violence; it is known that boys enjoy and learn well in this competitive context while girls neither enjoy nor learn well in this context. (9) Eighty percent of a school's sports budget is spent on male sports and only 20 percent on female sports; every year some closet feminist points out the inequity of this situation, but every year the feminist is outvoted by the majority, who feel it is self-evident that male sports are more important than female sports.

These examples are all particularly distressing exactly because the dominance theory seems to explain them so well. It is, of course, not the only theory capable of explaining them. I will suggest later that it might in some contexts be quite reasonable to call upon one of the other major theories. In fact, I would argue further that these theories are not mutually exclusive, but may operate in concert. The examples are all, however, instances for which the dominance theory appears to be a reasonable explanatory candidate and it is in that sense that I turn to them now. We tend, at this time, to be embarrassed to admit that we approve of male dominance; the fact that this is so is itself an indication of significant progress. Just over a hundred years ago (1896), Lewis Carroll argued that in considering the admission of women to the university, the authorities ought not lose sight of the *real* goal of the university—namely, the provision of an education to young men. Carroll's actual words were:

In the bewildering multiplicity of petty side issues, with which the question of granting university degrees to women, has been overlaid, there is some danger that Members of Congregation may lose sight of the really important issues involved. . . .

One of the chief functions, if not *the* chief function, of our universities, is to prepare young men. (Carroll 1991, 1068, author's emphasis)

It is possible to unconsciously endorse male dominance; that is, male dominance is not necessarily to be identified with male conspiracy, although it may be. Consider the school board example that I raised earlier, where board members are seeking to hire a principal for a school that has some male (as well as female) teachers. They plan to hire a man for the job because there are some male teachers on staff. The board members do not necessarily believe that men ought to rule the world and that women should always play roles subordinate to men. They *may* be consciously attempting to perpetuate this "male plot," but they need not be. They may simply hold relatively unexamined views about where the reins of power are appropriately held, such that whenever there is a choice, they will prefer the allocation of power to males over females. They may, like most of us, have grown familiar with a world in which males are valued and females devalued; hence they unconsciously replicate a system in which privilege and power are disproportionately directed towards males. In other words, they may have grown accustomed to a *skewed* context, which is subsequently perceived as the norm against which current practices are evaluated. If, for example, we attended schools in which boys received nine tenths of the teacher's time and attention, then a context in which they received *only* two thirds could very well be perceived as a situation is which the boys were shortchanged. When awareness has been raised, however, and the data make it clear that it is girls who are receiving less than equitable treatment, those who still persist in directing more time and energy to boys may now be numbered among those who are intentionally promulgating a male supremacist plot.

One might think that the day of male dominance went out with Lewis Carroll, if not with the dinosaurs, but this is unfortunately not the case. Contemporary biological determinists and many fundamental religious adherents continue to propound such a position. Not all men hold such views, of course, nor do men exhaust the numbers of those who hold such views. "Real Women" continue to advocate philosophies of male supremacy.

One *could* advance a theory of *female* dominance, although this would seem to fly in the face of any real-world empirical evidence. Sometimes scholars appeal to Amazonian societies in their attempts to provide examples of female dominance. Although there is some anthropological evidence that, prior to the era of European invasion, certain North American Native societies were matriarchal, the gendered organization of these societies appears not to have survived colonialism.

Others have argued a somewhat different version of the female dominance hypothesis, i.e., they have advanced some form or other of "the hand that rocks the cradle rules the world" hypothesis. Such people appear to believe that "real" power lies in the apparent eschewing of power, and that the "real" decisions are those made behind the scenes rather than in the spotlight of public attention. Although there may be some truth to this claim, as a political ideology we must be very suspicious of it. For when the hand that rocks the cradle has asked for fair financial recompense, it has all too frequently been slapped. And when people have put themselves forward from behind the scenes into the spotlight, they have frequently been derided. One of the most extreme instances of this was the televised coverage of John Crosbie's reference to Sheila Copps as a "slut" during a sitting of the Canadian parliament. The account of power that identifies "real" power with the apparent eschewing of power is not particularly persuasive, although it is an account that might well be used to fob off a yoke of bondage on the unsuspecting and allow those who secure the shackles in place a sense of self-righteousness.

Male dominance works well for the moral argument I wish to make. I believe that it is in part because it works *so well* with the moral argument that many theorists have been led to reject an account of language or any other data which is based on a hypothesis of male dominance. There is a reluctance on the part of people who analyze linguistic and other social data to blame men for the oppression that has characterized women's lot. This is understandable. It is distasteful to blame people, and being the object of blame may feel even less acceptable. But if the issue is a moral one, then however distasteful positing or accepting blame may be, it is nonetheless a crucial part of the analysis. In such circumstances, the refusal to engage in "blame-talk" is always suspect. There may be good reasons for particular instances of refusal to engage in "blame-talk"—but if blaming simply means assigning moral responsibility where it belongs and holding people to account for failing to meet their responsibilities, then blaming is a crucial part of any moral analysis. When people persistently neglect to locate moral responsibility, we must ask why. Are they concerned about offending people, in particular, offending men? Do they fear their scholarship will be dismissed as man-hating? Do they think that laying blame in this way will diminish the chances of editorial boards and granting agencies approving their work? Do they worry that their reputation with students and colleagues will suffer? Each of these concerns is realistic, but far from trivializing the import of the male dominance theory, goes a long way towards establishing the truth of the theory. History has provided us with a glut of instances of moral atrocities committed under the auspices of the dominance of one social group over others. The enslavement of Black people, the internment of Japanese Canadian citizens during the Second World War, the Jewish Holocaust, and the European and West Indian witchhunts are all chilling examples of the extreme consequences of dominance. The mistreatment of children is another instance of what happens when we invoke dominance theory, although it must be admitted that the case of children is not *identical* to the cases cited above, insofar as children are different from adults in certain significant respects.

Although there are exceptions (I have cited proponents of biological determinism and members of some fundamentalist religious groups as examples earlier), the "natural" dominance of one group over another will not as often be called upon today as in former times to *justify* the differential allocation of power and privileges. I believe this is because we have learned that while dominance may explain power differentials, it does not justify them. Nevertheless, I believe, as I have argued earlier in this chapter, that male dominance still serves to *explain* many of the observed features of our language as well as other aspects of our society. Any attempt at moral accounting will need to focus on justification rather than explanation—white patriarchy may have explained the enslavement of Black peoples, but it never justified slavery.

In fact, moral codes will have to be relied upon most strongly in those instances where dominance is the most exaggerated. If two individuals both in need of a limited resource are similarly situated with regard to status, personal finances, and professional categorization, we are less likely to feel a sharp necessity for appealing to basic concepts of fairness than in those instances where status, finances, and professional categorization are strongly skewed in favour of one individual. In this second case we worry (aptly) that the individual with more money, higher status, and a more prestigious profession is likely to receive better treatment, and we feel compelled to appeal to *moral* precepts to ensure that the weaker party is not cheated in the distribution of resources.

By and large, dominance theory is no longer regarded as a strong contender in explaining gender patterns in language. The sex roles socialization theory is regarded as a much stronger contender by many theorists, and I turn my attention to that theory now.

Chapter Three

The Sex Roles Socialization Theory of Gender and Language

Pamela Fishman provides a very clear characterization of this theory, although it is a theory which she herself rejects. She says,

> Discussions of the way women act, including the way they talk, often rely on some notion of a female "personality." Usually, socialization is used to explain this personality. Women are seen as more insecure, dependent and emotional than men because of the way that they are raised. (Fishman 1980, 127)

Among those whose writing on the topic of gender and language appears to fit fairly smoothly into the socialization theory[1] are Robin Lakoff (1976), Philip Smith (1980), Judy Pearson (1985, 44), and Deborah Tannen (1990). Lakoff refers specifically to a "socialization process" (1976, 5) which keeps a female linguistically "in line, in her place" (ibid.). Tannen claims that "boys and girls grow up in what are essentially different cultures" (1990, 18).

Language patterns into which women are most frequently seen as having been socialized include hesitance, insecurity, indirectness,

---

The note to this chapter is on p. 58.

weakness, deviousness, politeness, and hypercorrectness, which is itself sometimes appealed to as an indication of a feeling of inferiority with one's own way of speaking (Lakoff 1976, 10, 15, 17-19; Pearson 1985, 185-187; Sankoff 1980, 14; Smith 1985, 55,78). Men, on the other hand, are perceived as having been socialized into strong, dominant, forceful, and direct ways of talking. In an account consistent with that of socialization theory, French and French perceive gender differences in speech as part of a display of one's gender identity. They claim that

> some aspects of women's and men's usage may operate simply to display gender identity. . . . [For example,] men used high level tones as their neutral, or unmarked, contour on statements, whereas women's neutral contour was a rise. There is no functional significance attaching to this beyond the display of gender identity, however; . . . It is quite possible that women's frequent use of, for example, qualifiers . . . has little to do with the meanings 'hesitant' or 'tentative' . . . but serves simply to mark out their speech as 'female speech'. (1984a, 58)

Peter Trudgill explains the social difference between men and women by pointing to the fact that "society lays down different social roles for them and expects different behaviour patterns from them. Language simply reflects this social fact" (1974, 94). Pat Kincaid's account of spousal abuse in Ontario is based almost totally on a socialization theory. She claims that if the abusive husband

> has been brought up to believe that his wife should cook and clean for him and she is not performing those tasks to his satisfaction, what he believes should be happening is, in fact, not happening. . . . The viewing of and reacting to the situation will be highly dependent on his own sex role socialization and on what he has learned about the use of violence and its relationship with the achievement of what he believes are desirable goals. (Kincaid 1982, 157)

It is important first to be clear that theories of male dominance and sex role socialization are not necessarily mutually exclusive. In fact, they may be mutually sustaining. Some scholars perceive a strong link between sex role socialization and male dominance; Cline and Spender (1987, 42-65) discuss their perception of this link in a paper appropriately titled "Schooling for Subordination." Researchers such as Cline and Spender thus rely on male dominance as the *basic* explanation of the data, where socialization itself is part of the data explained by male dominance. Dale Spender perceives schools as performing an important part of the socialization process for the patriarchy. Although presenting themselves as meritocracies, in reality schools judge males as having more intellectual ability than females because males "are the ones who decide what constitutes ability" (1982, 88); those in power ensure the perpetuation of the system by carefully choosing "their successors in their own image" (ibid., 91). Furthermore, views that threaten this skewed arrangement are judged to be radical and subversive: "While almost the entire curriculum is about men, the inclusion of a few women can be perceived as political and subversive" (ibid., 100).

Esther Greif's account of interruption patterns also involves a combination of the socialization thesis and the male dominance thesis. She says,

> Males are typically socialized to be dominant and to take charge of situations. Therefore fathers may demonstrate their high status and show their children who is in charge by controlling the conversations with their children, and interrupting and speaking simultaneously are two ways of doing this. (1980, 257)

Greif believes that children learn what behaviour is considered appropriate for them both from the way adults treat them and by modelling the behaviour of same-sex adults. From both of these sources, they learn that "males and females behave differently, and that males are more dominant" (ibid.).

Other researchers see the link as more tangential, focusing on the socialization, but deemphasizing any link with male dominance, and rejecting in particular any notion that socialization practices have been *intentionally* designed in such a way as to perpetuate and exacerbate the oppression of females. Those who hold this form of the socialization view are likely, therefore, to see the dissemination of information and education as a large part of the solution to the problem. If males are not intentionally grabbing power, but simply behaving in ways that disadvantage females as a consequence of the way they are socialized, then awareness of these patterns would seem an almost sufficient condition to altering them. In her discussion of the different ways in which women and men listen, Melanie Booth-Butterfield exemplifies this position. She says,

> there are very few *innate* differences in the listening ability of males and females. The diversity develops from indirect sex role socialization, that

is, the mistake of teaching roles thought to be appropriate for each sex rather than teaching skills equally to both genders. . . .

These learned patterns can be modified with education and training programs. Merely causing and increasing awareness of listening habits may be enough for some people. For example, if people learn that men are more likely to interrupt a female colleague, that information may be enough to change the tendency. Most listening habits are not conscious and, when brought to consciousness, can then be improved. (Booth-Butterfield 1984, 41, author's emphasis)

Those who adhere to the socialization theory but *deemphasize* any link with male dominance are also likely to see males and females as equally victimized by the roles into which they are cast, and may argue for androgynous roles as the solution to the problem. Mary Ritchie Key (1975), for example, holds such a view. In fact, Key claims that although the linguistic examples that she cites may suggest that

the language problem is worse for females, this is not the whole picture. Men's lives have been shortened by burdens too great for them to bear alone. The perpetual struggle has been harder on men than on women who have received their benefits and pensions, and now 'enjoy' them alone. (1975, 145)

Many theorists, such as the biological determinist Steven Goldberg (1977, 203-204), have argued for the importance of socializing females into those roles that the patriarchy deems appropriate for them. Goldberg claims that if females fail to aspire to and fail to excel at those roles for which nature has rendered them well equipped, and if they insist on competing with males on male turf, then they will lose those benefits they are now allocated and gain nothing in return. In other words, a patriarchal world in which male dominance is a fact will be a kinder world if it promotes socialization patterns that make females more satisfied with and better at the subservient roles allocated to them (ibid.).

The influence may also work in the other direction. If generations of girls and women are socialized to be subservient and submissive, this will help to shore up the bastions of male dominance. Fishman makes this point when she says that "Socialization is seen as the means by which male-female power differences are internalized and translated into behaviour producing properly dominant men and submissive women" (Fishman 1980, 127). It is this observation which has led many feminists to look to radically altered socialization patterns as a means of establishing a chink in the armour of patriarchy, leading some to argue that the solution lay in the direction of socializing females into the same patterns that had been traditionally reserved for males.

There are, in fact, many possible responses to our current system of socialized sex roles, some of which involve retaining and some of which involve abandoning *sex* roles, although none involve the abandonment of *roles per se*. The position that sex roles ought to be rigidly retained has enjoyed significant historical endorsement, although its contemporary support is waning. According to some of the major proponents of this position, while both roles as they have been historically defined are necessary, and each complements the other, role switching should not be encouraged. Rousseau argued for this position (1911, 321, 324, 335), as have two of his contemporary "kindred spirits," Goldberg (1977) and Bettelheim (1984).

One could also argue a reformist position, although I have not seen this argument made in the context of retaining sex roles. In other words, one could argue simply for a redefinition of the current *sex roles*, while still insisting that the male/female roles be strictly differentiated. On the other hand, one could imagine many possible reformist positions—for example, a multiplicity rather than a duality of roles, with five or ten or even more roles corresponding to the level of estrogen (or testosterone) in one's system. One could imagine the attribution of roles to a particular individual being fluid, rather than fixed forever at the moment of one's birth on the basis of external genitalia. Interestingly, the gender change literature suggests that even where there is sufficient ambiguity in the appearance of the external genitalia to render an attribution of one role or the other at best uncertain, that attribution has still been made, and *that decision* has frequently been sufficient to determine long-term role and sex identification, even when ultimately contradicted by the emergence of physiological data.

Money and Ehrhardt, for example, argue that the impact of the early socialization up till the initial age of language acquisition (approximately eighteen months) is so powerful that any sex reassignment after that time, even if based on the emergence of physiological data, will prove difficult if not impossible (1972, 176-179). Much the same point is made by Money and Tucker, who state that "whatever the status of your chromosomes, hormones, sex organs, and individuality, their directional push was no match for social pressures when it came to differentiating your gender identity" (1975, 87). Money and Tucker also speak of the importance of male/female pronouns in establishing a child's gender identity (ibid.); they refer to the first eighteen months of life as a relatively plastic period for gender identity formation (ibid., 91), but perceive that "the gender identity gate locks tight once it closes" (ibid., 98).

One *could* imagine, as Ursula LeGuin did in *The Left Hand of Darkness* (1969, 81-87), that sex roles and even sex identity were never permanently ascribed, but that an individual slipped in and out of the available sex roles according to hormonal balance, or mood, or choice, or any other imaginable criterion. As a society, we are a long way from any such fluid depiction of sex roles. We refuse to admit any exceptions to our strictly binary classification of sex identity, even though the hormonal, chromosomal, and even genital evidence *against* a strictly binary classification is overwhelming; we insist on classifying everyone as one or the other, with the result that there is a huge demand for the sorts of surgery that will restructure bodies so that they appear to conform to one or other of the two choices available. Perhaps because heterosexuality is perceived as a central component of *each* of these sex identities, we are equally tunnel-visioned about sexual preference, preferring to label a full 10 percent of the world's population sexually deviant rather than expanding our binary classification.

A quite different set of responses to our currently identified sex roles involves arguing that although roles may be appropriate, the defining of and socialization into these roles according to sex is inappropriate. The third major theory attempting to account for the purported gender patterns in language (which I shall discuss in the following chapter), the appropriate registers theory, basically adopts the position that looking only to gender as an explanation of these speech patterns results in far too narrow a perspective. Many factors inform how people speak, and gender is only one of these factors. Supporters of this theory would urge that much of our speech and other behaviour emerges from our roles *rather than* our sex. For example, people who nurture children, whether female or male, are likely to exhibit a particular set of linguistic and other characteristics.

A recommendation to abandon *sex* roles could take any of several possible forms. One, which I have referred to briefly above, is that the male role, because it is much more likely to lead to success and satisfaction, ought to be promoted; however, instead of being promoted only for males, it ought to be promoted for females too, and little girls as well as little boys should be taught the skills required to succeed in the traditionally identified male role. Feminists who urged assertiveness training for girls and women frequently endorsed this position.

Others have argued an androgynous position, claiming that we ought to select the best features of the female and male socialization patterns and initiate all people into these preferred features. Key is one of the proponents of this position, describing the ideal androgynous language as a language that

> will be complementary rather than divisive. It will find balance and harmony in its completeness. It will establish an equilibrium in its unity rather than invidious separation. It will combine the abstract with the concrete; feeling with logic, tenderness with strength; force with graciousness. It will be a balanced tension—supporting rather than opposing. It will be exuberant and vibrant, leaving out the weak and the brutal. It will not tolerate the simpering, helpless, bitchy sweetness of the "feminine" language. Nor will it tolerate the overwhelming smash of the opinionated and blustering "masculine" language. It will move away from the cruel distinctions that have wounded both male and female human beings. (1975, 147)

Philip Smith conducted research which indicated that androgynous speakers were perceived to be both more competent and more attractive or likeable than high masculine style or high feminine style speakers (1980, 124-125). The feminine woman was rated second to the androgynous speaker for competence, and the feminine man rated the least competent of all (ibid., 125). These results are fascinating, but plagued by the sort of inconsistency that characterizes much of the writing on androgyny. For if the androgynous personality is, in fact, a combination of both high masculine and high feminine attributes, it is difficult to see how such a personality could exist, save on a schizophrenic level, when it is expected to incorporate, for example, the masculine quality, "hides emotions" (ibid., 123), together with the feminine qualities "expressive of emotions" (ibid.) and "emotional" (ibid.). (For a critique of the concept of androgyny, see Morgan 1982; Morgan and Ayim 1984.)

Still others have urged that it is the female roles, with their focus on nurturance and caring, that are life-sustaining and community oriented, while the male roles, with their focus on aggression and dominance, are life-threatening and individual oriented. Trudgill, for example, claims that "men's and women's speech . . . is not only dif-

ferent: women's speech is also (socially) 'better' than men's speech"
(1974, 94). Many of the claims that I will make in Chapters Five and
Six of this book correspond to this particular version of the *sex* roles
abandonment position. That is, I will argue that the male sex role, as
it has been traditionally defined, is not generalizable without contradiction. One could not have a cohesive society if each individual's primary motivation was to dominate others, to achieve the highest
rungs of the hierarchy ladder, just as one cannot have a conversation
if all parties are strictly interested in having their own say and are
unwilling to listen to or offer linguistic support to other participants.
The traditionally defined female sex role, described in terms of nurturing and supporting others, is, I will argue, generalizable without contradiction. That is, it is perfectly logical to imagine a society in which
nurturance and support are forthcoming from all of society's members.
Hence I will argue that it is the female identified roles that ought to be
taught to everyone, and that ought to be consistently rewarded. A huge
part of the problem, from my perspective, is that as a society, we continue to reward most generously those very roles which, if adopted by
everyone, are guaranteed to destroy the social structure.

One could also argue that while traditional roles may have served
society well at a former phase in our development, we have now out-
grown these roles and should abandon socialization practices that
promote them. We are told by countless scholars that in a world
populated by large predators, it was male aggression that saved the
species and the day. The aggressive males not only survived themselves, to pass on their aggressive dispositions to the next generation,
but they also protected the females and the young who, shorn of the
benefit of such male protection, would have been in imminent danger
of extermination. It is always difficult to unravel these accounts from
assumptions of male chivalry which seem to colour many of the
scholarly theories that attempted to justify male dominance and male
aggression in the name of survival of the species. In spite of my scepticism concerning the scholarly merit of these theories, I do concede
that there could have been a time in our history when hierarchical
jostling, pushing against others so that one could oneself be centre
front, may have had survival payoff for the community as a whole. If
there ever was such a period in history when aggression, dominance,
and hierarchical structures benefited far larger segments of society
than the particular individuals involved, that period is long gone,
however. For in the world we live in now, our survival is far more

closely calibrated to our ability to listen carefully to other people, to understand them, and to coexist peacefully with them. One could argue that it is not only socialization into the traditional *sex* roles which is seriously flawed, but that socialization into these roles even without any rigid adherence to sexual differentiation is a mistake; thus one might argue that we ought to be looking for new and superior roles to match a new and rapidly emerging society, rather than continuing to twist and pull at the old roles in a futile attempt to make them fit a radically different social design. To use a seamstress metaphor, such pulling and twisting goes against the grain of our social fabric, and is certain to result in a misshapen garment when it is constructed.

Regardless of the many possible views that one could hold concerning socialization into sex roles, it is patently obvious that we live in a society which by and large endorses rather than rejects roles defined according to sex, and which punishes those who deviate from the roles considered appropriate to their sex. There is, of course, a set of roles that lies outside those which are sex-defined and which may consequently be adopted by anyone; whether or not a particular role belongs to the female-coded set, the male-coded set, or this "other" set will vary from one historical era to another and from one culture to another. The midwife role, for example, as the word itself suggests, was and continues to be exclusively female identified; it is a role that has virtually disappeared from many cultures, but in those where it does exist, it remains female identified. The obstetrician role, however, was for a long period strictly male-defined, as women were not allowed to attend the educational institutions that bestowed the title. Now, in most areas of the world, the obstetrician role may be occupied by females as well as males, although many would argue that it is still essentially a male role, and that those women who do adopt it do so on male terms. In contrast to the opening up of the obstetrician role to include females, the midwife role, which is making a somewhat limited comeback, remains linked exclusively to females. One cannot help but wonder whether this is a consequence of the continued perception of the role as essentially female identified and hence beneath the professional aspirations of males.

The same point as that concerning the obstetrician role has been made about academia in general—namely, that while females are no longer precluded from participating, they are expected to accept the criteria and aspire to the standards of excellence that have been pre-

scribed by males and for males. The language of the classroom in secondary schools, colleges, and universities is the language of hierarchy,
of dominance, of debate, not the language of intimacy; in other
words, the classroom language past the primary years is the language
that little boys use when they play together and is almost totally alien
to the language that little girls use in their chosen games. (See Sachs
1987 and Gleason 1987 for a discussion of these differences in the
talk and play of girls and boys.) Indeed the school system in general,
not just in its language, but in its grading system as well, promotes
hierarchical structures. The struggle of the British Columbia elementary school system to remove all forms of competitive grading of its
students and the outrage with which this has been greeted in many
quarters of the country give us some sense of the primacy that we
attach to competition and hierarchical evaluation in the educational
system. It is interesting to think about alternatives. Could we, for
example, establish a set of necessary and sufficient conditions for
completing grade twelve history, or passing first year university introductory psychology, or gaining admission to a faculty of education,
such that people either satisfy the set of conditions, or they don't—in
other words, they either pass or fail. For those worried about lowering
standards, this is by no means a necessary consequence, for the conditions could be made as stringent as desired or required. Admission
criteria to a faculty could also be made very stringent, and if there
were still more applicants who met the conditions than could be
admitted, then perhaps a lottery would be as fair a mechanism as any
for making final selections.

I do believe that in certain respects, there has been some opening
up of socialization patterns and sex roles compared to former times.
Women may now choose to be physicians and lawyers, and my experience suggests that men are choosing to participate in the nurturing
of young children to a greater extent than in the past. But even so, sex
roles and the corresponding socialization patterns continue to exert
an iron grip over our choices and our lives. Nor is it the case that
males universally benefit from this fact. Those males who don't fit
smoothly into prescribed male sex roles, particularly young and adolescent males who are not athletically inclined, suffer enormously
from the imposition of those sex role standards that they are expected
to live up to. Some time ago while walking through a large shopping
mall, I encountered two "oddities"; one was a man with only one ear
and the other was a man sitting on a bench knitting. I would be hard

pressed to say which of the two received more stares or which generated more expressions of shocked amazement from the passersby.

It is important to be clear that not all men buy into the prescribed male sex role, just as many women refuse to participate in the prescribed female sex role. As a society, we do make it difficult for people to reject their "appropriate" roles, however. One wonders what prompted the man I referred to earlier to engage in a very public place in such a stereotypically female-defined activity as knitting. Was he attempting, perhaps, to challenge and erode the stereotypes? If so, then I would judge from the expressions on the faces of people who passed by, to use a knitting metaphor, that he had his work cast on for him!

How many young boys do we find taking ballet or figure skating lessons? How many young girls do we find signing up for junior league hockey teams, even in those cases where girls are "permitted" to play on the teams? These are rhetorical questions, for the answers are obvious. What is less obvious is why these stereotypically sex-defined boundaries have persisted over the years.

I have a young friend (now fourteen) who lives in a small community outside London, Ontario. He is an avid hockey player, and a fairly skilled one, who plays on the local hockey team. This is not surprising, as there is essentially no other form of organized winter recreation for the children; hockey constitutes a large part of these children's lives, and many of them attend hockey school in the summer. There are, of course, no girls on the team. In the games that I have watched, the girls sit on the wooden benches in the cold arena beside their parents and other younger siblings, cheering their brothers on.

This is in perfect conformity with the historically prescribed socialization patterns, insofar as the boys are engaged in a very active sport, and the girls are engaged in supportive behaviour. (See, for example, Sachs 1987 and Gleason 1987, who suggest that girls' play and language respectively, in contrast to the boys' play and language, involve high levels of supportiveness and solidarity.) It may seem as though I am making a mountain out of nothing here, and that I am reading villainy into something as innocent as child's play. I think not, however, and I would worry much less about this example were it not for at least three accompanying circumstances.

First, the "cheering on" that is engaged in by the parents is morally troubling, to say the least. I have heard boys as young as six or

seven urged to "go for," "get," or "kill" players on the opposing team
till the parents were too hoarse to holler any further "encouragement." I realize that the parents do not literally want their little sons
to murder the competing players, but I am not naive enough to
believe that this is merely a manner of speaking or that it is good
clean fun which has nothing to do with real aggression. My young
friend of whom I spoke earlier has had his collarbone broken twice
while playing hockey, for example. For all that it may be our national
sport, hockey is a violent aggressive game, and we should think twice
before we attempt to initiate a whole generation of little boys into it.
This "support" of the parents for their young sons reminded me
uncomfortably of a news coverage of a group of young American
males receiving military training for combat in the Gulf War. Hundreds of these soldiers-in-training filled the television screen, and as
they practised their manoeuvres, they screamed the words, "Kill! Kill!
Kill!" One worries about the safety of living in a society that will reab-
sorb these people into its midst when they have retired from the official war zone.

Second, the boys who are not skilled are the butt of a range of
responses that extend from unpleasantness to outright cruelty. On
driving past a newly constructed Olympic-sized swimming pool in
London, Ontario, a very pleasant cab driver once initiated a conversation with me about sports. He remarked that he had two children,
one a baby whom his wife took to the pool occasionally for "kin-
derswim" sessions, and the other an eight-year-old son, whom the
father had decided ought to be a professional hockey player. This man
spoke kindly of his son, and the reasons he gave for wanting his son
to be a hockey player all had to do with his son's own happiness and
success; they were the kinds of reasons one would attribute to a concerned and caring parent. The father explained to me that he himself
might have made it into professional hockey if only he "hadn't been
so stupid as to smoke," and that he was going to see to it that his son
had a real chance to earn the kind of salary and bask in the kind of
respect that Wayne Gretzky enjoyed. "A lot better life than being a
cab driver," he assured me. I couldn't help but wonder how many of
those parents shouting themselves hoarse on the wooden benches had
similar dreams of glory for their sons, how many of them saw little
Wayne Gretzkys in the making if only they got enough "encouragement." I think, in fact, that this vision loomed so large it blocked out
the more troubling picture of many little boys who didn't want to play

hockey, who were not aggressive, who were not athletic, and who might have much preferred to take figure skating or ballet lessons instead, if society permitted.

But society does *not* permit. My experience of being a spectator at even a few hockey games made this abundantly clear. Girls' things were not for boys. To emphasize this, when parents shouted out "corrective" words to boys who "goofed" on the ice, these words were frequently couched in the most insulting language available for males—language that likened them to females. Parents would frequently shout, "Your sister could play better than that," "You're no better than a bunch of girls," or a simple, succinct "sissy." So I worry, not only for a generation of girls, who are held up as that to which boys could degenerate if they don't take heed, but also for a generation of boys who are pushed into an aggressive, and often violent and dangerous competition, which many of them don't enjoy and which by definition most of them can't win. Goldberg claims that the inability of most girls to win at boys' games and boys' competitions is a reason for maintaining the two separate streams of sex role socialization (1977, 202-204); what he neglects to add, however, is that most boys cannot win these games and competitions either, because they are *defined* to ensure precisely that. My worry extends beyond females and males specifically to the entire society, approximately half of whose members have been socialized into violent and aggressive forms of "sport" and "entertainment."

Third, the hockey example concerns me, not because the little girls are supporting their brothers, which I think is a good thing and something to be encouraged, but because it is simply one more example of unidirectional, non-reciprocal support. Female cheerleaders at male sports events is another example. Auxiliary women's groups that perform support functions for male groups is another. The institution of co-ed classrooms for the purpose of "civilizing the boys," as I have heard one chairperson of a secondary school mathematics department express it, is another. Mixed-sex "conversations" in which female participants are judged by the males to be good conversationalists insofar as they encourage the males to talk about themselves is another.

If sex roles were immutable, there could obviously be no moral argument against these roles as they are currently defined and no alternative to socialization practices that endorsed such roles. But history makes it very clear that the roles have in fact evolved considerably, thereby demonstrating that they are mutable, and that the weight of moral pressure can legitimately be brought to bear on them. Our highly sex-defined socialization practices are in great need of change. The female role of support and nurturance needs to be rendered reciprocal, such that the caretakers are also cared for; otherwise the females who engage in these roles are not moral agents, but little better than cleverly socialized servants, and unpaid ones at that. The male role has a different shortcoming, namely, it *cannot* be generalized, at least without risk of considerable dissatisfaction if not disaster. Part of the nature of a hierarchy is that only a few reach the top, so for everyone to devote their lives struggling to reach the apex is to guarantee a few winners and many more failures.

While it is clear that both sets of roles are in need of change, this is much easier said than done. As a parent who has tried to resist sex-role stereotyping in such simple things as selecting toys and clothing for my children, I have learned the hard lesson of the power of these stereotypes. An individual is virtually powerless against them. I have shared these tales of woe with many other parents who have had similar experiences and similar failures. The Barbie Doll industry and the manufacturers of little boys' war toys perceive that they have much to lose by any challenge to current socialization practices. Schools could make a difference more easily because they operate in a context in which peer pressure, that critical element in many young children's choices, can be influenced.

The socialization theory, while more popular with current researchers than the male dominance theory as an explanation of the facts of gender and language, is not as strongly endorsed as the appropriate registers theory; I turn now to the next chapter and a discussion of the appropriate registers theory.

Note

1 In this and the remaining chapters, I shall use the terms "sex roles socialization theory," "sex roles theory," and "socialization theory" as though they were interchangeable.

Chapter Four

The Appropriate Registers Theory of Gender and Language

U nlike the male dominance theory and the socialization theory, which presuppose *that* there are gender differences in language, the appropriate registers theory does not necessarily make this assumption. According to this theory, if we believe that sex alone accounts for observed differences in language patterns, our perspective is far too narrow and our account likely to distort the reality. The body of literature critical of the gender-based speech differences claims, such as those postulated by Lakoff (1975), has paved the way to the appropriate registers theory. (See, for example, Schultz, Briere, and Sandler 1984, 334.) Some of the proponents of this theory are Fishman (1980), Jose, Crosby, and Wong-McCarthy (1980), Leet-Pellegrini (1980), Maltz and Borker (1982), Pedersen (1980), and Tannen (1990). Pamela Fishman suggests that we look to the situation itself for an explanation of the language behaviour before we resort to explaining the behaviour in terms of how the speaker was socialized. Fishman believes that many features of female speech, including the far more frequent use of questions as well as the phrase "you know," are used by women as attempts to solve the problem of carrying on a conversation when they are receiving no help from their male conversational partners (1980, 128, 129, 131).

Maltz and Borker describe male-female language differences as cultural. They say:

> We place the stress not on psychological differences or power differentials, although these may make some contribution, but rather on a notion of cultural differences between men and women in their conceptions of friendly conversation, their rules for engaging in it, and, probably most important, their rules for interpreting it. (1982, 199-200)

Tannen also emphasizes what she describes as the different cultures in which girls and boys grow up and she identifies understanding as the most important requirement in resolving the problems engendered by the constant proximity of members from these two radically different cultures (1990, 17-18).

Just as the socialization theory is not independent of the male dominance theory, so the appropriate registers theory is not independent of either the male dominance or the socialization theory, and hence it is not surprising that several names occur on my lists as proponents of more than one of these theories. If oppression, accompanied by limited access to power, defines one of the "appropriate" contexts, the link to male dominance is self-evident—Kramarae's research suggests that there is indeed such a connection. She says, "The strategy framework encourages us to look at women's and men's verbal interaction as indications of and responses to a differential distribution of power" (1981, 153). The word "appropriate" is itself somewhat worrisome—when we say that language in a certain context is appropriate, we must be careful to ask, "Appropriate for whom?" Furthermore, after assuming sole responsibility for the interactional aspects of a conversation for a long enough time, the result may be the same as though one had been socialized into an affiliative personality. Women may well come to feel "insecure and hesitant in such conversations" (Fishman 1980, 131). Donald MacKay also admonishes us to take people's interpretive frameworks into account when we ask ourselves how language influences thought. His research shows that "different evaluative frameworks can give completely opposite results" (1980a, 95). Fox claims that "conclusions about the relationship between gender, reading, and writing need to be situationally specific, for neither men's language nor women's language is stable across contexts" (1990, 51). Similarly, Aries claims that gender differences in speech style are influenced by the outside culture, the status, the social role, and the social opportunities of the speakers (1987, 158).

Sex is perceived as one factor only, and sometimes not a particularly important factor, in explaining individual differences in speech styles. Philips summarizes this theory clearly when she says that

> gender differences in language form derive from differences in speech roles and speech genres, which in turn are related to gender role differences in activities, with no awareness of those linguistic differences or association of those differences with the activity itself rather than with the gender role. (1987, 25)

The differences may extend beyond how people speak to include what they understand words to mean. Donald MacKay's research, for example, showed that men and women had different interpretations of the meaning of the pseudo-generic "he" (to be discussed in more detail in Chapter Seven), and also that those sympathetic to and those unsympathetic to the women's movement had different understandings of the term (MacKay 1980a, 91-94).

Whereas the socialization theory attributes the language differences to a general sexual bifurcation which pressures all of us to behave in ways that conform to our particular sex role, the appropriate registers theory is much more casual about the importance of our consciously striving to live up to sex-role expectations. Our sex is a determining factor in the roles we play, which in turn are a determining factor in our language styles, and supporters of the appropriate registers theory want us to stop glossing over this intermediary factor—the roles we play—for we do not simply move from sex to language style.

Many of the more current publications on gender and language criticize the writing that emerged in the sixties and seventies, because this writing assumed that gender was the single operant factor, and ignored all other categories. Tove Pedersen captures the spirit of this criticism:

> A study of language/communication and sex has to be a study of the relationship between characteristic features of verbal communication and sex as *one* important variable in the social context. . . . Only through analyses of actual situations is it possible to determine whether sex represents an important variable in any particular situation and whether sex *covaries* with other factors. (1980, 106, author's emphasis)

The author criticizes many of the writers on gender and language for oversimplifying (for example, making sex the *only* pertinent variable) and overgeneralizing (for example, designing research around situations that were "peculiar and atypical" (ibid.), and then generalizing from these observations to conclusions about ordinary language interactions). Elinor Ochs, for example, claims that much of the research on language acquisition paints a picture of mother-child interactions that is peculiar to white, middle-class society, and that seriously misrepresents the language learning milieu of the rest of the world (1983, 185).

Frequently the role or context in which the speaker operates is considered to be *more* important than sex in accounting for speech patterns. Thus those who spend much time nurturing young children would be expected to develop a certain style of speaking, or register. Gleason makes precisely this point in discussing Child Directed Speech (CDS). Gleason says that "CDS is clearly a separate style, or register. It appears in the speech of women who are not mothers, in the speech of fathers, and, indeed, in the speech of all speakers, child and adult, who are addressing young children" (1987, 191). Gleason believes that CDS is a critical factor in the emerging language of the child, and that its importance has been seriously underestimated as a result of the virtual unquestioning acceptance of Chomsky's thesis— a thesis which suggests that the quality of language heard by the child is of only trivial importance compared to the child's own Language Acquisition Device.

Those who spend their days scrambling to maintain their position at the top of the corporate ladder could be expected to develop a quite different register. The former group just happens by and large to be female and the latter group male, but it is the context itself and not the sex of the speaker that is the determining factor in the speech style which will be selected, according to this theory. Hence Maltz and Borker emphasize the consistency between women's speech styles and life styles, which focus on egalitarianism and affiliation, as well as the consistency between men's speech styles and life styles, which focus on competitiveness (1982, 205, 208). They liken the language differences between men and women to cultural differences (ibid., 199-200).

A wide range of research supports this particular account of gender differences in language. Research on courtroom language conducted by Erickson et al. indicated that generally speaking, individuals with low social power adopted the language features that are frequently identified as female, such as the frequent use of intensifiers, hedges, formal grammar, question intonation in declarative statements, and polite language (1978, 267-268); they claimed that according to their research, these features were in fact "more closely linked to social power and status than to . . . sex" (ibid., 268).

Not all research supports this point of view, however. The research of Fisher and Groce on doctor/patient talk, for example, indicates that "the voices of women patients are consistently stifled" (1990, 242) by male doctors. Furthermore, women patients

> are more likely to be heard if they do not upset the asymmetry in the medical relationship, if they insert information into a conversation controlled by doctors, if they accept their doctors' accounts, if they provide social [as opposed to medical] information, and/or if they offer excuses. (Ibid.)

Whenever female patients appeared to threaten the powerful position of the doctors by "presuming" to offer medical reasons of their own or challenging the doctors' accounts, their claims were very likely to be rejected. Male patients fared better. They were less than half as likely to have these same sorts of accounts rejected as were female patients (ibid., 245). In fact, in their language, "male patients seemed more like doctors than patients" (ibid.). It is unfortunate that no female doctors were included in this study. Even so, the contrast between female and male patients may give us cause to hesitate before rejecting sex as a very powerful determining factor in language style.

Zimmerman and West's work illustrates that difference in professional rank is sometimes not as important in determining speech patterns as gender is—in one of their studies "a male undergraduate . . . repeatedly interrupted . . . [the female teaching assistant's] attempts to explain a concept" (1975, 116). Research done by Crosby and Nyquist, which examined the language interactions of police personnel and clients indicated that *both* role *and* sex were important determining factors in speech style. In the Crosby and Nyquist study, clients used "the female register more than police personnel" and females used "the female register more than males" (1977, 319).

Evidence of very negative evaluations of cross-sex talk—that is females speaking in stereotypically identified male ways, or vice versa—also undermines any claim that sex is not *the* central feature to be taken account of in any analysis of language. Rasmussen and Moely's research showed that "subjects rated males who spoke women's language as homosexual; they tended to rate females who spoke men's language as uppity" (1986, 149); Rachkowski and

O'Grady document "a pervasive tendency to stigmatize the female clients displaying masculine sex-typed behaviours in comparison to male clients displaying these same behaviours" (1988, 771). Furthermore, Abbey and Melby's research revealed that males interpreted particular non-verbal cues in females as indicators of seductiveness, sexiness, and promiscuity, although females made no such parallel interpretation in the case of males (1986, 283).

It is interesting to examine the feminist research dealing with educational administration from within the context of the appropriate registers theory. This research suggests that there is not one style (a male style) adopted by educational administrators and a different style (a female style) adopted by their staff, but rather that administrators themselves exhibit very different styles of leadership, depending on their gender (Shakeshaft 1987). The differences in leadership style postulated by Shakeshaft are correlated by her to the differences in speech documented by the gender and language research (ibid., 179-186). Shakeshaft's research, to be discussed in more detail in Chapter Ten, essentially posits that in their administrative style, female administrators are more participatory, interactive, democratic, and student-oriented than their male counterparts. Shakeshaft's research on educational administration thus challenges the view that the professional context may be more telling than gender in determining speech styles and behaviour patterns generally; for her work shows that among those in an *identical* professional context, the gender differences in style are enormous.

Support for the appropriate registers theory is found in some of the research on young children's language; Goodwin and Goodwin (1987), in their study of Black working-class children in the Philadelphia area, argue that the language patterns of the girls and boys, although not without differences, are highly similar (205); they challenge the claims of researchers who characterize female language as sweet, kind, and considerate, arguing instead that the language of the girls in their study was *more* brusque and combative than the language of the boys (205, 239-240).

Other research arrives at outcomes different from that of Goodwin and Goodwin (1987), however. Abrahams, for example, in describing the language of Black people, says that "women are expected to be more restrained than men in their talk, less loud, less public, and much less abandoned. They speak in a register closer to standard conversational English than do the men" (1975, 70).

"Silence is also highly valued in children (especially in the presence of Momma)" (ibid.).

> That is not to say that there is no interaction between mother and child, only that interactions are nonreciprocal. Imperatives are given, informational questions asked, but seldom is either used to instigate verbal communication so much as to produce action on the part of the child. (Ibid., 70-71)

> The value placed on silence in the home (on the part of children) is one facet of an elaborate ideal of deference, which includes learning proper modes of address, how and when to act in the presence of adults, and how and where to look (mutely) when being addressed by an older person. Thus, one of the most important routines by which a woman defines her respectable sex-role is by speaking little with the mouth and a great deal with the eyes, the arms and shoulders, the whole set of the body. (Ibid., 71)

> We know something of the importance of women being able to answer a rap with a rap and to maintain self-respect through a control over the speaking going on in their presence through such means as smart talk and maintaining silence. (Ibid., 79)

In a different paper more conducive to acceptance of the appropriate registers theory, however, in which he discusses the language patterns of "one Afro-American peasant community in the West Indies" (1972, 15), Abrahams addresses to some extent the interplay between gender and role. He says that *"talking sweet* has come to be identified not so much with the Euro-American world as it has with peasant household values. In contrast, *talking bad* is identified with male life away from home" (ibid., 17-18, author's emphasis).

> This identification of language variety with a social dichotomy does not mean that women always speak sweetly nor that men always talk bad. These varieties are associated with the value systems of the two groups and do come into conflict occasionally. But most important for our purposes, the *sweet* varieties are associated with ceremonies that celebrate household values, while *talking broad* is stylized for licentious performances.
> As part of the training in household values, then, one of the responsibilities of the head of the household is to assure that each of its younger members develops some competence in *talking sweet*. (Ibid., 18, author's emphasis)

Other research conducted with young children casts doubt on the appropriate repertoires theory. Jacqueline Sachs (1987) studied a play situation with children whose ages ranged between twenty-four and sixty-four months. The children were left alone in a room in same-sex pairs to play together. Prominent among the toys left in the room was doctor paraphernalia—toy stethoscope, bandaids, syringes, and so forth. The pair was then observed through a one-way mirror and the behaviour videotaped. It is interesting that the observations from one pair of two-year-old girls could not be used because they were afraid to be left in a room without an adult present, and the observations from two pairs of boys had to be scrapped because their behaviour was too aggressive. A third pair of boys discovered that there were people behind the one-way mirror, so their interactions were also dropped from the study. In each case, the two children constituting the dyad were within four months of each other in age and were acquainted with one another, having come from the same preschool class (1987, 178-179).

Sachs' study showed that the boys would tell their partners which role to take (ibid., 180), and that the boy issuing such instructions invariably wanted the high status role of doctor for himself (ibid.). The girls, on the other hand, asked (rather than told) their partners which role they wanted (ibid.), were themselves as likely to express an interest in playing the patient, mother, or baby role as the doctor role (ibid.), and, something the boys never did, frequently suggested that they could both be doctors or both be patients (ibid., 181). In fact, in one argument that Sachs recorded between two boys, one boy ordered the other to remove the stethoscope on the basis that "Just one person can be the doctor. One person" (ibid., 185). Given the hierarchical arrangement of boys' play, it is easy to understand why two doctors in a game is inconceivable; if the structure of the play is such that the participants have more egalitarian roles and their relationship to one another is more cooperative, then the possibility of more than one doctor arises naturally. The boys showed a distinct preference for giving orders or directions, thus issuing many direct imperatives (ibid., 183), while the girls showed a preference for a much more cooperative style, issuing almost no direct imperatives, but many joint utterances, such as "Let's sit down and use it" (ibid., 184) and lots of tag questions of the sort that gave the play partner an opportunity to agree with or dissent from the proposed action, for example, "Oh yes, she needs the little pill, right?" (ibid.). Sachs inferred from the far greater preponderance of this sort of tag question and of joint utterances, together with the far lower preponderance of direct imperatives, that the little girls' language was more cooperative than the little boys' (ibid.). The more polite (ibid., 183), softer (ibid., 185) language of the little girls was an indication of a greater concern to include the other child in the decision-making process according to Sachs (ibid.), foreshadowing, perhaps, the claim that "women may be more responsive than men to situational demands" (Halberstadt, Hayes, and Pike 1988, 599) and the research in educational administration discussed earlier, which suggests that female administrators are more consultative, male administrators more dictatorial (Shakeshaft 1987, 187-188, 206; see also Aries 1987, 154-155; Beasley 1983, 15).

Sachs examined a potential objection to her claim that the little girls' and boys' speech styles differed along the lines she suggested. A critic might point out that more deferential, polite language is developmentally more mature than brusque imperative language; such a critic would draw support from the fact that very young children who can understand direct imperatives (such as "Pick up your toys!) cannot understand embedded imperatives (such as "Would you mind picking up your toys?"). Add this to the commonly made claim (Harris 1977, 81-83; Maccoby and Jacklin 1974b, 75), but nonetheless criticized by some (Fairweather 1976, 256-266; Macaulay 1978, 361) that girls are developmentally ahead of boys in their language, and the critic appears to have grounds for challenging the style differences, and explaining Sachs' observations in terms of the boys not having yet acquired the more developmentally mature style of polite cooperative language. In other words, this critic could attempt to explain Sachs' observations on the basis of level of linguistic development that differs with sex, rather than with sex per se.

In her response to this would-be critic, Sachs points out that the boys in her study did indeed exhibit more mitigated language upon occasion, thus illustrating that their characteristically ruder language was not imposed by developmental immaturity, but was a style choice. In one of the examples, a little boy's partner had become very angry at him, resulting in attempts on the little boy's part to make up. His language in this context contains no direct imperatives and it teems with conciliatory tag-questions. I shall cite the interchange between the two children recorded by Sachs. The italics in this passage is used by Sachs to flag the mitigated language style.

CH: *You wanna be the doctor?*
JA: No.
CH: Why?
JA: Cause I hate you.
CH: Please, I won't do that anymore. *Never, never again, all right?*
     Let's be friends. Now let's get up, right? You wanna do something?
     You wanna be the doctor forever and never change? Wanna do
     that? (Sachs 1987, 185)

Research conducted by E. Ochs Keenan suggests that contrary to typical Piagetian claims, very young children are quite capable of engaging
in genuine conversational interchanges. Keenan studied two twin
boys, aged two years and nine months, analyzing 257 of their conversational exchanges; of these "only 17 or 6.6 per cent appear to be
unequivocally not addressed or adapted particularly to the co-present
interlocutor" (1983, 4). In the case of the educational administration
research referred to earlier, it is more difficult to make the argument
that it is the developmental immaturity of the male principals that
accounts for the observed differences rather than differences of style
based on sex!

Nor could Sachs' recorded differences be explained by the boys
more often playing the more dominant role of doctor, which might
itself determine a more brusque imperative speech style. For even
when Sachs totally eliminated all the speech that was uttered in the
role of the doctor, the number of direct imperatives used by boys was
still much higher than the number used by girls (Sachs 1987, 183).

Jean Berko Gleason (1987) claims that the adult differences
between female and male speech may be present in the speech of children as young as four years old. Her research suggests that even in
children that young, girls' language is more polite and boys' language
ruder (ibid., 198). One of the issues Gleason's research addresses is
whether the ways in which adults, particularly parents, interact with
young children, provides us with part of the explanation for these differences. She suggests that the greater aggression of boys over girls,
one of the few very strongly supported sex difference claims, could
very well be responsible for adults talking more sharply and using
more direct imperatives in their speech to little boys than to little
girls, thus providing little boys and little girls with dramatically different models of speech (ibid., 189-190). This explanation is supported
by some of the educational literature, which suggests that boys are
more boisterous than girls in schools, frequently causing more problems for their teachers (Cline and Spender 1987, 58).

As I have discussed in Chapter Two, there is an abundance of research demonstrating incontrovertibly that male students, young and old, receive *far* more than their fair share of the teacher's time and attention when compared with female students. Many educational researchers, particularly practitioner-researchers, are understandably sensitive about these sorts of observations; they feel that they, as teachers, are being cast in the role of sexist villains, responsible for perpetuating sexist arrangements. They urge the reader to be reasonable and to consider the reality of the teacher's role. The teacher has a class of perhaps thirty students, an agenda she is required by law to cover, some boisterous male students who are an impediment to her doing her job, and female students working quietly at their desks on precisely the curriculum she has been prescribed to teach. Any reasonable person's attention would be diverted to controlling the behaviour that is interfering with the teacher's job, and if nearly all of that behaviour emanates from the boys, then most of the teacher's attention will logically be directed to the boys. It is important to point out here that while nearly all of the disruptive behaviour emanates from the male students, many of the male students do not pose behaviour problems for the teacher and they too are disadvantaged by the disproportionate amount of time demanded of the teacher by the disruptive male students.

As discussed in Chapter Two, Cline and Spender claim that boys become more obstreperous when they fail to obtain the bulk of the teacher's time and attention (1987, 58). This is one of the realities of coeducational classrooms, providing us with an enormously powerful moral premise for reverting to single-sex schools; but it does *not* justify our blaming the teacher for perpetuating sexist arrangements. Such perpetuation is basically unavoidable so long as we continue to have student-teacher ratios as high as thirty to one, and so long as the social context into which the school fits is itself one that values males and devalues females. We can understand that what goes on in elementary schools does foster sexism, but we can do so without blaming the elementary schoolteacher for the consequences. For even if she attempts to alter this schema, broader social impediments out of her control may make this impossible. I don't want to suggest here that teachers never act immorally with regard to the perpetuation of sex-role ideology, or that there is nothing teachers can do to raise students' awareness and promote a fairer society. To the contrary, I think there is *much* that teachers can do. At the same time, I agree with those practitioners-researchers who are horrified to learn that they are being blamed for directing most of their time and energy to the boys in their classes, when not to do so would mean that they couldn't teach at all. Blaming these teachers is like mother-blaming, a too-easy identification of the cause of the problem, an identification that ignores the broad social context into which the school and the family fit.

As mentioned earlier, one possible explanation for the emergence of different speech patterns in even very young boys and girls is that they are *spoken* to by adults in very different ways, and that their own speech mirrors the style of talk that is directed towards them. Another account, also discussed by Gleason, is that little children pick up on the speech patterns of their same-sex parent, with little girls learning softer, more polite language from their mothers and little boys learning ruder, more brusque language from their fathers. A study conducted by Gleason offered some support for this second hypothesis as well. The study involved a situation in which either a mother or father had participated, with their child, in a laboratory setting. At the end of the session, a research assistant came into the room and presented the child with a gift. Although male and female children were equally urged by their parents to thank the research assistant, the mothers were much more likely to add their own "thank you" than were the fathers (1987, 196).

In addition, Gleason found that fathers' speech to their children contained a higher proportion of direct imperatives (e.g., "Close the door!") than mothers' speech, whereas mothers' speech contained a higher proportion of polite imperatives that were embedded in question forms (e.g., "Would you mind closing the door?") (ibid., 198). In one study, the number of direct imperatives uttered to their children by fathers was approximately double the number produced by mothers (ibid., 195).

Gleason also suggests that fathers' speech is less well tuned to their children than mothers' speech. Mothers tend to match the average length of their sentences (MLU) very closely to their children's ability, but fathers do not (ibid., 194). In one instance, a father used longer sentences with a three-year-old daughter than a five-year-old son. Fathers also tend to use vocabulary items beyond the child's level (ibid.,195). Furthermore, fathers' understanding of their children's speech was not as good as the mothers' understanding (ibid.,194). (Stein argues that mothers' speech to normal children is cognitively superior to fathers' speech, but that the reverse is true in the case of language-deficient children [1976, 118, 123-125, 130-131].)

These two factors, that children model the language patterns of their same-sex parent, and that children respond to the highly sex-specific language directed to them by parents, are not mutually exclusive. It may both be true that fathers and mothers talk differently, thus modelling very different language to boys and girls respectively, and that mothers and fathers alike engage in different kinds of talk with their female and male children. Greif's research on interruptions in parent-child language supports this double hypothesis, showing that little girls were interrupted by both parents more than little boys, and also that fathers in general interrupted their children more frequently than did mothers (Greif 1980, 253, 256, 257); in addition, Greif's research showed that contrary to the stereotype of children persistently interrupting their parents, the truth was that parents interrupted their children far more than vice versa (ibid.).

One might expect that if little girls are interrupted more than their brothers by parents, that they will also be the recipients of more direct imperatives. But this appears not to be the case. Gleason's research shows that little boys receive more direct imperatives than little girls, particularly from their fathers (1987, 194-195). In fact, Gleason thinks it is this factor that accounts for the case discussed earlier of a father who used longer sentences in talking to his three-year-old daughter than his five-year-old son. Direct imperatives characteristically constitute very short sentences (consider "Shut the door!"), and since fathers include many more such imperatives in speech to their sons than to their daughters, this would obviously shorten the average length of sentence uttered by a father to a son (ibid., 195).

Gleason's research also indicated other more disturbing aspects of fathers' speech as it was directed to their sons. Fathers were more likely to disparage sons in particular, by referring to them with names like "Dingaling," and "Wise guy," and they were more likely to overtly threaten their children, especially sons. One example of such a threat presented by Gleason is "Don't go in there again or I'll break your head" (ibid.). (These features of fathers' language documented by Gleason will be discussed in a more critical vein in Chapter Six.) As mentioned earlier, Gleason claims that mothers' speech tends to be more in tune with their children than fathers' speech. Nonetheless, both fathers and mothers, as well as other adults who interact with children, modify their language in the presence of children (ibid., 191-192). All of us, regardless of our gender, speak differently to children than we do to adults.

This is true of children as young as four, who exhibit clear modifications to their normal speech in addressing two year olds. These modifications in the speech of four year olds include using direct imperatives to two year olds, but indirect or softened imperatives to adults (Schatz and Gelman 1973, 32); "shorter, simpler utterances to 2-year-olds than . . . to adults" (ibid., 2); smaller M.L.U.s with younger children (4.0) than with adults (5.4) (ibid., 9,11); moderating language output such that "the younger the listener, the more the S[ubject] used short utterances" (ibid., 14); more "concrete verbs with their younger listeners and abstract verbs with their adult listeners" (ibid., 32-33); and frequent repetition of utterances when speaking to two year olds (ibid., 33). Furthermore, the four year olds' language was similar to adult language in that it did not simply revert to the two-year-old level in these discussions, but reflected a level slightly above that of the two year olds (ibid., 34).

This suggests that the role of interacting with children in itself determines some patterns of speech, regardless of the sex of the speaker. At the same time, other observations indicate that the sex of the speaker determines some speech patterns, including some of those that emerge in parent-child interchanges. This is not surprising. It would have been much more surprising if either the sex or the context of the speaker made no difference in the speech patterns adopted. It seems a matter of common sense that sex as well as other aspects of the context will influence how we speak.

Leet-Pellegrini adopted essentially this position. She conducted a study which she believed illustrated that both sex and context were necessary features in accounting for speech patterns. Specifically, Leet-Pellegrini observed the evidence of dominance in pairs of people, some of whom had been made "instant experts" on the topic they had been asked to discuss—television programming—by having been provided with a "fact sheet" immediately prior to the discussion. On the basis of the study, she concluded that "the interaction of gender and expertise (and not the single factor of being male *or* being expert) accounted for the major proportion of findings" (1980, 97, author's emphasis). I agree with Leet-Pellegrini's general hypothesis regarding the importance of taking both gender and context into account. I am sure that most people have had first-hand experience of instances that defy the stereotypes, of the arrogant upper-class woman who inherited privilege and dominance from her parents' income level, as well as the deferential submissive man who earns his living by sweeping ivory tower floors trod upon by the intellectually elite.

Even so, I disagree with Leet-Pellegrini that this general hypothesis is strongly supported by her study. Although she claims her study shows that "it was the interaction of expertise with gender" (ibid., 101) that accounted for the conversational dominance as well as submissiveness, I disagree. I believe there are two aspects of her findings which in fact controvert her claim. First, when the conversational pair consisted of a man and a woman with the expert male, the male retained dominance throughout the conversation, from beginning to end. When the male expert was paired with another male, however, the expert male "did not maintain a dominant stance" (ibid.) throughout the conversation; rather,

> it was the expert who structured the conversation initially, but by the end it was not clear which male partner, the expert or the non-expert, was structuring the conversation's exiting moves. What we may be observing is an instance of conversational jockeying for power, or an attempt by non-expert males to recoup status lost from having been placed in the one-down position. (Ibid., 101)

I think this is a clear contradiction of Leet-Pellegrini's hypothesis, indicating dramatically that in this instance, the context of expertise *was not* required at all to explain the male dominance patterns, as *both* the expert and the non-expert males struggled to achieve dominance.

Although I have not conducted empirical research on this topic, I have noticed the same sort of phenomenon in an introductory philosophy of education course that I teach. The students' term work for this course consists of three major assignments—an analysis of an argument in one of the articles they are responsible for reading, a critique of an analysis written by other students, and finally a revision of their own original analysis utilizing the feedback they have received from other students and myself. The students are encouraged but not required to work in groups of three, and most do. Most of the groups turn out to be same-sex groups, but there are many mixed-sex groups as well. Those who work in groups are graded as a group on all three assignments. My observation, after using this format for approximately one hundred students a year over an eight-year period, is that the mixed-sex groups have the most complaints about working in groups—there are very few complaints and the students on the whole give me only positive feedback on their experience of working in the group—but those who do come to me to discuss problems in the group dynamics, usually one or two per year, are overwhelmingly mixed-sex groups.

In the same-sex groups, the tone and style of the feedback provided to the other students varies enormously according to the sex of the critiquing groups. This interchange of papers among the students is conducted anonymously, so the students don't know whose paper they are commenting on, or which students are commenting on their work. Nor do they know the grade I assigned to the paper they are commenting on. My observations are that the all-female groups are very supportive in the feedback they provide, even to very weak papers. They do provide lots of helpful comments to the group to enable them to improve their paper, but always in a highly supportive tone, and taking care to identify the strengths of the paper they are commenting on, even though they often have to scrape very hard to find strengths. This supportive style runs through the feedback of students whose own papers range the whole spectrum from weak to very strong, and regardless of where on the range of weak to very strong the papers they are working on fall. For example, very strong critiquing female groups couch their corrections to weak groups in kind, supportive language. Weak critiquing female groups commenting on strong papers often say things like "Well done! We wish we had thought of this idea ourselves!" The style of the all-male critiquing groups is very different. They never make comments like the one above, and they tend to "tear apart" the paper they are working on, pointing out problems in a style that verges on insulting; this is equally as true of the very weak all-male groups commenting on very good papers as it is of any other group. Furthermore, even though their language is couched in a supportive style, the all-female groups provide as much or more relevant commentary on the weakness of the paper they are working on than do the all-male groups.

My observations accord with the second point I wish to make about Leet-Pellegrini's findings—namely, when female experts were paired with male non-experts, the females exhibited submissive assenting behaviour and no dominant behaviour. The expert women, "in the presence of nonexpert men, responded with *even more supportive, collaborative work than usual* (ibid., 103, my emphasis); furthermore, women experts assented more with male partners . . . than with female partners" (ibid., 102).

In the same vein, Charol Shakeshaft claims that when working with male subordinates, females "try to look less authoritarian, less in charge, and less threatening in an effort to be effective" (1987, 204). Hence "women administrators often down play their power, intelligence, and skill . . . [making] themselves more tentative and less threatening" (ibid.). When working with female subordinates, on the other hand, female administrators might engage in either a power-disguise or a more traditional power-display style (ibid.). Shakeshaft claims that men perceive less threatening women as more competent (ibid.). Research indicates that more hostility is directed towards female than male leaders (Kahn 1984, 274-275), that female leaders receive more disagreement at the hands of both females and males than do male leaders (Alderton and Jurma 1980, 59), and that male executives are listened to by their staff more closely than their female counterparts (Booth-Butterfield 1984, 40-41). Not surprisingly, the problems of being heard and taken seriously are even greater for Black women (Doughty 1980, 170; Ihle 1990; Pollard 1990). Arnold Kahn's research indicates that men perceive a weaker man's helping a powerful man in a very different way from a weaker man's helping a powerful woman; "helping a powerful man raised the weaker man's power and status, while helping a powerful woman kept a powerless man without power" (1984, 243). Furthermore, some research indicates that even if particular status characteristics have not been associated with a task, those differences in status will nevertheless "determine the observable power and prestige order of the group" (Berger, Cohen, and Zelditch, Jr. 1972, 253).

I maintain therefore that Leet-Pellegrini's study, contrary to what she claims, does not controvert the traditional view that "male-female interaction is different from female-female or from male-male interaction" (1980, 101). Leet-Pellegrini's claim that "men may pre-empt forms related to power [while] women may pre-empt forms related to support or nurturance" (ibid., 103), is far more useful in explaining her findings than the actual hypothesis that forms the basis of the study—namely, that "it was the interaction of expertise with gender which produced clear and consistent findings" (ibid., 101).

Tannen's comments on Leet-Pellegrini's work are particularly interesting. A superficial interpretation of Leet-Pellegrini's research might lead one to believe that "women are getting a bum deal," that "they don't get credit when its due," because "men are bums who seek to deny women authority" (1990, 128), according to Tannen. Tannen suggests that a more enlightened interpretation of this data could be that men's persistent challenging of the women's authority is "a sign of respect and equal treatment, rather than lack of respect and discrimination" (ibid., 128-129). Tannen bases this more positive explanation on the fact that the men behaved similarly to women as to other men—in each case, the men struggled to challenge authority and to take power for themselves. In other words, according to Tannen, if men treat women as they treat other men, they are being respectful—if a woman is treated like "one of the boys," she has no basis for complaint. What is left out of Tannen's account is any sense that persistent challenging of those who clearly do have more expert knowledge than oneself is not respectful, no matter which gender it is directed towards; persistent jockeying for power and persistent linguistic domination do not become acceptable because they are ubiquitously applied—such behaviour is inherently problematic. (These issues will be dealt with in more detail in Chapters Five and Six of this book.)

In spite of the reservations that I have expressed with Leet-Pellegrini's study, I do accept the hypothesis that gender must normally be coupled to other aspects of the context in providing any coherent explanation of speech patterns. Whether gender has more explanatory power than other aspects of context is not clear, nor is it clear whether the research will ever be capable of giving us a definitive indication, for gender is almost always correlated to these other contexts, making it very difficult to ascertain which factor is the more powerful. Expertise is an interesting case in point to consider, given that males tend to be credited with more expertise than females, whether or not this is actually the case. Goldberg's research documents the fact that even female readers perceived an article attributed to a male author to be more authoritative and knowledgeable than the same article attributed to a female author (Goldberg 1974, 40-42). Dale Spender discusses her own research in a faculty of education in which she worked with students who were both aware of the problem of sexism (1984, 134) and claimed that they were concerned to eradicate it from their own behaviour as educators (ibid., 134, 136). All Spenders' students were given a report card which they were then asked to evaluate; the report cards were identical, except that half had the name "Jane Smith" and the other half the name "John Smith" at the top (ibid., 134). The students' responses to Jane and John were dramatically different. They believed Jane would probably drop out of school, that she would make a good secretary or receptionist, and that she would need to be closely managed (ibid., 135); John, on the other hand, was perceived as able to do anything he wanted, not understood by his teachers, and capable of managing people (ibid., 136).

Other research shows that the competence of male professors who succeed in encouraging discussion in their classrooms is not questioned by their students, whereas female professors who accomplish the same feat are judged incompetent (Richardson and Macke 1980, 90-91, 176). Insofar as the maintenance of classroom discussion is understood by most teachers to be a mark of good teaching, actual good teaching may well be a liability for female professors who wish or need to obtain high student evaluations on their teaching. Gruber and Gaebelein's research (although it does controvert the claim made above that women are automatically judged inferior to men) indicates "that when a male and a female say the same thing, more attention will be paid to what the male says than to what the female says" (1979, 307).

The context—knowledgeable, expert, worth listening to, authority—is shown in these studies *not* to be independent of sex; rather, knowledgeability or expert status is *assumed* on the basis of sex. As a factor in determining how well professors are evaluated by their students, and consequently, how likely professors are to be granted tenure, the difference between male and female, far from being negligible, dictates to a great extent the students' impressions of teaching excellence and expertise.

An interesting study conducted by Bambi Schieffelin on the speech patterns of the Kaluli in Papua New Guinea provides evidence that appears to contradict both the socialization theory and the appropriate registers theory. According to Schieffelin, sex-role differences in the socialization of Kaluli children are enormous, with no discernible language differences resulting. Girls are taught to

> assist with the care of infant siblings, . . . to give up things they like, especially foods, to please a begging brother or a younger sibling. . . . Boys, on the other hand, are given food preferentially and are rarely asked to help with domestic chores. . . . The boys are encouraged to be more aggressive than their sisters, especially in games. Little girls are encouraged to be submissive when their brothers make demands on them. In games they are instructed and encouraged to let their younger brothers chase and hit them. However, for all the differences in the

ways in which boys and girls are treated, there does not seem to be any significant linguistic reflections of these differences. (1987, 256-257)

The roles of the adult Kaluli women and men, on which the differences in children's roles are based, are similarly "clearly demarcated" (ibid., 258), although "this does not affect the ways they use language in the sense of traditional studies of language and gender" (ibid., 259). Schieffelin's research suggests the very radical hypothesis that neither the highly differentiated socialization patterns, nor the differences in the typical contexts in which Kaluli males and females operate have any discernible impact on their language in terms of any of the traditionally noted gender differences.

But whether we agree with Schieffelin that context and gender differences do not *explain* speech patterns, or we accept the more popular position that context as well as gender must be accounted for in *explaining* speech patterns, we still have not taken a single step towards *justifying* speech patterns. The appropriate registers theory is equally as guilty as the sex roles theory in letting us off the moral hook too readily. Tannen's position (1990) that men and women are simply talking at cross-purposes to one another because they operate within contexts totally foreign to each other is guilty of ignoring the applicability of the moral parameter to these speech patterns. As Kramarae points out, an explanation that focuses strongly on individual choices and contexts, as the appropriate registers theory does, may underestimate the power of the "social structure" (1981, 140) in controlling and manipulating people's behaviour.

There may be no particular features that are a necessary part of a specific context or of either sex role—hence the components that constitute sex roles as well as the image and status of particular contexts (the role of doctor, for example) vary dramatically from one society to another. In contrast, there are specific features of moral analyses that are both necessary and that will be common even across cultural differences. Suppose, for example, as some of the research indicates, that both men and boys show less concern for others in their language than do women and girls. This does not cancel, or even diminish the fact that showing concern for others is an important moral good, and that behaviours which exhibit a paucity of such concern ought to be corrected. Suppose also that being in a certain role, for example, a socially prestigious role such as physician, is correlated with rude brusque speech patterns toward one's patients. This does not diminish the fact that doctors ought to treat their patients with respect and consideration. Some research indicates that physicians may, in fact, be particularly intransigent in terms of eliminating sexist usage from their language; Harrigan and Lucic (1988), comparing University of Cincinnati psychology students, English students, medical students, and faculty members, along with the members of a local chapter of National Organization of Women, found that the medical students, followed by faculty members, were the least concerned about sexism in language and about attempting to avoid it in their own usage. National Organization of Women members, followed by the psychology students, were the most concerned about eliminating sexist language (ibid., 132-133).

Not unrelated to my physician example, if one lives in a society where male dominance over females is a fact of life, it does not follow that such dominance is justified. Might does not make right in the moral realm. It is obvious that the moral rules are still applicable, even if we live in a society that makes it easy to ignore such rules. In other words, all three of the theoretical accounts of language and gender—the male dominance theory, the sex roles socialization theory, and the appropriate registers or context theory—could be true, without at all alleviating the necessity of our judging behaviour, including verbal behaviour, by moral standards. I suspect, in fact, that all three theories are true, and furthermore that all are necessary to account for the behaviour we see and hear in our everyday lives. Far from ruling out a moral analysis of behaviour, these theories require us to perform just such an analysis.

Chapter Five

The Moral Criteria of Language

The past twenty-five years have not been silent on the topic of conversational styles; to the contrary, as Chapters Two, Three, and Four have indicated, this quarter-century has produced an enormous literature on the topic. The focus of the literature, however, has been *perceived* gender differences in conversational styles. Although fascinating and important, I believe that this focus has masked underlying moral considerations. When researchers identified women's speech as being more interactive and more tentative, and men's speech as being more brusque and more authoritative (Fishman 1977, 99-101; Key 1975, 35-36, 76-77), for example, the discussion tended to end at that point. It seemed as though the gender difference claim regarding speech patterns was perceived as an ample explanation, and the linguistic data then abandoned as not requiring further elucidation. Lakoff, for example, admonishes us "to remember that neither of these two styles [i.e., female or male] is good or bad" (1975, 74). Neither, in her opinion, is one "more socially useful than" (ibid., 83) the other. I believe that Lakoff is mistaken in both these claims, and I

The notes to this chapter are on pp. 117-118.

shall argue later that on one level traits of both moral worth and social usefulness can be identified within the genderdized language patterns.

The gender difference claim is rich in its explanatory capacity, and is absolutely necessary to an understanding of the phenomena of language interactions. In other words, the gender differences research on language patterns has succeeded in explaining a great deal; at the same time, it has failed to justify anything. Morally, we remain at the "So what?" posture. For when we have completed the gender analysis, we are still left with the question as to which sorts of language patterns enjoy moral worth and hence ought to be endorsed and promoted. It is my purpose in this chapter to focus on this moral issue, and to identify and discuss some possible moral considerations.

I shall begin by discussing some of the aspects of Grice's and Habermas' writing relevant to my account. Paul Grice's work on conversational implicature provides an extensive discussion of the logic of ordinary discourse. His focus is on a *logical* rather than a *moral* analysis; nevertheless, there is some overlap between these two focuses, and his analysis is too important to be overlooked. Grice suggests (1981, 184-185) that the logic of ordinary conversational exchanges is governed by four maxims, namely—Quantity: Say as much as, but no more than necessary; Quality: Say only what is truthful and only what you have adequate evidence for; Relevance: Be relevant in what you say; Manner: Be perspicuous, succinct, and direct in what you say. He suggests furthermore that many apparent exceptions to these maxims can be understood if both speaker and listener analyze the discourse according to certain rules of inference— enter conversational implicature. Consider Grice's own example (1981, 184). Smith is requested to write a letter of reference for Jones, a former philosophy student of Smith. In the letter of reference, Smith notes that Jones has good manners and legible handwriting. This appears on the surface to be a clear violation of the first maxim, that of quantity, according to Grice. One would have expected the referee to say as much as was necessary, which in the context of a letter of reference should be a good deal more than that the candidate has good manners and legible handwriting. The letter of reference also appears to violate the third maxim—that of relevance. Why doesn't the referee discuss the candidate's clarity of thought, rather than clarity of handwriting?

Grice suggests that both the recipient and the sender of the letter will do well to examine this communication within the parameters of the conversational maxims; only thus can they understand one another. Accordingly, the recipient, noting the apparent violation of the first maxim, will assume the sender was striving not to violate any of the maxims. This suggests in turn that a more obviously relevant communication, such as that the candidate had a keen logical mind, would violate the maxim of quality or truthfulness. According to Grice, we must assume that the referee has some reason for not providing a sufficiently detailed account of Jones' philosophical strengths, i.e., we must assume that Smith has some reason for violating the maxim of quantity. "That reason is likely to be that the things he would say would either be untrue or else bad and he doesn't want to say those things. So the explanation then would be that he had a low opinion of the candidate" (Grice 1981, 185).

Thus Smith will be able to communicate the relevant information about Jones indirectly to the potential employer, on the assumption that both understand the letter to be an attempt to obey the four maxims of conversation as fully as possible. This analysis explains the power of damning by faint praise. It also illustrates, I believe, that the maxims are not parallel, but hierarchical, with the maxim of truthfulness occupying a position of more prominence than the others. Thus, while it is expected that one will say as much as is necessary, one is allowed to say nothing, or next to nothing, if the providing of details would push one into deceitful talk. It is interesting to note here that Smith's concern for truthfulness seems to extend only to the potential employer; a more truthful response to Jones, under the circumstances, would have been for Smith to tell Jones directly that it wasn't possible to write a strong letter of support.

Grice's maxims approximate closely the joint criteria of soundness exacted of premises in an argument, namely, that they be true (maxim of quality), relevant (maxim of relevance), and adequate (maxim of quantity—say at least as much as necessary); of somewhat lesser importance is what might be called the criteria of elegance—that the premises be non-repetitious (maxim of quantity—say no more than necessary) and unambiguous (maxim of manner—be direct and clear). Grice's account of *conversational* implicature would thus appear to be heavily influenced by a fairly traditional notion of argument soundness.

I believe that Grice's choice of example betrays that in his discussion of conversational implicature he was *not* primarily interested in *ordinary conversations* at all. The provision of a reference for a former student falls much closer to the formal end of the communication spectrum than it does to the informal end exemplified by ordinary conversation. In fact, the example is about as far as one can get from a conversation. It implies no give-and-take, no exchange. It implies someone's telling something to someone else, a strictly one-way communication, rather than people conversing with one another. It is instructive that on Grice's own account, Smith's comments take the form of a letter and do not even occur within a conversational setting. Conversations typically involve two distinct but related facets—the actual content of what participants say and the interactions among the participants. Grice's analysis, and the example of the letter of reference in particular, illustrates that he understands the primary function of ordinary conversations to be the conveying of information, a situation in which one party has the information that a different party requires, suggesting in turn an asymmetry in their relationship, at least in the context of this particular communication. Grice's conversational maxims apply only to the first of these facets, and not to the second.

Suppose that the conveying of information is not perceived (or not always perceived) as the primary function of a conversation. Suppose instead that the primary purpose of the conversation is construed in terms of forging links, of sustaining relationships, or of exploring interpersonal themes among the conversational participants. In other words, suppose, as Wolfram Bublitz claims, that "maintenance and development of satisfactory social relations between the participants play a more important role than the exchange of as much new information as possible" (1988, 135). Grice's maxims will have little application here. In fact, some of Grice's discussion of the letter of reference example makes this clear. Remember the inference that Grice suggests the recipient of the letter will make about the referee—namely, "the things he would say [if he obeyed the maxim of quantity] would either be untrue *or else bad* and he doesn't want to say those things" (Grice 1981, 185, my emphasis). The writer's reluctance to say something bad is totally unaccounted for by Grice's maxims exactly because the maxims basically mirror the soundness criteria of arguments. What Grice needs here is a maxim that reflects the old adage "If you can't say something nice, don't say anything at all." "Don't hurt people unnecessarily in what you say," comes close. Presumably Grice imagined the writer of the reference letter feeling some kind of affection, loyalty, or responsibility for the student and hence a reluctance to shatter more than necessary the student's chances of getting a job. Otherwise, it is difficult to understand the referee's reluctance to simply tell the whole truth, thereby obeying the maxim of quantity, damning as it would be to the candidate.

Furthermore, if we focus not on the information we transmit, but rather on the way we treat the other conversants when we communicate, then our criteria for "good talk" will have to be extended beyond the content of what is said to include the interactive features of the conversation as well. In particular instances, conflict may emerge between our attempts to satisfy both sets of criteria. Lakoff (1990, 169-171) discusses the tension we frequently feel between being clear and direct when we speak to people (Grice's fourth maxim) and skirting delicately around issues that might hurt their feelings. Although Grice does not directly address this conflict in terms of his maxims, his concern about the referee saying something "bad" (1981, 185) indicates that he is assuming something like a maxim that one should not hurt others unnecessarily in one's discourse. Typically, we have been charged with maintaining moral conduct in our language only in terms of content, not interaction.

Habermas' discussion of communicative competence (1970) comes the closest to providing a moral analysis of the interactive realm in ordinary conversational exchanges; according to Habermas, a speaker must possess communicative competence "in order to participate in normal discourse" (ibid., 367). He speaks of the importance of three symmetries—namely, "unrestrained discussion" (ibid., 371), mutual "unimpaired self-representation" (ibid., 372), and "full complementarity of expectations" (ibid.). Clearly underlining his own sense of the moral parameter of these symmetries, Habermas continues in the same paragraph to describe them as "a linguistic conceptualization of what are traditionally known as the ideas of truth, freedom, and justice" (ibid.). In his discussion of critical inquiry, Sirotnik[1] cites Habermas widely, attributing to Habermas two different sets of criteria required for the occurrence of competent communication—these criteria govern what may be loosely described as the conditions of *truth* of the communication and the conditions governing the *process* of communication among the participants. The first set of criteria is fairly close to the list of conversational maxims stipulated by Grice (1981, 184-185); the second set is much closer to the moral criteria that I specify later in this chapter. As described by Sirotnik, the first set of conditions defining communicative competence are:

1. *Comprehensibility*. Utterances must be understood; misunderstandings must be clarified, exemplified, illuminated, etc., before further competent communication can take place.
2. *Sincerity*. The speaker must be honest and the hearer must trust the intentions of the speaker; both parties must show good faith through their actions.
3. *Fidelity*. All available and mutually recognized pertinent information must support the truth of utterances. Inquiry methods will not be limited to traditional empirical techniques, but will be expanded to include the variety of phenomenological methods and, importantly, the critical evaluation of all information.
4. *Justifiability*. Utterances must be recognized by all parties as not only appropriate or legitimate for the speaker but, more importantly, appropriate in relation to explicit moral and ethical commitments. Critical inquiry is thereby explicitly normative and focuses on underlying values, beliefs, interests, intentions, etc. (Sirotnik 1991, 238, author's emphasis)

While these four conditions roughly parallel Grice's conversational maxims, there is a more explicit cognizance of the *moral* underpinnings of communication in Habermas' account; this is particularly evident in the discussion of justifiability and even more explicit in the conditions specified by Habermas as governing the *process* of competent communication. Such a process must embody "the essence of social justice, i.e., fairness, in the rules for discourse and dialectical methodology" (Sirotnik 1991, 248). What this means is that each participant in the conversation "must have (and believe they have) equal opportunities to" (ibid.):

1. initiate and/or enter the discourse;
2. refute or call into question the comprehensibility, sincerity, fidelity, and/or justifiability of the utterances by others;
3. express their values, beliefs, attitudes, sentiments, intentions, interests, etc.; and
4. regulate (i.e., command, oppose, permit, forbid, etc.) the discourse. (Ibid., 249)

As I stated earlier, these conditions describing the requirements of a fair process of communication are fairly close to the moral criteria of conversation that I specify later in this chapter. I do have some serious reservations, however, about Habermas' requirement that the participants not only have, but also *believe they have* equal opportunities in terms of achieving these four conditions. My reservations stem from the fact that people's sense of what is equal is frequently highly inaccurate, because it is skewed by trends and patterns that usually embody significant levels of inequity. While there was some discussion of this issue in Chapter Two and there will be a more extensive discussion in Chapter Ten, let me say a few words at this point to clarify what I mean. Our judgments about whether social conditions are equitable are often arrived at by comparing these conditions to the traditional status quo. So if, for example, we note that a large corporation has 5 percent more members of visible minorities in positions of upper management than it had five years ago, we may be tempted to relax into satisfied approval, believing that this state of affairs indicates that the corporation is truly egalitarian. Others may note with dissatisfaction the drop in the percentage of white managers, and claim that the current proportions are strong evidence of bias against whites, in other words, of reverse discrimination. Proponents of both perspectives are basing their appraisal of the current proportions on a comparison with a traditional breakdown by race of management positions, however, while providing no analysis whatsoever of that traditional breakdown, and hence pay too little attention to the fact that while the proportion of visible minority managers may have increased by 5 percent, the proportion nevertheless remains at an unjustifiable low of 7 percent. The representation of visible minorities in upper positions, although less racist than in the past, is still racist. In other words, the traditional status quo is simply accepted without any extensive critique, while ignoring the sexist, racist, and classist forces that have been defining factors in the formation of that status quo and hence in the usurping and allocating of power. In particular, people who are accustomed to dominating discourse may believe that they have had a less than equal share in the conversation when, in fact, they have received more than their fair share of the conversational segment. The empirical literature supports this claim, as is evident from several studies discussed earlier in Chapter Two. Let me very briefly review the pertinent aspects of this research. Dale Spender documented many situations in which teachers believed that in their attempts to redress gender inequity against the females in their classrooms, they (the teachers) had inadvertently ended up discriminating against the males. Yet when the classroom interactions of such teachers were videotaped, it was "often found that over two thirds of their time was spent with the boys who comprised less than half the class" (1982, 54). In other words, more than two-thirds of the time to less than half the class felt like a "raw deal" to the teachers *not for the group receiving less than a third of the teacher's time, but for the group receiving more than two-thirds of the time*! The research of Myra Sadker and David Sadker (1985, 54) reveals that in analyzing videotapes of classroom situations in which the boys outtalked the girls at a ratio of three to one, administrators and teachers alike *perceived* that the girls had done the bulk of the talking. They all interpreted the interactions as skewed towards the girls, and were unable to see the male bias until the researchers explicitly pointed it out to them. Furthermore, there is evidence that male students who are favoured less dramatically than they are accustomed to become obstreperous in class, requiring an enormous amount of teacher attention in order for the teacher to maintain control in the classroom (Cline and Spender 1987, 58; Spender 1982, 54, 56-58). As a result of the factor of contextual skewing, I believe that Habermas' stipulation that all the conversational participants must *"believe they have"* (Sirotnik 1991, 248, my emphasis) equal opportunity is seriously problematic. I do, however, support his stipulation "that all participants must have" (ibid.) equal opportunity in terms of the four conditions he outlines.

I shall now attempt to answer, at least in part, an important potential criticism of subjecting conversational exchanges to moral analysis and censure—namely, that to subject our linguistic interactions to moral scrutiny would be to overmoralize.[2] According to such a critic, too much of our lives would be subject to moral evaluation; conversing would become tiresome, losing much of the sense of joy and spontaneity that now characterize it. Furthermore, if we believe that language is intimately and inextricably bound up with our feelings and thoughts, we will be even more reluctant to extend the moral realm to language, for this would smack of making ourselves morally answerable for our feelings and our thoughts, which is ridiculous.[3] I acknowledge that it will often be difficult and even unpleasant to find ourselves constrained by moral rules where previously our behaviour felt free and untrammelled. However, I offer three observations which in part answer the criticism.

First, perhaps there are certain aspects of our linguistic behaviour that *ought not* to be free and untrammelled. There are many contexts in which the plea for unselfconscious behaviour is itself suspect. Michael Levin, for example, argues against the term "Ms." on the grounds that its use will make our language self-conscious and awkward (Levin 1977, 217). But this plea begs the very moral question at issue, by *assuming* that our language cannot have moral dimensions. For if it *does* have moral dimensions, then it follows that we *ought* to be self-conscious about it, even if this self-consciousness is unpleasant or inconvenient. It seems evident to me, as I have argued in Chapter One, that some aspects of language have moral dimensions—for example,[4] the use of racist or sexist slurs which sustain and exacerbate ideologies, interactions, attitudes, and political/economic relations that underpin a reality that is sexist and racist. In other words, language practices that endorse abuses of power and the maintenance of an unjust distribution of privilege are morally problematic because they interfere with the achievement of respect and connectedness among persons. By "respect," I include, like Kant, the notion of treating other people as ends in themselves and never merely using them as a means to achieve our own ends—this rules out much of the repertoire of so-called respectful behaviour surrounding the custom of chivalry and "treating a woman like a lady." In cases involving the use of racist or sexist slurs, the applicability of the moral issue must outweigh our reluctance to be made self-conscious about our language patterns. Furthermore, people whose language embodies racist and sexist slurs should be made to feel self-conscious and uncomfortable about such ways of speaking, *just because* such ways of speaking are *morally* objectionable. In other words, there are some contexts in which a person's desire to continue freely in established habits is itself morally suspect. In terms of the criticism that applying moral standards to our language entails applying them to our thoughts and feelings as well, I would deny that this is true. I have argued in Chapter One that it is because our language is under our control and because it has the potential to affect others for good or for ill that we ought to subject it to moral evaluation. In *most* contexts, we would not perceive our feelings as subject to control, thus rendering any moral judgments of them moot; so far as thoughts are just thoughts, we would not usually see them as having palpable effects on others in the way in which language does. A thought may exist in the privacy of one's own head, but language is in the public forum, and this is a very relevant moral difference. *If* the conditions of control and impact on others *were* met, however, it would make sense to apply moral standards even to feelings and thoughts. If thoughts are translated into action, for example, when a racist employer discriminates against Native applicants for jobs, then a moral judgment is applicable. Similarly, a sadist's pleasure in torturing children, if amenable to therapeutic treatment that the sadist refuses, also becomes a moral matter.

Second, perhaps a reason for believing that language need not be governed by moral rules is that much of the self-consciousness and labour required for our language to measure up to such criteria is in fact being performed by a large number of the linguistic participants without the other participants even realizing this. If this were so, then our language could appear to naturally achieve the standards, and hence it might seem as though introducing the criteria on a moral level would be both extraneous and tiresome. I propose that this is precisely what has happened. In other words, women have historically assumed personal responsibility for maintaining a context in which conversations could flourish, in which other speakers felt "cared for" linguistically. I hypothesize that the caring was so much a part of the fabric of the conversation that its presence was seldom noticed and its need seldom felt. Like housework, interactional linguistic labour was noticed only if women neglected or refused to contribute the elements required to maintain this context, and indeed, in cases where this has happened, the *women* have been blamed for being hostile, angry, and uncooperative, illustrating that on some level, we have laid responsibility for the maintenance of these factors on the shoulders of women all along. As Lakoff points out, a man who fails to engage in social conventions of politeness will usually be "indulgently overlooked" (1975, 55), whereas for a woman "it's social death in conventional circles to refuse to go by the rules" (ibid., 56). Aries also reports that it is "more important for employee morale for women than men to appear friendly, express approval, promote happy relations, and show encouragement, concern, and attentiveness" (1987, 155). In other words, it may appear unnecessary to subject language to moral criteria on the grounds that our language has proceeded smoothly without such moral criteria actually being in place; whereas in fact we have been assigning responsibility for the maintenance of these features to one particular group of participants who are given no credit for this labour, but who are subject to severe criticism when they refuse or fail to perform it.

Third, the extension of moral criteria to language need not be as overpowering as one might initially suppose. As Susan Shimanoff says, just because behaviour is open to evaluation does not mean that it will always be appraised, as "there are factors that inhibit sanctions" (1980, 91). As a linguistic and moral community, we will have to decide when the context calls for moral evaluation and when it does not. Furthermore, the moral criteria themselves may be more or less compelling. Shimanoff, for example, although she does not discuss the moral criteria of language specifically, does describe positive and negative evaluations in ways that are helpful to the development of the ideas in this book. She speaks of three sorts of rules—obligatory rules, which prescribe behaviour that must be obeyed, prohibitive rules, which specify behaviour that one must not engage in, and preferential rules, which specify behaviour that, although it is recognized as valuable, is not to be strictly required of us. If it turns out that many of the moral parameters of discourse are governed by rules that fall within this third category, then the yoke fashioned by imposing moral criteria on our language use may not be nearly as onerous as our critic feared. Furthermore, even when moral criteria apply, it does not necessarily follow that there will be anything like legal compulsion to behave in the desired ways. We would all probably agree that while offering to help someone on crutches across an icy street is morally desirable, any attempt to *legislate* such helpful behaviour would be wrong-headed. In some cases, of course, we would expect legislation to accompany moral desirability, but for the most part this would not happen.

Whether onerous or not, however, if language, like any form of behaviour, impinges on other people, if, as I have indicated above and shall argue in more detail below, it is a factor in the formulation of attitudes and perceptions, then it needs to be governed by moral criteria. If, like other forms of behaviour, language is capable of doing harm to other people, then it needs to be governed by moral criteria. The new genre of "chilly climate" research strongly suggests that non-inclusive, trivializing, and demeaning language does indeed do harm to those victimized by it. As I have argued in Chapter One, MacKinnon's *Only Words* (1993) makes a compelling argument that the language of pornography harms women in serious ways. It is only possible to imagine language incapable of doing harm if we look at each particular linguistic occurrence in isolation from the broad context against which it occurs. As Van de Wetering claims, however, such isolation makes no sense—racially derogatory language, for example, cannot be disassociated from "a long and dreadful history of rock-pelting, derision, and segregation" (1991, 100). This argument will be further developed in Chapter Nine. Furthermore, the implications of *not* evaluating linguistic behaviour by moral standards would include indifference to slander, deceit, and access of potential speakers to the discourse, all of which are clearly undesirable.

It would be particularly interesting to examine conversational interactions from within the framework of the ethical theories of Carol Gilligan (1982) and Nel Noddings (1984), for these moral theorists take as their starting point and root their notions of morality in the sort of realm that I have described earlier as the private realm. Such an investigation, although it will not be carried out in any detail in this book, would augment in useful ways the discussion of the moral parameters of linguistic interactions.

There are several different frameworks through which language could be perceived and evaluated. One could judge conversational interactions against standards of etiquette or health, as well as morality. Indeed, one of the focuses of the research on gender differences in language has been on etiquette, with many of the researchers claiming that women's language surpasses men's language in politeness (Key 1975, 75-77; Lakoff 1975, 17-19, 55-56). Concerns of politeness are not totally independent of moral concerns, of course, as the use of rude language is likely to hurt feelings and cause embarrassment; hence one who deliberately uses rude language is deliberately causing harm to others, and this is a matter of moral concern. In Chapter Nine, which focuses on the issue of political correctness, I shall develop the distinction between moral consideration and matters of etiquette, arguing that many of those who oppose fair language policies do so on the grounds of reducing moral issues to mere matters of etiquette.

So far as I know, there has been no attempt to evaluate language from the point of view of health. I envisage such an evaluation, if it were done, focusing on mental health—taking account of factors such as stress and anger. If this concept of health is broadened to community or global proportions, then it is clear that it too is interrelated with moral concerns. Some researchers do indeed envisage health from within this broadened community perspective, claiming that

for several decades, social scientists as well as health planners and prac-
titioners have perceived the need to return to the premodern conception
of disease as a sociocultural phenomenon, and of health as a multi-
dimensional *process* involving the well-being of the whole person in the
context of his environment. (Ahmed, Kolker, and Coelho 1979, 8-9,
authors' emphasis)

The authors add that their notion of health "takes into account
the specific roles the individual is expected to play in his cultural
milieu. . . . In particular, effective functioning in two social roles, the
familial and the occupational" (ibid., 13). This entails, they suggest,
that "health . . . must be viewed not merely as a state desirable in
itself but as a means toward the fulfilment of strategic role obligations, and illness as an obstacle to such fulfillment" (ibid.). Defined
in this broad way, the concept of health has obvious connections with
my discussion of language, and the relevance of applying moral criteria to both health and language appears to be straightforward. Stress
and anger at a global level spell danger of a kind we are regularly
inundated with on world news coverage. It seems reasonable to
assume that each of us, particularly those in positions of power, has a
moral responsibility to engage in patterns of behaviour and conversation that will minimize such danger.

I have argued elsewhere (Ayim 1987a; Ayim 1988) that our language, like our value structure and our way of life, is saturated
through and through with violence and aggression. I shall not reiterate these arguments here, but shall assume that such a description of
our language is widely accepted and not in need of further discussion
at this point. This position will be developed in more detail in Chapter Eight.

In what follows, I will examine the evidence which suggests that
the learning of language is a very powerful agent in shaping the sub-
stance of the roles we learn and the values we assimilate. I will then
turn to an exploration of language patterns, investigating what particular qualities might reasonably be held up as moral virtues of language itself, particularly conversational interactions. In the following
chapter, I will use these criteria to reexamine some of the empirical
claims about gender differences in language, paying heed to the
important role that evaluation and interpretation have played in this
literature. The importance of the ideas emanating from this research,
as well as the limitations and paradoxes to which the research gives
rise, will be addressed.

It is evident that language is not the whole of reality, and that even if we were to succeed in bringing about wholesale linguistic reforms, the world would still confront us with other inequities and injustices. I have no desire to contradict this view. Nevertheless, language is a part of reality, and not a trivial part. In fact, there is some evidence that it is the single most important part of the social structure, particularly in terms of shaping attitudes and expectations. Some theorists claim that young children's knowledge of gender is in large part a knowledge of how gender operates in language. Money and Ehrhardt refer to "the gender forms of personal reference embedded in the nouns and pronouns of the language" (1972, 15) as a source of constant affirmation to children of their gender assignment; Money and Tucker also speak of the importance of male/female pronouns in establishing a child's gender identity (1975, 87, 116, 118, 127). Gleason suggests that it may be the sex-role prescriptions that the child has assimilated through acquiring language which explain the claim one finds in the transsexual literature "that after the age of 18 months it is very difficult to reannounce the sex of a child if there has been an initial misidentification" (1987, 198). It seems reasonable to believe, furthermore, that the linguistic dominance and the linguistic caring that males and females engage in respectively is a model for the dominance and caring repertoires that come to characterize other aspects of their behaviour as well. Perhaps sex-role "lessons" are easily taught to school-aged children because they have learned them already, in learning how to speak the language. Whether we could learn better, more altruistic moral postures through learning better, more altruistic language patterns is a fascinating question.

This raises a question which up till now has loomed large throughout these pages, namely, What is the nature of the relationship between language and perceptions of reality? The question has been of interest to philosophers at least as far back as Plato. Interest in the question was rekindled in the 1920s and 30s through the work of Sapir and Whorf; Whorf argued that grammatical systems *determined* people's perceptions of reality with the result that speakers of such dramatically different languages as Hopi and English, for example, organized their experiences and perceived their realities in very different ways. In the words of Whorf, "in its constant ways of arranging data and its most ordinary everyday analysis of phenomena . . . we need to recognize the influence it [language] has on other activities, cultural and personal" (1956, 135).

To a certain extent, I have begged the question raised, and I will continue to beg it to a large extent because it is not possible to assemble incontrovertible empirical evidence in favour of either of the two major candidates (namely, the opposing views that language determines reality or that language is determined by reality) that have been offered as answers. Scholars who attempted to garner empirical evidence to support the Whorf hypothesis of linguistic determinism achieved at best inconclusive results. However, as I will point out in Chapter Seven, MacKay argues that the reason for these disappointing results was that the researchers focused exclusively on linking *descriptive* features of language, such as its mechanisms for coding colours and shapes, to speakers' perceptions; such research thus ignored the relationship between language and *evaluative* features, that is, "subjective or personal judgments concerning the *value* of concepts or events" (MacKay 1983, 45, author's emphasis). MacKay's own research, he argues, provides strong supportive evidence for the link between language and evaluative thought (1980a, 94-96).

As I will indicate in Chapter Seven, I am persuaded by MacKay's argument. I am not committed to a radical version of the Whorf hypothesis, however, which sees our perceptions and attitudes as strictly limited to and by the conventions governing the language that we speak (or sign). That is, I think people can (and some have) risen above the limitations of their language to formulate ideas that are revolutionary given the context of that language. The emergence of feminist ideas against a context of patriarchal, misogynist language is an example. What I am committed to is the much weaker claim that our perceptions and attitudes are *influenced by* the strengths and limitations of the language available to us. Notice that this thesis is totally compatible with the view that language is shaped by the context of community attitudes and perceptions—in other words, we would expect that those whose ideology included an abhorrence of racism, for example, would consciously attempt to eschew racist terms from their vocabulary. One would expect a mutual influence to exist between attitudes and language, and the weakened version of the Whorf hypothesis that I adopt, as it is totally compatible with this two-way influence, is not undermined by the "chicken or the egg" issue of which came first. Whether the influence of language on perceptions and attitudes is stronger than the influence of attitudes and perceptions on language is not even particularly germane to my thesis; so long as language has some appreciable effect on attitudes and perceptions, I am able to argue that language should be subject to moral criteria.

My critic might now charge that I have not established that language does influence attitudes and perceptions, and such a charge would, on the whole, be accurate. My references to MacKay's work in Chapter Seven go some distance to answering the critic. Nevertheless, this does not constitute what one could call satisfactory proof. I am, however, sceptical that it is possible to control the relevant variables, i.e., language, culture, history, geography, life style, etc., to an extent permitting proof. I believe that in the last analysis, Khosroshahi is correct in claiming that those who accept or reject the Whorf hypothesis do not do so on the basis of compelling evidence, but rather on the basis of subjective preferences (1989, 523, n. 2). Even in its weakened form, the Whorf hypothesis is too sweeping a claim to receive any decisive empirical authentication. In spite of the lack, if not the impossibility of empirical validation, people continue, often with passion, to accept or reject the Whorf hypothesis. I am no exception to this trend, and join the ranks of many other feminist researchers in particular who do not believe that common sense permits any other view than that language does influence attitudes. How could it not influence attitudes?

I offer the following, not exactly as evidence, which would be wrong-headed, given the preceding discussion, but more as illustrations of why I endorse the weak version of the Whorf hypothesis. How could children grow up surrounded by racist terms and not be influenced by the common parlance in formulating their attitudes and perceptions? Teachers are quite aware, for example, of the power of labels on children—label a child exceptional and you have stacked the deck in favour of exceptional behaviour. Label a child deviant and you have stacked the deck in a different direction. In a fascinating paper on demonology and styles of reasoning, Allen[5] cites the following sentence from a letter written to the Supreme Court of Spain in 1610: "There were neither witches nor bewitched until they were talked and written about" (1993, 95). Notice that I have not claimed that these labels *guarantee* the stipulated behavioral patterns, but only that they are a strong factor in encouraging such behaviour. Again, on a personal level, I find it mind-boggling that anyone could deny such a claim. What I find mind-boggling does not constitute proof, however, and I concede that there is no compelling empirical evidence to validate the claim that language influences perceptions and hence real social circumstances of people's lives. (See Graddol and Swann 1989 for an excellent discussion of this issue.)

So even though I have no decisively established, empirically grounded answer to the question raised earlier, namely, what is the nature of the relationship between language and perceptions of reality, I have answered the question, and the way in which I have answered it has shaped every chapter of this book. However, I believe it is possible to muster a persuasive argument for the importance of judging language by moral criteria even given the abysmal failure of researchers to validate the Whorf hypothesis. My argument is based on the straightforward claim that simply because people engage in language, linguistic interactions should be fair, inclusive, and non-prejudicial. Consider a somewhat analogous example of voting. To say that the criminally insane may not vote is one thing, to say that female people, Black people, or Native people may not vote is quite another. Race and gender are rightly seen as not merely irrelevant, but illicit criteria in selecting members of the voting population. Laws that outrightly enshrine racist or sexist voting policies are thus straightforwardly seen to be immoral. One doesn't need to go as far as laws proscribing certain segments of the population from voting to identify moral problems, however. An atmosphere that makes it threatening for particular groups of people to vote easily qualifies as morally problematic. I argue that the extension of these features to language are all that I require to make the case for the application of moral criteria. Laws that proscribe certain groups of people from speaking (and voting may actually be seen as a *form* of speaking) are morally problematic in an obvious way. An atmosphere that makes it threatening for particular groups of people to speak easily qualifies as morally problematic. There is bound to be disagreement about whether any particular "atmospheric conditions" are in fact threatening, but open and honest discussion will provide the best format for identifying worrisome conditions. What is crucial to remember is that *all* relevant persons must not only be *allowed* to contribute to this discussion, but must be *invited and welcomed* to participate. As MacKinnon points out, one of the great flaws of the debate surrounding pornography is that it excluded the voices of women entirely, focusing only on the perspectives of the male producers and consumers (1993).

I turn now to the particular features that I believe constitute the moral criteria against which conversational interactions should be judged. Let me say first that I believe these are genuinely *moral* criteria, and that they cannot legitimately be dismissed as mere matters of etiquette or as mere descriptions of language patterns. I do believe that these criteria are a fairly close match to many of the descriptive claims made about women's speech patterns (as will be discussed in more detail in the following chapter), but we should not be sidetracked by this away from the more important moral considerations. Let me also be clear that I do not perceive morally good language as a merely extrinsic good, whose worth lies in its achievement of some other end, namely, some extra-linguistic moral end. Morally good language is an intrinsic good, something to be valued for its own sake. While it obviously doesn't exhaust the pool of moral goodness, good language is both a legitimate and an enormous part of that pool. We live for the most part not as recluses, but in community. The moral criteria take account of this fact and attempt to regulate, in as fair a way as possible, community interactions. In this regard, the moral criteria of language are no different from moral criteria generally.

I perceive these moral criteria as prima facie requirements of good conversations. Upon occasion, there may be powerful and legitimate reasons to override any of them, but normally, unless exceptional circumstances were established, one would expect all of the criteria to be operative. This is an initial exploration, and I make no claim to completeness. I offer the following as important criteria which should be included in any list of important moral considerations of language interactions. First, morally good language is caring; second, morally good language is cooperative; third, morally good language is democratic; fourth, morally good language is honest. I shall discuss each of these criteria in turn.

(1) Language as Caring: Disregard of and indifference to others are the alternatives to caring. If language is caring, it will begin by displaying a readiness to *listen* to the other speakers, and to pay attention to them in verbal and perhaps non-verbal ways, such as making eye contact, as well. By these means, such behaviour invites others to speak and exhibits a positive valuing of their linguistic contributions. If we believe in the importance of caring as a criterion, we will do well to take heed of Hare's advice that we develop "the ability to discern the feelings of others and how our actions will impinge upon them" (1973, 161). Caring language will attempt to include these others as full participants, and in its inclusion of them, it will be concerned about their sense of being valued participants in the conversation,

their self-esteem, their level of comfort, and their desire to participate. Because it attempts to include others fully, caring language will not attempt to dominate them, nor will it normally confront them—it is anti-dominant and anti-confrontational. Caring language will acknowledge the right of others to participate in the conversation, but its focus will be on a positive valuing of those others rather than a neutral acknowledgement of their right to speak.

(2) Language as Cooperative: Self-centred individualism and egotism are the alternatives to cooperative language. Cooperative language works *with* others. It *engages* them. It facilitates their speaking and builds upon what they say. Whereas caring language values others by inviting them to speak and then listening to them carefully, cooperative language values them through interaction or exchange— by making a follow-up comment or asking a question at a strategic point. Cooperative speakers are those who have learned to monitor their own input into the conversation in such a way as to take seriously the contributions of the other participants. Without this monitoring, we all speak in monologue even when we speak in company. Conversation presupposes a genuinely social context, and it is the cooperative feature of language as exhibited in the responsive monitoring of what we say that provides this social context.

(3) Language as Democratic: The unfair allocation of privilege, even bullying and silencing of the unprivileged, are the alternatives to democratic language. Democratic language is predisposed to include and value equally other participants in the conversation; it is at heart anti-hierarchical. Democratic language will not tolerate the silencing of particular people or particular groups of people except in circumstances where those individuals or groups insist on silencing others. Democratic speech will strive, so far as possible, to see that everyone has a turn, and that no one is excluded from the conversation. In the microcosm, such as a particular conversation, the democratic criterion will insist that no individual be excluded on the presumed grounds of that individual's lesser right to speak. In the macrocosm, racism, sexism, and classism which silence individuals or groups will themselves be eschewed by this criterion; as well, a historical account which excludes the perspective of all but the politically dominant group will be judged undemocratic. Hence a history of the "discovery" of North America portrayed exclusively from the perspective of the European colonialists will fail the democracy criterion, as will an account of women's winning the franchise which depicts this event

through patriarchal eyes as "men giving women the vote" or an account which fails to point out that not all women and men won the vote at the same time—in Canada, for example, women in Quebec[6] and Native people with Indian status did not win the right to vote until the 1940s and the 1960s respectively.

Many educational and other institutions are now taking cognizance of the importance of fair and equitable language by designing and implementing guidelines for "inclusive" language. The notion of "inclusive" captures much of the sense of "democratic" as the term is used in this discussion. Democratic speech will not simply refrain from preventing an individual from speaking; it will overtly invite those who have remained silent to contribute to the conversation.

(4) Language as Honest: Morally good language is not devious; it is straightforward and honest. It can be sensitive (and indeed, if it is caring, it must be sensitive), but it will not normally deceive in order to protect. Deceitful exchanges normally involve a violation of either the cooperative or the caring principle. I cannot be genuinely working together with someone to whom I am dishonest in my conversation. Deviousness on my part normally suggests either that I do not trust the person in question, in which case there is no genuine cooperation and our conversation is a mere charade, or that I do not value the person, in which case I have violated the principle of caring.

I have described this fourth criterion as one of honesty rather than telling the truth. This choice of words is deliberate. Truth-telling (and truth-preservation) is closer to Grice's analysis of conversational implicature. My emphasis is quite different from his and much closer to Habermas' conditions of sincerity and fidelity, as described by Sirotnik (1991, 248). Hence I focus on being honest as opposed to saying what is truthful. The notion of telling the truth frequently suggests to people that there is one truth, clear, unambiguous, and unique, a truth in the possession of some privileged people and at least temporarily beyond the grasp of others. A corollary of this view is that the epistemically privileged have the right and perhaps even the duty to carry this truth to the epistemically underprivileged. Because I want to be careful not to suggest any such simplistic point of view, I speak in terms of honesty rather than truth. Among other things, honesty commits us to admitting that there is very little that is either worthy or interesting which is clear, simple, and unambiguous.

It is important to note that these four criteria are committed to a positive valuing not only of the other *participants* in the conversation, but also of the *conversation* itself. These features, particularly the first three, but also to some extent the fourth, all contribute to keeping the channels of communication open, to maintaining the discussion rather than permitting it to degenerate into monologue or allowing it to expire altogether.

Notice that there seems to be a rather uneasy fit between my first three criteria and my fourth criterion. This is, upon reflection, not surprising. The first three criteria are of a different kind than the fourth criterion, in the sense that they have a quite different focus. The fourth criterion is akin to the conversational maxims proposed by Grice (1981, 184-185) insofar as its primary focus appears to be on the preservation of truth; by being honest in what we say, we allow others to make valid inferences based upon our remarks. The first three criteria, on the other hand, appear to focus not so much on the preservation of truth as on the preservation of relationships among the speakers that enhance the full and equal valuing of each participant. Grice, in providing us with a *logical* analysis of language, makes the conveying of reliable information the yardstick against which the maxims are ultimately measured. My goal is to provide a *moral* analysis of language, and hence it is respect for persons that becomes the ultimate yardstick for my criteria. The logical and the moral are not disconnected, of course; hence I argue that being dishonest in what we say to people entails on some level, a lack of full respect and concern for them. I advocate the fourth criterion insofar as it is an essential ingredient for building a moral society, not because it is an essential ingredient for acquiring the truth.

In his article entitled "Why Dialogue?" Bruce Ackerman "proclaim[s] dialogue as the *first* obligation of citizenship" (1989, 6, my emphasis). He further argues that dialogue enjoys this privileged place only in the public arena of morality—that of citizenship—and that in the private arena "a morally reflective person *can* permissibly cut herself off from real-world dialogue" (ibid., author's emphasis). Ackerman believes that the reason why dialogue is so important in the public realm is that the future of the human race depends upon our coming to understand one another as well as possible. This entails that we learn to talk to one another, "to strangers as well as soul-mates" (ibid., 22); he admonishes us to "consider whether, despite the stranger's strangeness, we might still have something reasonable to say to one another about our efforts to coexist on this puzzling planet" (ibid.). I argue that it is equally urgent for us to apply Ackerman's advice about maintaining dialogue to the personal level; we should not assume that at the personal level we are all soul-mates who understand one another clearly, for all too frequently perfect strangers may share the same house for decades. The level of misunderstanding between men and women in the most intimate of contexts may be more profound than the misunderstanding between alien nations. One of the great strengths of Tannen's book, *You Just Don't Understand: Women and Men in Conversation* (1990), is the insight that she brings to this level of misunderstanding. The current epidemic levels of familial violence and abuse might be diminished in direct proportion to a reduction in levels of misunderstanding.

Although I acknowledged earlier a difference in kind between my first three criteria and my fourth criterion, I wish to develop further my sense of the connection between these two sets of criteria. I have already pointed out that lack of honesty in our dealings with others signals ultimately a lack of respect or caring for them. There may be some exceptions to this, of course, such as a decision not to disclose to a patient that they have a terminal disease, but the exceptions are few and far between, as the extreme nature of this example suggests; even in this extreme case, there are many circumstances that would prompt us to tell the patient the painful truth. Generally speaking, then, to be honest with someone is an indication that we care about that person.

The connection between my criteria works in the other direction as well, however. If honesty (or truth) is our goal, then silencing others is most definitely proscribed. We cannot achieve honest communication with one another if we do not allow everyone to participate in the discourse. Undemocratic language in particular mitigates against achieving an honest or truthful linguistic result in much the same way that hiding or not taking full account of the available evidence predisposes scientific conclusions towards partiality and even falsehood. Inviting everyone to speak, creating a context in which it feels safe for them to speak, and then listening carefully to what they say (the caring criterion), building on their contribution through further interaction and exchange, such as follow-up comments and questions (the cooperative criterion), and refusing to tolerate the systematic silencing of particular groups of people (the democratic criterion) are as essential to achieving an honest (or truthful) conversation as a full inclusion of all the relevant data and an open mind towards new or unusual forms of evidence are to the achievement of scientific truth. Leaving people out of the conversation not only strains the fabric of caring; it also jeopardizes our attainment of truth.[7]

It will not have gone unobserved that my criteria, particularly the first three, are by no means neutral; they embody a very particular "slant." I would characterize my criteria as, first, anti-dominant and anti-confrontational (hence the caring criterion); second, anti-hierarchical (hence the democratic criterion); and third, anti-self-centred individualism (hence the cooperative criterion). I will conclude this chapter with a detailed discussion of each of these three features.

(1) *The criteria are anti-dominant and anti-confrontational*: My criteria contain a clear bias against dominant and confrontational styles. I will turn now to a discussion of why this is so. I believe that there are strong logical reasons to support an antipathy to certain forms of dominance and confrontation. Not all confrontation or dominance is undesirable. Confronting a liar with a harmful lie may be a positive good; notice that this instance honours the fourth of my criteria—namely, that language should be honest. Dominance and even aggression directed towards a wife-batterer may be similarly positive; again, notice that this behaviour may represent an act of caring—caring for the batterer's actual and potential victims, and that caring is the first of my four moral criteria. I have been careful to use the modal verb "may," not because I am afraid to take a definite stand on this issue, but because I do not believe there is one simple obvious solution to any social problem, including spousal abuse. I believe that in many instances a criminal charge and a prison sentence are appropriate responses to wife-battering. In other instances, I believe that providing counselling for the batterer would constitute a much more appropriate response, and an appeal to the criminal justice system would be seriously mistaken. These two "remedies" are not theoretically incompatible, although the nature of our penal system often renders them practically incompatible.

The point I am trying to make about the anti-dominance stance of my criteria is that dominance may be justifiable and even required in many contexts. Any adult who has ever protected a child from abuse at the hands of another adult will understand this. It is dominance for its own sake, dominance for the fun of it, dominance as a means of bolstering the unjust distribution of privileges, dominance as a style of living and expressing oneself that is troublesome.

Males, male roles, and male styles tend to be positively valued in our society, while females, female roles, and female styles are devalued. The deepest insult that one can give a man or a boy is to suggest that he is like a female. A book by the well-known mystery writer Elspeth Huxley (1938), demonstrates this in the clearest way possible. The novel, entitled *Murder on Safari*, is constructed around a white hunting safari in East Africa; the native Blacks are painted with every colonialist stereotype one could imagine. One of the central characters, a white male named Gordon Catchpole, who is engaged to be married to Cara, a female member of the party, is depicted as weak, cowardly, and insipid (his fiancé Cara eventually runs off with *a real man*—one of the white hunters). The reader recognizes these despicable features in Catchpole's character because Huxley has given him female speech patterns and female body language. When he is eventually killed—gored to death by a raging buffalo—the reader is made to feel that it is no great loss.

Of the male styles that our society has glorified, dominance and aggression are high on the list. Even our portrayal of animals reflects this. I watched an otherwise excellent televised documentary on caribou which illustrates my point. The documentary examined the life styles of the caribou, and demonstrated how these life styles, indeed the caribou's very existence, are being threatened by humanity's ever-extending greed for physical resources. The caribou was portrayed as a noble animal, the mother-infant bonding, the protection of the young by the adult females, and the fighting of the males with one another were all given dramatic footage. The documentary could have ended with a female suckling its infant, or a female helping its young in the dangerous fording of a treacherous river, or the members of the herd in the midst of their seasonal marathon trek of several thousand miles; what was chosen instead as the final and lingering image of the caribou was two males locking horns.

Males locking horns has become symbolic of that which is strong and admirable and worthwhile—the noble warriors who hone their strength to a fine point and use that strength to protect the weak—their females and their young. The actual facts about the animals whose habits have served to inspire this picture are then conveniently forgotten—the male caribou, for example, spend their lives fighting with each other and impregnating the females—but their aggressive dispositions are never used to protect the herd. In fact, aside from the breeding season, the females and young travel alone with no adult males present. It is the adult females who protect the young and who teach them how to protect themselves from danger.

Yet we continue to act as though male aggression were for the benefit of the species. We even talk as though we believe that it has evolved for precisely that reason, and we reward it.

As women, many of us have bought the Little Red Riding Hood myth, together with its dream of a strong competent woodsman who will protect us from the world's big bad wolves; our myth has not included any sense of the possibility that the woodsman's axe could be turned against us. We have rewarded, even glorified the woodsman, but we have not thought it necessary to give Little Red Riding Hood lessons in self-defence so that she could protect herself from both wolf and woodsman. In her book, *Lost in Translation*, Hoffman recalls a young boy on whom she had a childhood "crush." This boy, among other things, had dropped a heavy book on her head while she was walking under his window and had attempted to push her into an excavation made by the Germans which could well have contained mines (1989, 18-19). In spite of such behaviour, Hoffman recalls holding the "deep belief that his greater physical strength is there to protect me" (ibid., 19). The statistics on date and wife abuse make me less sanguine about sharing Hoffman's childhood belief, at least on any general basis.

Tannen believes that by-and-large, however, women are wary of aggression, and that sex differences in interpretation of aggression are the source of one of the most fundamental misunderstandings between men and women (1990, 150-160). Tannen assumes that very little male aggression is real—most is ritual, and it is a ritual that they enjoy, particularly with intimate others. They therefore engage in metaphorical wrestling with their wives, finding themselves constantly frustrated and disappointed, because the wives fail to recognize that they are being complimented by being selected as sparring partners in the ritual combat—there is after all no contest, not to mention no fun, in wrestling with a weakling. Intimacy is characterized in a totally different way by women, who, instead of being complimented and exhilarated by the wrestling match, feel hurt. Men would like the women with whom they are intimate to be more aggressive, to return push with push according to Tannen (1990, 160). I am not sanguine about the truth of this claim either. Research on wife abuse indicates that husbands frequently "justify" battering their wives because of a show of dominance or even independence in their wives' behaviour (Kincaid 1982, 162-164). One of the most critical lessons a male-to-female transsexual has to learn is submission—

i.e., an erasure of dominance from one's repertoire of behaviours (Garfinkel with Stoller 1967, 146-148). Tannen herself, in a different passage, speaks as though she might agree with this when she describes dominance, aggression, and pushiness as "qualities that are perceived as far more negative in women than in men" (1990, 209).

In a similar vein to Tannen, Ong (1981, 29, 119-121, 146-147) argues that historically, ceremonial or play aggression drained off much of the real hostility of students towards teachers. Since the aggressive mode is no longer tolerated in classrooms, the students' aggression is now expressed in a real rather than play form, with the result that teachers now face real violence at the students' hands. I am very sceptical of this analysis because it presupposes the validity of the catharsis model—that mock violence offers an outlet to and hence prevents the eruption of real violence. If this were true, then we should have expected to find a superfluity of real violence in girls' and women's lives for generations, given that the play violence of the debate and many forms of sport was not open to them as it was to males. The reality, of course, is that the enactment of real violence most strongly characterized the lives of males, for whom ritualized aggression was an acceptable form of behaviour, thus suggesting that *it is not the closing off of ritualized aggression* that is responsible for real aggression, but *something else entirely*.

The linguistics literature does not provide us with universal agreement that female language is supportive and affiliative, while male language is dominant and aggressive. The dissenting voice frequently emerges from those researching children's language. Corsaro and Rizzo's research on children's disputes in Italian nursery schools would seem to support the claim that the little girls took as much delight in a no-holds-barred argument as the little boys did (1990, 38-64).

Goodwin and Goodwin, in their study (referred to earlier) of working-class Black American children from the Philadelphia area, claim that the language of the girls they studied was dramatically not the sweet, sugary, supportive style that the standard linguistics literature attributes to females, including young Black females (1987, 239). Contrary to this standard picture of "sweetness and light," the Goodwins claimed that the "girls use of dispute structures was quite similar to those of the boys" (ibid.). In fact, the authors believe that any analysis of these children's speech based on sex differences would have seriously misrepresented their speech (ibid., 205); the Goodwins caution us to be wary of research that characterizes all females one way and all males another, paying no attention to even such basic factors as race (ibid., 241). It is not that there are no differences between the boys and girls they studied, but that *focusing* on these differences to *explain* the children's speech would have seriously misrepresented it (ibid., 244-245, n. 4), for the speech structures were far more similar than different. Much the same point (also referred to earlier) is made by Bambi Schieffelin who claims that the Kaluli children of Papua New Guinea, do not exhibit much difference in their language based on sex. Schieffelin says that "for all the differences in the ways in which boys and girls are treated, there do not seem to be any significant linguistic reflections of these differences" (1987, 257).

Several of the differences that the Goodwins did document challenge the stereotypes: they claim that the girls' arguments were more complex than the boys, embodying multiple embedded claims and perspectives, while the boys' more often took the form of simple opposition (Goodwin and Goodwin 1987, 238, 248, n. 42); their research also indicates that while the boys' arguments were of relatively short duration, it was not unusual for an argument among girls to last for weeks (ibid., 240); two further differences are documented, but these reflect rather than challenge the stereotypes. The first has to do with the content of the arguments—whereas boys tended to dispute about their relative rank orderings in skill and ability, the girls' disputes centred around their relationships with others and with their appearance (ibid., 229). Secondly, when boys argued with other boys, this often took the form of one boy directly confronting another with an alleged offence, such as having broken the complainant's skate board. The girls' arguments seldom involved this direct form of confrontation, but much more often involved talking "about offensive actions of others in their absence" (ibid., 230). Ironically, the offensive action most frequently attributed to the absent girl was that of talking about the complainant behind her back (ibid.). It is interesting to ask whether this observation involves a violation of my first criterion of caring—is it uncaring to make disparaging remarks about someone behind their back? On the other hand, it could also involve a violation of the fourth criterion of honesty—is it dishonest to make comments behind a person's back that one would not normally make to their face?

Reading the delightful accounts of children's language provided by Goodwin and Goodwin as well as Corsaro and Rizzo calls to mind my own personal delight with argument, engendered in part by a background in philosophy and probably in equal part by a very argumentative father; a world of discourse that refused to tolerate any form of argument would be, in my eyes, sadly diminished. Am I being inconsistent here?

I think not. To proscribe disagreement would not only be foolish; it would also be reckless. There is much about our world that morally exacts our disagreement. To proscribe argument would be reckless, for arguments will often serve us well both in condemning immoral structures and in supporting moral ones. Part of the problem has been that by historical tradition, the argument turf has been relegated only to men. Goodwin and Goodwin express surprise that society has so thoroughly condemned arguments, while their research has revealed much that is creative and delightful in children's arguments (ibid., 226). I think that it is not the argument per se that society has appraised negatively, but the use of arguments by children and women; children, like women, were to be seen and not heard, and arguments were thus exclusively the territory of adult males.

The point of an argument is supposedly to get at the truth, not to best one's opponent. So long as arguments reflect this purpose, they are perfectly acceptable, even welcome, and sometimes mandatory. Three caveats are important for us to bear in mind. First, arguments need not be negative; they may be positive, and used in support of positions and ideas. This feature of the argument has frequently been lost sight of in our actual use and understanding of arguments. Second, arguments are *one* avenue among many for getting at truth; feelings, ordinary discussion, and gossip are examples of other avenues, perhaps more efficient than argument in many contexts for getting at the truth. Third, truth is seldom singular and is mostly plural; it is seldom simple and is mostly complex.

(2) *The criteria are anti-hierarchical*: It is frequently observed that male language as well as male play tends to be hierarchical and power-based whereas female language and female play tend to be egalitarian and solidarity-based (Fishman 1980; Gleason 1987; Sachs 1987). Dale Spender claims that traditional education—i.e., male-centred education—is very hierarchical and competitive, in sharp contrast to feminist education, which is in essence cooperative (1981, 169). In Barbara Johnstone's research based on an analysis of her students' conversational narratives (1993), she claims that in their stories her male students glorified a world of struggle, a world in

which an individual protagonist who was always a male and usually the writer himself, was pitted against a hostile world which he conquered through a physical, verbal, or intellectual contest (ibid., 1993, 69). By contrast, her female students glorified a world of cooperation and helpfulness, a world in which the community norms and conformity to these norms were of paramount importance (ibid., 69-70). The protagonists in the females' stories included males as well as females, and frequently involved group action rather than focusing on the struggle of an individual against the group (ibid., 70-71). This brings to mind some aspects of Nel Noddings ethical theory. In contrast to traditional ethical theories, which see the individual as primary, and the moral law a mechanism for maximizing the good and the autonomy of individuals collectively, Noddings perceives relationships as primary and the moral law (caring) as a mechanism for promoting people's capacity to sustain relationships. She says:

> we are irrevocably linked to intimate others. This linkage, this fundamental relatedness, is at the very heart of our being. Thus I am totally free to reject the impulse to care, but I enslave myself to a particularly unhappy task when I make this choice. As I chop away at the chains that bind me to loved others, asserting my freedom, I move into a wilderness of strangers and loneliness, leaving behind all who cared for me and even, perhaps, my own self. I am not naturally alone. I am naturally in a relation from which I derive nourishment and guidance. When I am alone, either because I have detached myself or because circumstances have wrenched me free, I seek first and most naturally to reestablish my relatedness. This is my basic reality. (Noddings 1984, 51)

As models for moral behaviour, I have qualms about aspects of both the male and female storytelling styles documented by Johnstone. The female stories seem to suggest that conformity to community norms is always a good thing and deviance from these norms is to be universally condemned (Johnstone 1993, 69-70); this is a very worrisome belief for any community whose norms fall short of moral perfection. Goodwin and Goodwin's observation that girls (unlike boys) make negative comments about other girls in the absence of those girls, rather than confronting them directly (1987, 230), is similarly worrisome, from a moral point of view; this behaviour suggests a kind of underhandedness or dishonesty. I have also been very careful to stipulate that I do not believe that dominance and confrontation are always reprehensible, and that they may, upon occasion, be morally mandatory.

The male stories worry me on several counts, however. The preferred stance of struggling against rather than working with the group must confound the requirements of community living (Johnstone 1993, 69-71). Sometimes of course, as I have argued above, it will be morally incumbent on us to confound the community norms, in instances where the norms themselves are racist, sexist, classist, or morally problematic in other ways. But if the point of the struggle is the struggle itself, rather than the improvement of the community, then this pitting of the individual against the group is self-defeating. If all of us glorified and acted out this stance, there could be no community and that is the heart of the problem. Individualism and confrontation are not generalizable in a social context. They *cannot be general models* for our behaviour, although they can be justifiable and even required in certain contexts.

If we live in a racist society, it is morally incumbent on us to refuse to foster the norms of that society, to stand up and be counted as individuals in opposition to the community standards; the point of the opposition here is not the glory of doing battle, but rendering the society more social, more inclusive of all peoples, and more egalitarian. The sorts of speech styles attributed by many linguists to males (see Fishman 1980, Gleason 1987, and Sachs 1987) are the very opposite of egalitarian; they are *at heart* hierarchical (this empirical literature will be discussed in more detail in the following chapter). Hierarchies, by definition, have room for only a few at the top, forcing most of us to the lower rungs. The hierarchical arrangement can offer each person a chance for happiness and satisfaction only if many people *actually desire* to be situated "below the salt," as it were. Fox's research with student writing described one of the male students as almost fixated on his own suffering incurred as a result of constantly being pushed to the bottom of the hierarchy (1990, 60-64). In spite of this suffering, however, the student consistently struggled to turn the classroom into a competition, and expressed contempt for those students who were, in his opinion, too weak or too timid to pull themselves to the top (ibid., 69-70).

Leet-Pellegrini claims that her research supports "the view that male experts pursue a style of interacting based on power, while female experts pursue a style based upon solidarity and support" (1980, 97). Sachs' research on young children's games suggests a similar gender pattern. When the boys played together, nearly all of them wanted the prestigious role of doctor, and furthermore, they structured their playing in such a way that there could only be one doctor (Sachs 1987, 181, 185), a setup determined by logic to generate dissatisfaction in all the players except the head "honcho" who made it to the doctor role. The girls in Sachs' study, on the other hand, often expressed a preference for roles other than doctor, such as mother, baby, or patient (ibid., 180); furthermore, they structured their games in such a way that more than one player could be the doctor (ibid., 181).

It is interesting to speculate on whether the fact that the girls tend to play and talk in small, rather than large groups like the boys, influences the greater levels of solidarity and supportiveness documented by researchers in the play and talk of the girls they studied (Gleason 1987; Sachs 1987). There is a possible link to male fear of intimacy, leading to a preference for large rather than smaller groups, thus making it more unlikely or difficult to establish supportive interactions. Tannen's claim that "more men than women are comfortable holding forth to a crowd" (1990, 136) is probably a close match for most of our informal observations of women and men talking. Aries' research supports this view, claiming that whereas men prefer to address their remarks to groups as a whole, women prefer to address individuals (1987, 154). Carol Mitchell's research on joke-telling suggests that women are more reluctant than men to tell jokes in a setting outside the home and that women have a strong preference for a small audience, unlike men, who prefer larger audiences (1985, 168). Mitchell also notes that men told "more obscene jokes, more racial, ethnic, and religious jokes" (ibid., 166-167) than women, and that "on the whole, men told a considerably higher percentage than women of the openly hostile and aggressive jokes" (ibid., 167). Not only is the content of the male jokes included in Mitchell's study more hostile, but the ways in which they use the jokes are also more hostile (ibid., 185); for example, the males in her study are reported as more likely to use jokes "to deride someone whom they dislike . . . [and] are more likely than women to tell jokes that they think might be offensive to some members of the audience" (ibid., 167-168). Matsuda indicates "that in researching hundreds of incidents of racist violence . . . in virtually every case the perpetrators were men" (1993, 23).

One cannot help but wonder why the men studied appear to prefer joke-telling that leads "to hurt feelings and hostility" (Mitchell 1985, 167) over women's style of joke-telling, which "seems to conciliate opposing views" (ibid.). Is there a connection between this and boys' inclination to design their games in such a way that almost all the players turn out to be dissatisfied with the role they play? Would the game be no fun for them otherwise? If there could be more satisfied players than one, would this rob the game of the challenge that made it interesting? If the top role in the game held room for more than one player, is it no longer worth the struggle to achieve in these little boys' minds?

I don't know the answers to these questions, but they remind me of a conversation I had with a male student of mine early in my teaching career. I was teaching an evening course in logic and philosophy of science and the student was a senior administrator with a major Canadian business. He was very affable, extremely pleasant in class, and generally an asset to class discussions and dynamics. We had both arrived to class early, and were chatting informally about our day. He expressed excitement with his day, which he had spent interviewing candidates for a middle management position. He shared with me his formula for making the second to last set of cuts—in an interview with the candidates he would ask them outright if they wanted his job, rejecting all but the ones who answered affirmatively. If they didn't want his job, he didn't want them working for him, he told me. I was puzzled. They weren't applying for his job, and if hired, wouldn't be hired to do his job. Why was it a necessary condition that they want to do a job they weren't even being considered for, I asked him? He looked at me pityingly and did his best to explain that this firm wanted only the highest calibre of administrator, and that automatically excluded anyone whose sights weren't set on the upper echelons. My student believed so thoroughly that this kind of competitiveness was necessary to the job that he was willing, indeed he intended, to hire someone who would represent a real threat to his own position. Like the little boys struggling for the doctor role, did he believe his position not worth occupying unless the rules were defined in such a way that he had to struggle constantly to protect it from ambitious competitors?

The sense that competitiveness is a positive good, a trait worthy of inculcation in all responsible people, is one that enjoys widespread acceptance. Contemporary critiques of the Canadian and American educational systems bemoan the fact that we have fallen behind the Japanese and the Germans. There is less sense of panic that our schools are graduating illiterates who can barely read at the grade five level and who depend on others to tell them how to think than that we have lost the competitive edge with other nations; I also suspect that much of the critics' consternation emerges from the fact that North American students are being bested by Asian children—the bitter pill of inferiority would be easier to swallow if it were British children, for example, particularly white British children, who were found to perform at a higher level. The comparative focus is always on mathematics, not surprisingly, as mathematics is one of the few areas which allows such a simplistic comparison. The perceived duty of the schools to socialize a competitive spirit into its students is at least as old as schools themselves. Sometimes this point of view is explicitly defended, although this is less frequent in an era of feminist critique of education; sometimes it is implicit.

It is also frequently assumed that assertiveness is an appropriate mode for classroom interactions. A careful reading of the following text will reveal that the authors have *presumed* the desirability of assertiveness in the classroom. In their paper on androgyny and conversation, Jose and his coauthors described the structure of the study on which the paper was based as follows:

> Half of the subjects role-played a class-room [*sic*] situation *where assertive behaviour is appropriate*, and half role-played a party situation where non-assertive behaviour is appropriate. . . . They were instructed to role-play the discussion *very assertively in a classroom situation* (instrumental condition), or *with primary emphasis upon understanding the other person's choices in a party situation* (expressive condition). (1980, 116, my emphasis)

Notice the assumption, which the authors do not even discuss, that assertive behaviour is appropriate to a classroom situation. Notice also the even more startling assumption that *understanding* other people's choices is appropriate to a party situation, and that this *distinguishes* the party from the classroom situation, where the focus is on *assertive discussion*, instead!

I have some concerns about the structure of the girls' games in Sachs' research (1987), even though their structure seems to make more logical sense than that of the boys. If we assume that the roles of mother, baby, and patient are in fact less desirable than that of doctor, the fact that some girls actually want these roles *seems* to solve everything nicely. Everyone can have their choice of role because not everyone wants the "head honcho" role. This looks like a wonderful resolution to the hierarchy paradox, yet it leaves me uneasy. My uneasiness reminds me of another anecdote, a joke about a dialogue between two little boys that was told to me as follows: Tom has just divided a chocolate bar into two uneven pieces and given Bob the smaller piece.

Bob: You gave me the small piece! That's not fair!
Tom: What would you have done if you'd been giving out the pieces?
Bob: Why, I'd have given you the bigger piece and taken the smaller one myself.
Tom: Well you got the smaller piece. So quit complaining!

Besides assuming that reapportioning the chocolate bar is not a possibility, which it clearly is, this dialogue makes another false assumption—that a situation which one accepts, and maybe even embraces, out of politeness and consideration for others is indistinguishable from a situation one would choose simply with one's own selfish motives in mind. It gives no credit for and takes no account of altruism.

If little girls are choosing inferior roles out of consideration for the desires of the other players (and Sachs suggests that a concern about including the other players could indeed distinguish much of the girls' behaviour from the boys' behaviour which she studied [1987, 185]), then they may be badly taken advantage of when playing with those who show no such reciprocal consideration—i.e., particularly when playing with boys. Not only will they miss out on the more desirable roles, but they will get no credit for relinquishing these roles, on the assumption that they had their chance to choose, like everyone else, and they chose not to be the doctor.

A different possibility is that the little girls *do not* perceive the doctor role to be more prestigious, but express a preference for the other roles simply because they find these roles more attractive. Consideration for the other players is not required as part of this explanation. This hypothesis also seems to offer a resolution to the hierarchy dilemma—an escape between the horns almost, by abolishing the hierarchy itself. All roles become equally good, with none better than the other. Isn't this the perfect resolution? If hierarchies are the source of the problem, and this setup removes the hierarchy, why does it, too, leave me uneasy? I think my uneasiness stems in part from the very real possibility of a merely apparent egalitarianism bolstered by a socialization of females to prefer their own inferior status, a vital component in the perpetuation of the oppression.[8] Two adults participating in the traditional patriarchal family may say and believe that they are equals—the man is breadwinner and the woman home-maker, but both are nonetheless equals in the relationship. I do not think such equality is ruled out by logic, but the empirical counter-evidence is abundant in the case of many marriage dissolutions, when the man's income will go up and the woman's down, when his salary will reflect his continued years in the work force, and her employer, if she can find one, will not recognize child-care as relevant experience, when the typical man will quickly default on his child-support payments, if he pays any at all, while the typical woman struggles to afford even minimal food and accommodation for the children. This hierarchy is a fact of life for essentially every heterosexual couple whose relationship ends, and if little girls have been led to believe that this is not so, they will be ill-prepared to cope with the reality of the situation, should it occur to them.

There are, of course, some contexts where hierarchies are necessary, and need to be built into the social structure; if every passenger had the same right as the pilot to decide upon flight manoeuvres, the airlines industry would be in a great deal of trouble. There are many other contexts where the necessity of the traditional hierarchy is less evident, marriage providing us with one example, and school administration with another. Why do we need one dominant party in a marriage? Why can't the two be partners in the full sense of the word? Why can't teachers run a school themselves, or at least have equal say with the full-time administrators? Some of the literature on educational administration indicates that the most efficiently administered schools are also schools that stress cooperation rather than authoritarianism and are work places that foster high staff morale and commitment (Shakeshaft 1987, 200). Mary Beasley claims that in the new management trend which extols cooperation and communication rather than confrontation and control, "women are ahead of the trends. They do not have to learn those leadership and management skills. They have been practising them most of their lives" (1983, 15). There are some contexts in which hierarchy is necessary, although I believe that these contexts are far fewer than we have traditionally believed. But hierarchy *for its own sake is antisocial*. It is this perceived desirability of hierarchy in male life styles rather than the mere presence of hierarchy that I believe is cause for concern.

(3) *The criteria are anti-self-centred individualism*: Two additional features of the male storytelling described by Johnstone are, in my opinion, problematic. First, and this is closely related to my dis-

cussion of hierarchy, the men's stories almost always featured a single individual protagonist (Johnstone 1993, 70-71), unlike the women's stories, which often featured groups of people working together (ibid.). Second, the protagonists in the males' stories were always males, and almost always the speaker himself (ibid., 69-70). The protagonists in the females' stories, by contrast, included males as well as females (ibid., 70). The female storytellers thus show themselves willing to try to envisage the world from a point of view other than their own, to put themselves in other people's shoes at least for a fictional moment; this is important because such a "trying on" of other vantage points is a first and necessary step for achieving the moral principle of universalizability (that is, acting on a principle of treating other people as we would like to be treated ourselves, *if* we were like them in relevant respects). The male storytellers, by comparison, have not looked beyond their own perspective.

There could be a positive as well as a negative explanation of this phenomenon. It could be that the males simply assume their perspective is the true one, perhaps the only possible one such that it doesn't even occur to them to write in another voice. Many of the feminist critiques of science (see Harding and Hintikka 1983; Harding 1986; Merchant 1980) accuse male scientists of confusing their own particular subjectivity with objectivity, because they are either unwilling or unable to give serious credence to a point of view that does not accord with their own. A more positive explanation would suggest that the storyteller knows there are other perspectives, but does not presume to be able to speak with authority in a voice other than his own. There are too many instances of middle-class caucasians who visited countries in Africa for a few weeks, and then produced "authoritative" texts on Africa for us to be unsympathetic to this wariness to stray into other people's perspectives. Writers sometimes describe a greater difficulty in "getting at" a character whose gender does not match their own and a much greater sense of confidence in the reality of their same gender characters. The writing and telling of stories within one's own perspective could be indicative of either a highly arrogant stance that there is only one perspective—one's own—or a humble stance that one cannot possibly speak for other people, and must let them speak for themselves if their voices are to be authentic.

This introduces an interesting moral quandary. If one lives life in a white skin, one will experience things differently and experience different things than if one's skin is brown. Even this is a matter-of-fact claim rather than a necessary truth. For if our society were totally non-racist—if society took skin colour to be as trivial a component of self as eye colour in the sense outlined by Wasserstrom (1979, 6-7, 14-15)—then the distribution of privileges based on skin colour would simply not occur. But our world is not colour-blind, and I cannot assume that the privileges I take for granted are available to First Nations people or Black people, or people of Asian ancestry, or members of any other racial groups. What follows from this? It follows that I should not be dogmatic in attributing the parameters of my life to everyone. But it also follows that *precisely because* my reality does not apply to everyone, I should exert extra energy to try to understand their realities as best I can. I need to talk to individuals within these groups, associate with them, try on their shoes, put their perspective as I understand it into my words so that they can correct, criticize, and augment my understanding until I get it right, or as close to right as any of us can get in understanding anyone else's perspective. There are some people in the world so totally self-centred that they couldn't even understand a sibling's perspective; we have no right to assume that their account of even a member of their own racial group will be the least bit veridical. There are others who have struggled to look at things in different ways, who have imagined other realities than their own, who, perhaps because they have loved other people, have managed to almost see the world through those other eyes. So long as we live in community with others, we must do everything we can to foster this kind of understanding; silencing its expression will not foster the understanding. Like the women in Johnstone's study (1993, 70), we must tell our stories in other people's voices as well as our own, with the double proviso that we struggle to achieve the greatest accuracy possible in presenting those voices, and that we always remain ready to correct our version of the story according to the narratives of the people themselves.

I turn now to a more detailed analysis of many of the empirical claims concerning gender and language, discussing these claims from within the framework provided by the four moral criteria introduced in this chapter.

Notes

1 See also Meehan 1995.
2 Barbara Houston pointed this problem out to me and provided useful feedback for the discussion that follows.

3 I am also indebted to Barbara Houston for pointing out this particular criticism.
4 This discussion owes much to feedback received from Leslie Thielen-Wilson on an earlier draft of this chapter.
5 I am grateful to Martha Ayim for bringing this article to my attention.
6 I am indebted to Leslie Thielen-Wilson for this example.
7 I am grateful to Andy Blair for raising this point in an informal discussion with me.
8 I am indebted to Leslie Thielen-Wilson for this point.

Chapter Six

Morality and Gender in Language

//The limits of my language mean the limits of my world," Wittgenstein claimed (1961, 115). "My language is the sum total of myself; for the man is the thought," Peirce declared (1931-1958, 5.314). I propose to apply moral standards, such as those we exact of our world, to language, and then to explore the implications of so doing. In other words, I shall link the discussion of the four moral criteria of language postulated in the previous chapter with some of the claims emanating from the research on gender differences in language as well as some of the standard interpretations and evaluations of these purported differences. I do this somewhat warily, perfectly aware of the danger of falling into the very trap that I described earlier, namely, permitting these empirical observations to hide the underlying value considerations. This literature does offer us an important message which I shall attempt both to summarize and to distinguish from the moral issues.

The fit between the moral criteria and the empirical claims is not a perfect one. It is at best, loose, but even so, it should be exceedingly rich in enabling researchers and social reformers to generate helpful and realistic guidelines for exploring avenues and developing strategies of linguistic reform. The discussion of any one of these particular criteria under the auspices of the research on gender patterns in language could easily occupy a book onto itself. My brief discussion will necessarily scratch the surface, but hopefully, it will succeed in capturing the flavour of that research. I shall discuss the empirical literature on gender differences in language under each of the moral criteria listed above.

A (1) Gender Differences and Language as Caring: The literature is very clear that it is women's language in particular that exemplifies features of caring. Studies I discussed earlier indicate that in general the interaction patterns of female managers are more accommodative, whereas those of male managers are more exploitative (Brenner and Vinacke 1979; Shakeshaft 1987) and that male verbal behaviour together with behaviour generally is more aggressive than that of females (Maccoby and Jacklin 1974a, 110). An investigation carried out on adolescents indicated that the females offered more comfort and support in their language than males although the males offered more physical support (Zeldin, Small, and Savin-Williams 1982, 1495, 1497). Studies also indicate that in their language, women demonstrate "greater concern with internal psychological states" (Barron 1971, 24, 39) than men, and that they pay more attention to the speaker, if eye contact is any indication (Eakins and Eakins 1978, 150). Furthermore, women have greater skill than men at decoding and understanding non-verbal cues; Hall's analysis of the relevant research indicates that 84 percent of sixty-one studies performed support this claim (Hall 1979, 38).

Particular instances of caring patterns in women's speech have frequently received negative evaluations from the language specialists, however. Consider, for example, women's tendency to use fewer direct imperatives or commands than men do, and women's preference for sentence structures that make requests rather than issue edicts (Gleason and Greif 1983, 143; Key 1975, 76-77; McMillan et al. 1977, 545, 547-548; Thorne and Henley 1975, 16). I offer this language pattern as an example of caring on the grounds that making a request appears more deeply concerned with the self-esteem and comfort of the other conversational participant(s) than issuing a direct command. Key, noting that women's speech contains more modals (such as "can," "could," and "would," which are instrumental to making indirect requests) than men's speech suggests that women's speech is thereby rendered indefinite, inconclusive, and uncertain

(1975, 75-76). Newcombe and Arnkoff's research (1979, 1299) indicated that the inclusion of tag questions (e.g., the "isn't it?" of "It's warm in this room, isn't it?"), qualifiers, and compound or indirect requests in speech render the perception of that speech as less assertive. Gleason and Greif suggest that mothers' indirect imperatives to their young children are misleading insofar as "the mothers tend to couch their directive intent in question form" (1983, 148). In Pearson's discussion of these findings, she warns the reader against the female tendency to use the less aggressive compound request form—e.g., "If you don't mind, would you shut the door?" as opposed to the more aggressive direct command, "Shut the door!" Pearson claims that "propriety and politeness are acquired at the expense of being misunderstood or not achieving your goal" (Pearson 1985, 188).

Many of these criticisms of women's language demonstrate the critic's assumption of the principle that male language is the norm, and female language, insofar as it deviates from the male standard, is deficient. Furthermore, I shall argue that for the most part, this negative evaluation is both misleading and unjustified. People who say, "If you don't mind, would you shut the door?" are generally perfectly well understood. McMillan et al. (1977), in their analysis of gender differences and direct imperatives, approach closer to the position that I develop here. While they describe direct imperatives as "simple and direct" (1977, 548) and as "direct and practical" (ibid., 555), they go on to suggest that "perhaps the syntactic categories that women use are a reflection of the greater value in women's culture on interpersonal sensitivity and emotionality, or perhaps their use reflects and sustains women's supportive role and minority status" (ibid., 557). I would go one step further, disagreeing even that the direct imperative is practical, particularly for women and particularly in a sexist culture. One who asks politely may in fact be more likely to have the door closed than someone who issues a rude, brusque order to that effect.

The understanding of indirect imperatives may falter with an audience of young children, who perceive only that they are expected to reply to a question (where either "yes" or "no" is a grammatically acceptable answer), and fail to realize that a direct request is being made of them. Yet even in this case, one wonders if the use of the direct imperative, "Shut the door!" is necessarily preferable. If the shutting of the door is of paramount importance, then the direct imperative seems called for. If teaching (and modelling) polite and caring language patterns form additional goals of the discourse, then the direct imperative is highly undesirable.

Engle points out the paucity of the father's language to the child, relative to the mother's, in terms of its educational value. Her research indicates that the father's language is not adapted to the speech level of the child in the way in which the mother's is. She claims that "Fathers appear to adopt a linguistic level when talking to children and then stick to it even when the children's language matures" (1980, 262). In contrast to this,

> the changes in the mother's language are a reflection or a prognosis of the changes in the children's language. The fact that this relationship is not found in the father-child language interaction implies that if language teaching is occurring, the fathers are not participating in it. (Ibid., 263)

Engle also notes a greater tendency for fathers, rather than mothers, to exert control over children in both their games and their language. The mother follows the child's choice of toy and tends to elaborate on the child's game, whereas the father, although he may include the child in the play, selects the toy of interest to himself rather than the child, and "control[s] the [play] interaction closely" (ibid., 264). Engle's research also indicates that fathers are much more likely to make direct suggestions to the child, while mothers are more likely to encourage the child to make her or his own choice (ibid.).

Gleason and Greif's research, as discussed above, revealed a similar tendency in parent-child speech. Their interpretations of men's and women's speech to young children is particularly instructive in this regard. They noted, as cited above, a much higher proportion of direct imperatives in men's speech to young children, with fathers using just slightly less than twice as many direct imperatives as mothers and male day-care workers using more than five times as many imperatives as female day-care workers (1983, 143). They also noted that fathers were much more likely to interrupt female children than male children (ibid., 147). Fathers were both less polite to their children in their language and less likely to exhibit or model polite language themselves (e.g., by saying "thank you" in appropriate circumstances) than mothers were (ibid., 146-147). The authors suggest that fathers "exhibit more control over the conversations with their children" (ibid., 147).

The most surprising feature of the article, from my perspective, is the summary. In the article, the authors indicate that in their interactions with their children, fathers frequently control and direct their children, are rude to them, threaten them (one brief excerpt of a father's speech to his son goes as follows: "Anthony, stay out of here before I break your head. Don't go in there again or I'll break your head" [ibid., 144]), that fathers misunderstand what their children say, and that they concentrate on what they (the fathers) want to say rather than interacting with their children and ensuring that the children understand them (ibid., 148); from this, Gleason and Greif conclude that the father's speech to his children is "cognitively and linguistically more challenging than the mother['s]" (ibid.), that it "has a positive effect on children" (ibid., 149), and that it "may serve special functions in their children's cognitive and linguistic development" (ibid.).

It is true that Gleason and Greif point out very clearly many times the greater sensitivity and understanding embedded in mothers' as opposed to fathers' speech to their children. They point this out again in their conclusion, along with the passages I cited above. But to infer, from the evidence which they assemble, that fathers' speech with their children is cognitively and linguistically more challenging than mothers' speech is worrisome from a moral point of view. For it suggests that the language that children must aspire to, the adult language that mothers fail to teach them well, is a rude, brusque language, more intent on giving the one speaking their say than on real interaction. It also suggests that caring, sensitive language is either unnecessary or trivially easy to learn. Otherwise mothers, in modelling polite language for their children long before the children engage in it themselves (ibid., 147), would be perceived as challenging their children cognitively and linguistically. In fact, politer language featuring indirect imperatives is developmentally more mature than brusquer language featuring direct imperatives. Ironically, the father's comparative lack of expertise in communicating clearly and interactively with his children is not interpreted negatively by the authors, but rather receives the highly positive interpretation of being "cognitively and linguistically more challenging than the mother['s]" (ibid., 148).

This inappropriate positive interpretation of fathers' language interests me for another reason. It is clear, I believe, that the actual data generated by Gleason and Greif's research indicates that fathers' language to their children, relative to mothers', is highly dysfunctional. Yet the fathers *are praised* for cognitive superiority! This illus-

trates, I believe, a characteristic reluctance to criticize the speech patterns of males. It seems to me self-evident that on *every* level, including the cognitive level, Gleason and Greif demonstrate the speech of
the mothers to be superior to the speech of the fathers. Is their taking
pains to include fathers in their allocation of praise an indication of
hedging on their part, a hedging of the moral issue? Are they reluctant
to claim straightforwardly that the fathers' language is rude, controlling, and threatening, although their data clearly support such a characterization, because this would commit them to holding a male
dominance version of parental language? Does this surprisingly positive characterization of the fathers' language, in the face of totally
contrary evidence in their own research findings, indicate a nervous-
ness, albeit unconscious, to generate hostility in journal reviewers
and readers, and does it therefore offer strong support for the male
dominance theory? These are real questions, to which I do not
presume to know the answers; they are also highly uncomfortable
questions to ask as well as answer. Nevertheless, if we are serious
about analyzing language within a moral framework, we must ask
these questions, and struggle to answer them. This very discomfort
illustrates, I believe, why a moral analysis of conversational patterns
has been resisted for so long and so thoroughly.

Pearson, as mentioned earlier, warns her readers that embedded
imperatives and indirect language may result in the speaker's being
misunderstood and consequently not having their imperatives carried
out (1985, 188). It may, in certain limited circumstances, be true that
one risks a greater likelihood of not having the door closed in uttering
the less aggressive sentence, but it is interesting that Pearson does not
consider it necessary to warn the reader that employing the more
aggressive direct command involves risk as well—risk of hurting the
feelings of the person being spoken to, risk of treating that person as a
mere means to achieving one's own ends, and risk of undermining
that person's sense of autonomy and self-respect. There are, of
course, contexts where the importance of the listener's obeying the
command outweighs the importance of offending the listener with
brusque, peremptory language. "Get out! Fire!" and "Don't cross yet!
There's a car coming!" are two such examples. Ordinary parlance,
however, will normally provide far fewer such contexts than it will
contexts where offending the listener with rude language and under-
cutting the listener's autonomy and dignity with direct imperatives
are realistic concerns.

(2) Gender Differences and Language as Cooperative: The literature on gender patterns in linguistic interactions is unambiguous in
attributing more cooperative features to the language of women.
Women don't simply attempt to bring the outsider into the conversation (as we shall discuss more fully under the next feature)—they
tend also to take cognizance of that person's contribution, once made.
Women interact more with the other participants than men do (Fishman 1977, 99-101; Fishman 1983, 94-96). Men are much more likely
than women to not respond at all to a speaker (Fishman 1983, 96), to
delay for a significant length of time before responding (Zimmerman
and West 1975, 118-122, 124), and to introduce radical changes of
topic when they do respond (ibid., 124).

Other studies indicate that in their interaction patterns with
members of the opposite sex, women are more concerned with fairness than men are; men are more concerned with winning and more
likely to engage in aggressive and competitive behaviour (Benton
1973, 435, 440). Other researchers claim that

> Males display a pattern of ruthless, cutthroat competition, with a
> strong orientation towards winning. Females, on the other hand, more
> often manifest concern for fairness, equalization of outcome, and a
> strong orientation towards the social-interaction aspects of the game.
> (Amidjaja and Vinacke 1965, 447)

Women are more likely to utilize discussion, while men are more
likely to utilize bargaining as the basis for deciding who should win
(ibid., 450). There is some evidence that when men do engage in
cooperative behaviour, they do so as a strategy "to maximize their
gains" (Hottes and Kahn 1974, 273). Furthermore, women are more
highly motivated by the prospect of bringing about a fair outcome
than they are of winning (Uesugi and Vinacke 1963, 78). Other
researchers whose work contradicts many of Vinacke's findings,
nevertheless claim that males have a "greater professed desire to win"
(Phillips and Cole 1970, 169) while "females tend to be more egalitarian" (ibid., 170). The current literature on women and educational
administration strongly supports the notion that women perform this
role in a much more collaborative way than their male colleagues,
systematically consulting with teachers and even with students in
setting goals and working towards the realization of those goals. (See,
for example, Helgesen 1990; Pearson 1981; Rosener 1990; Sergiovanni 1992; Shakeshaft 1987; Shantz 1993.)

(3) Gender Differences and Language as Democratic: Studies which investigated the formation of coalitions in small group interactions indicated that women were far less likely than men to "gang up" on a weak player; in fact, they would sometimes suggest helpful coalition strategies to weak players that were clearly disadvantageous to themselves (Uesugi and Vinacke 1963, 79).

> The women did not see the objective to be a matter of winning, so much as a problem of arranging a "fair" outcome, one that would be satisfactory to all three players. For example, there were frequent efforts to resort to rules which would make competition unnecessary. (ibid., 78)

When organized in groups of three, the women frequently formed a triadic alliance or no coalition at all, thus leaving out no one in these arrangements; when they did form two-person alliances, these were set up "predominantly on a 50/50 basis" (Amidjaja and Vinacke 1965, 450); they also tended to decide who should win on the basis of discussion as opposed to bargaining tactics.

In a study specifically investigating patterns of democratic leadership, it was found that "females contributed a significantly greater percentage of positive socio-emotional communication acts than male democratic leaders" (Fowler and Rosenfeld 1979, 76). Males were much more likely to insist on giving their own opinions and to engage in negative social interactions (ibid.). Women's language patterns thus appear to be more oriented towards facilitating the inclusion of all speakers than men's language patterns. Current literature on educational administration also documents a greater tendency of female than male administrators to follow democratic (rather than autocratic) procedures in carrying out their administrative duties. (See, for example, Gips 1989; Helgesen 1990; Lee 1993; Pearson 1981.)

Other research indicates that males and females divide rewards among group members differently. Leventhal and Lane suggest that when males perceive their work as superior to the other member of the group, they take more than half the reward, but when they perceive their work as inferior, they take less than half the reward. Females, however, take "little more than half the reward" (1970, 315) when they perceive their work as superior and substantially (compared to males) less than half the reward when they perceive their work as inferior. Leventhal and Lane postulate that while males operate purely with an equity principle in distributing rewards, females allocate rewards on the basis of "a tendency to behave accommodatively as well as a tendency to maintain equity" (ibid.). I suggest it is possible that equity is at work in both cases, but that the female notion of equity being appealed to here is more sophisticated than the male notion, taking account of more than merely the perception of quality of work output. Also, as cited in the previous chapter, in Matsuda's extensive research on racist violence, she found that "in virtually every case, the perpetrators were men" (1993, 23).

Even though women's behaviour and speech may be documentably more democratic than that of men, women are not necessarily judged more positively on that account. In fact, exactly the reverse appears to be the case. Richardson and Macke, in their research investigating student evaluations of university teaching, although they admitted that other studies controverted these results (1980, 177), indicated that female professors encouraged participation in their classrooms to a much greater extent than male professors (ibid., 173); nevertheless, female professors were judged by students to be less competent (even though they were considered likeable) the more they succeeded in developing student participation in their classes, whereas the competence ratings of male professors were not lowered when they encouraged greater student participation in their classrooms (ibid., 90-91, 176). Richardson and Macke claim that unlike women who have to work for positive student evaluations, "men are likely to be judged competent and likeable regardless of what they do" (ibid., 177). Similarly, while talking a lot is positively correlated to men making a good impression, it is negatively correlated to women making a good impression (Gall, Hobby, and Craik 1969, 873).

(4) Gender Differences and Language as Honest: The inclusion of the honesty criterion perhaps appears anomalous on the surface. Whereas the three earlier criteria all appear to be clearly met by women's speech patterns in ways in which they are not by men's, at least so far as the research on gender patterns in language is concerned, this fourth feature is not so readily attributed to women's speech. Women are often accused of being indirect (Jespersen 1922, 245-246), of embedding or disguising imperatives (Key 1975, 76-77; Lakoff 1975, 18-19) or even ordinary declarative sentences (Lakoff 1975, 15-17). Yet it remains far from clear that an embedded imperative actually is a disguised imperative, and hence a deceptive or dishonest use of language. If "Would you close the door, please?" is in fact a polite request to have the door closed, then the charge of dishonesty doesn't arise. Only if it is a categorical order, to which the

answer "No!" would be unacceptable and criticizable, does the charge of dishonesty apply.

The literature indicates that women use more qualifiers (e.g., such phrases as "about," "around," "approximately," "maybe," "somewhat," "sort of," "kind of," "I guess," "I think," and "in my opinion") in their speech than men do (Lakoff 1975, 53-54; Swacker 1975, 81-82) and this is characteristically interpreted as a timidity for taking responsibility for the content of the sentence (Lakoff 1975, 53-54). Kramer suggests that qualifiers provide a woman "an out," that they allow her to change her mind "without too much difficulty or fear of embarrassment" (1975, 48). In other words, the act of qualifying is interpreted as hedging. This is particularly evident in the work of Pearson (1985, 186), who uses the terms "hedges" and "qualifiers" as synonyms.

Yet hedging may not always or even often be an appropriate explanation of the use of qualifying terms. *Admission* of uncertainty may frequently be a much more accurate interpretation of what is actually going on; the alternative to this use of qualification is not directness, but bluffing, a particular form of deviousness. Other research indicates that self-honesty is much more a part of women's than men's communication styles. Female comedians engage in self-disparagement to provoke humour much more often than male comedians (Levine 1976, 174). Furthermore, men who engage in self-disparagement are viewed as "significantly less confident, significantly less witty and significantly less intelligent" (Zillmann and Stocking 1976, 156) than when they engage in disparagement of either friends or enemies. Females evaluate self-disparagement much more positively than males do, with females judging the self-disparager (regardless of sex) to be "significantly more intelligent, provocative and skilful than did males" (ibid., 161). The authors speculate that one may infer from this that "the female in our society seems to take the minor putdowns of everyday life in her stride, while the male struggles to project a spotless image of dominance and infallibility. He cannot easily laugh at his own expense. The cost in terms of image seems too high" (bid., 162).

Kramer claims, as pointed out earlier, that qualifiers permit women a way out, and allow them to change their minds without embarrassment (1975, 48). A more viable interpretation of qualifiers is that they legitimate or render acceptable a wide range of responses from the listener, an important consideration if the speaker fears negative consequences to herself from offending the listener.

Not only are women likely to be more honest about their own weaknesses or vulnerabilities, they are more likely to straight-forwardly reveal their true feelings and emotions. In her discussion of this gender difference in communication, Pearson warns women of the possible pitfalls of divulging their true feelings under conditions that are not safe (Pearson 1985, 251). I think this warning is entirely appropriate, yet I would like to supplement it with the introduction of an even bigger worry—a worry about the moral stature of a society in which it is not safe to express one's feelings, particularly one's weaknesses.

Several other studies claim that men are more likely than women to engage in deception and deceit in order to bring about the state of affairs they desire, including lying about the results of HIV tests (Christie and Geiss 1968, 963; Expline, Thibaut, Hickey, and Gumpert 1970, 62; Kaplowitz 1976, 383; Malone 1991, 18). Lakoff, for example, claims that women will engage in such friendly gestures as embracing and sharing confidences "only when there are real feelings of sympathy between them" (1975, 79), whereas men will exhibit "the markers of camaraderie . . . even when they can't stand each other" (ibid.).

On the other hand, some research done on children's language indicates that while boys will directly confront other boys, girls are much more likely to confront an *absent* subject, raising an objection about something the "culprit" has said or done to others who are present (Goodwin and Goodwin 1987, 230). This girls' pattern documented by the Goodwins appears to be not only dishonest, but also cowardly compared to the boys'. Carol Mitchell's research on joke-telling (1985) indicates a similar phenomenon—namely, that women may *disguise* their hostility (ibid., 173, 184). In particular, women may disguise their level of aggression in the presence of men (ibid., 184).

The bulk of the literature, with the exception of those two studies just mentioned, indicates that women's speech patterns better meet not only the first three criteria, but this fourth criterion of honesty as well. In the very instant in which we acknowledge this, however, it is crucial that we acknowledge as well that the empirical gender-based claims are morally trivial. To focus on and glorify the gender differences in speech patterns is to suggest that women use language one way and men another, and that's the end of the matter. Attributing centrality to the empirically observed gender differences involves us in a regression to the "Boys will be boys," syndrome, whereby we applaud male language as aggressive, authoritarian, and alienating, because that's the way males are. This "explanation" would also commit us to applauding female language as nurturant, inclusive, and other-oriented, based on the "kinder and gentler female nature." Both explanations preclude the assignment of moral praise or blame—if that's simply the way men are, then they can't be blamed any more than women can be praised for simply being the way they are. This approach makes it all too easy to eschew any moral responsibility for the way we speak.

By attributing centrality to the *moral criteria* of language, however, we accept moral responsibility for our linguistic behaviour. Precisely what we must do morally is to insist that people regard their conversational styles and practices as moral matters, to be governed largely by the same criteria as govern any other form of behaviour. In classrooms boys and men get *far* more than their fair share of the teacher's time and energy. Indeed, they have come to expect this as their due, such that when they receive two-thirds of the teacher's time, as I have pointed out previously, they consider they have not had enough (Spender 1982, 56-57). Students and teachers need to be confronted with this data and asked to evaluate it not primarily within a context of gender differences, but within a moral context. In this second case, the behaviour is seen for what it is—egoism of the grossest kind, which further exacerbates the condition of sexism in our society. As women, we must understand that in conforming without protest to the traditional linguistic division of labour, we are guilty of endorsing and strengthening discriminatory and immoral social arrangements.

Some research indicates that even at a preschool age, girls hesitate to ask for an adult's help in performing a task, whereas boys will nonchalantly ask for the help (Pellegrini 1982, 213). This same pattern continues with school-aged children, with boys making more direct requests than girls (Haas 1981, 925, 932-933). According to Haslett, girls "develop interactional strategies earlier" than boys, a reflection of the "differing patterns of sex-role socialization, where females are reinforced for being nurturant and other-directed . . . [whereas] males are reinforced for being aggressive and self-assertive" (Haslett 1983, 127). Haas' research indicates that in mixed-sex groupings, "Boys played the dominant role with girls by issuing the most direct requests and giving the most information. Girls were submissive, as seen by their greater Use [*sic*] of verbal compliance" (Haas 1981, 933). Females, unlike males, are punished for egocentric aggressive linguistic behaviour.

When we see this as a moral matter it is very clear that the egocentric orientation is highly problematic, and ought to be discouraged among *all* language users. Egocentrism is a problem in language for the same reason that it is a problem in any moral context—namely, that it is not generalizable without contradiction. Given that we live in a community, the rules governing our behaviour must commit us to fair and equitable treatment of other community members. Egocentrism only works if we assume special status for the egoist, which would justify overriding the interests of other people. Inside or outside language, the moral issue remains the same. The example of interruption illustrates clearly the failure of egocentric linguistic behaviour to generalize. If all conversational participants consistently interrupt one another, there can be no conversation. A conversation that occurs when one participant consistently interrupts the others presupposes that the other participants do not similarly engage in egocentric behaviour, but are committed to the conversation itself rather than to a display of their own dominance. Interruption cannot be generalized without contradiction. To generalize it is to undermine the possibility of a linguistic community. It can only be tolerated if we *assume* that a critical mass of community members will accept the indignity of being linguistically dominated in this way, without engaging themselves in such behaviour. Thus differential interruption patterns, for example, can only be tolerated if we are willing to accept on principle the notion of the appropriateness of one group of interrupters and another group of interrupted, in other words, if we are willing to accept on principle the notion of linguistic discrimination.

That men interrupt women more than women interrupt men (Key 1975, 130; Zimmerman and West 1975, 116-117), that male students assume they have the right to more than two-thirds of a teacher's time (Spender 1982, 56-57), that women and not men are willing to acknowledge and laugh at their own foibles and weaknesses (Levine 1976, 174; Zillmann and Stocking 1976, 161), that men are willing to engage in subterfuge in order to achieve their ends, including lying about positive HIV tests (Christie and Geiss 1968, 963; Expline et al. 1970, 62; Kaplowitz 1976, 383; Malone 1991, 18), that females perform more verbal support behaviour than males (Zeldin, Small, and Savin-Williams 1982, 1492), that females are more concerned with people's psychological states than males (Barron 1971, 24-39), but also that girls are more likely than boys to disparage an absent subject (Goodwin and Goodwin 1987, 130), these are not merely matters of empirical happenstance that divide along gender lines. They are matters of moral concern and involve violation of the most basic moral principles required for the sustenance of any kind of community.

They need to be perceived in this way and taught to young children from this perspective. If it is the case that "males are reinforced for being aggressive" (Haslett 1983, 127), then such reinforcement must be terminated. In the words of Dale Spender, cited in the introduction to this book, "The false logic of dominance demands too high a price and can no longer be afforded" (1982, 96). The consequences of adherence or non-adherence to the moral criteria of language should be made to fit the nature of morality, not handed out differentially as a set of privileges to one gender and a set of liabilities to the other. When our understanding of language centres around observed gender differences, then different sets of rules seem appropriate, even natural. When our understanding of language centres around a community in which interactions must be governed by moral principles, then such different sets of rules will be seen for what they are—not complementary, but blatantly oppressive and discriminatory.

We appear to be entering an era of "accountability" for teachers. If teachers alone were to be held accountable for ensuring that within the classroom setting, girls occupied half the linguistic turf and enjoyed half the linguistic privileges, while boys contributed half the linguistic labour, the impact would be phenomenal. It would, of course, be unfair to focus specifically on teacher accountability, for parents, the students themselves, and the administrative network of the school system would place serious roadblocks in the way of achieving this end. Nevertheless, if teachers *did* undertake the achievement of a moral proportioning of linguistic tasks and privileges, we would be a giant step forward in reaching a morally defensible linguistic community.

I am not naive about the vested interests that stand in the way of the achievement of moral ends. The egoists who can get away with counting on others to maintain the moral fabric while they continue to concentrate on number one are unlikely simply to relinquish their privileges when faced with the contradiction of generalization argument. It certainly looks as though the linguistic egoists can continue to get away with counting on others to maintain the conversation while they interrupt and dominate. This is depressing, but not surprising. What is surprising, however, is that we have tended not to even judge such linguistic behaviour on a moral axis.

I believe we have managed to avoid a moral interpretation of this data precisely because we have perceived it through the set of assumptions and expectations that accompany an explanatory emphasis on gender differences; that is, the moral nature of the issue may have been disguised by the very linguistic labour that females have contributed. So long as females keep the conversation going over the rough spots of male dominance and interruption, most of us will never notice that there is a problem, let alone a moral problem. If women facilitate the linguistic input of others, it may continue to go unnoticed that they themselves are frequently interrupted and silenced. If women, in Fishman's terms, persist in doing the "shitwork" (1977) then it may go unnoticed by men in particular, who don't themselves characteristically participate in this form of linguistic labour, that there's a lot of shit around. Hence the need for a moral analysis of the situation will not readily come to mind. Furthermore, so long as females are trained, socialized, and perhaps even indoctrinated to perform in caring ways even when their caring behaviour is strictly one-sided, then the egocentric linguistic behaviour of males will appear to be unproblematic and acceptable. So long as there are sufficient altruists in the world, egoists may never have to face up to the logical consequences of their egoism. Female-identified modes of behaviour, deeply ingrained into the females in our society, have averted the self-destructive outcome one would have expected from this sort of egoistic behaviour with the consequence that we have never been forced to confront the moral status of language patterns.

That females are, in fact, socialized or trained or indoctrinated to behave in precisely these sorts of ways is, I think, common knowledge. Haslett refers to society as reinforcing females "for being nurturant and other-directed" (1983, 127). The literature on transsexualism supports this claim in the most dramatic way. Agnes, a male-to-female transsexual, learned from her boyfriend Bill "how a lady should conduct herself on a picnic" (Garfinkel with Stoller 1967, 146). Bill recited to Agnes the failings of a female friend of one of his companions who had persisted in the following sorts of behaviour:

on wanting things her own way, of offering her opinions when she should have been retiring, of being sharp in her manner when she should have been sweet, of complaining instead of taking things as they were, . . . of acting bawdy instead of abjuring any claims of equality with men, of demanding services instead of looking to give the man she was with pleasure and comfort. (Ibid., 146-147)

From her women friends, with whom Agnes "exchanged gossip . . . [Agnes learned] the value of passive acceptance as a desirable feminine character trait" (ibid., 147). With regard to language patterns in particular, Agnes learned that the way to be perceived as an "interesting conversationalist" by men was to encourage "her male partners to talk about themselves" (ibid., 148).

A focus on sex differences has thus succeeded in masking the moral parameters of discourse. We need now to explicitly raise the moral question. This conceptual turnaround will be required to initiate the formation of a linguistic community in which people are expected to treat other people as ends in themselves, in which people will actually care about other people and their hopes and desires, in which people can truly cooperate with others in a democratic context that refuses to tolerate the oppression of particular individuals or groups of individuals, and in which people can find the courage and count upon the security required to speak with honesty about themselves, other individuals, and the community as a whole. The perspective for which I argue in this book—examining linguistic interactions and gender differences within linguistic interactions from a moral perspective—is a radical one. Taking on and speaking out in favour of radical perspectives is always a risky business. But the type of linguistic community that such a perspective would nurture is worth the risk. Perhaps, in the spirit of Wittgenstein's much quoted line (1961, 115), we can expand the moral parameters of our world by expanding the moral parameters and the moral worth of our language. We would do well to ask hard moral questions about our symbolic structures, for, in Peirce's words, "it is only out of symbols that a new symbol can grow. . . . A symbol, once in being, spreads among the peoples. In use and in experience, its meaning grows" (1931-1958, 2.302).

Chapter Seven

Feminist Critiques of Language[1]

The early 1990s have borne witness both to an official cognizance of the importance of non-stereotypic and inclusive language as well as to ongoing ridicule of the issue. Some research indicates that enforced inclusive language legislation has had a major impact on language use and that the language in official university documents has been influenced by feminist analyses of linguistic sexism (Markowitz 1984, 343). While large numbers of educational institutions officially adopt inclusive language guidelines, many teaching and administrative staff members of these same institutions continue to respond with the old adage that "sticks and stones can break my bones, but words will never hurt me"—in other words, language is trivial. On the whole, students appear to be more concerned about the impact of sexist language as well as excising sexism from their language than professors are (Harrigan and Lucic 1988, 132-133). I shall argue in this chapter that using gender inclusive language, that is, language that includes females equally with males, together with

---

The note to this chapter is on p. 153.

non-stereotypic language, is not only a non-trivial matter, but that it has profound moral implications.

Many people base their claim to language's triviality in the abject failure of researchers to come up with any convincing support for the Whorf hypothesis, that language determines or controls thought. In Chapter Five I have admitted, in agreement with Khosroshahi (1989, 523, n. 2), that acceptance or rejection of the Whorf hypothesis is based more on personal preference than on compelling evidence, with my acceptance of the Whorf hypothesis being no exception. Although the empirical evidence supports at best a correlation (rather than a causal relationship) between language and thought, I am convinced that if we weaken Whorf's original hypothesis from a view that language determines thought to a view that language influences thought, then it is unreasonable to deny its truth. Did the words of Hitler not augment anti-Semitic sentiment? Do patriotic songs not promote feelings of pride in and loyalty to one's country, school, etc.? As MacKay points out, virtually *all* of the research done to test the Whorf hypothesis concentrated exclusively on descriptive thought and ignored evaluative thought. That is, the research focused on examining such descriptive features as whether a language's mechanism for coding colours and shapes correlated to speakers' coding colours and shapes in a specific way. The results of such research have been consistently disappointingly negative. There was no effort to test for a correlation between the language and evaluative thought, however, that is, "subjective or personal judgments concerning the *value* of concepts or events" (MacKay 1983, 45, author's emphasis). MacKay claims that his research shows a *positive* correlation between language and evaluative thought (MacKay 1980a, 94-96). Similar findings emerge from the research of Khosroshahi (1989); these findings, along with MacKay's, will be discussed in greater detail below.

Feminist critiques of word choice in language have too seldom been carried out from a moral perspective, and too seldom appraised from that perspective even when there has been a strong hint of moral censure in the critiques. Even the most cursory analysis indicates that the impact of interpreting such feminist critiques from a moral perspective is enormous.

I will proceed to examine three separate but related feminist critiques of vocabulary choice in language—three segments of a spectrum of immoral linguistic treatment of women—namely, language that excludes women, language that trivializes women, and language that demeans women. These three features are highlighted in the analysis of speech patterns provided in the original "Chilly Climate" Report (Hall and Sandler 1982, 5, 6, 10). As I have said, the three complaints are segments of a spectrum, and as the discussion to follow will illustrate, they are significantly overlapping segments. The categories are very broad as well, and each encompasses many particular claims about language. Although my comments will be restricted to the English language, there is a burgeoning literature that advances similar critiques of other languages. I will argue that the standard way in which the language-using community distinguishes among excluding, trivializing, and demeaning language itself reflects a devaluing of women; I shall also compare some of the male devaluing terms (members of what I call the "plundering dick" family of terms) to female devaluing terms.

(1) Language that Excludes Women: This category encompasses the entire contemporary debate and concern around the issue of inclusive language, i.e., language that includes women equally with men and girls equally with boys. Of all the feminist concerns ever written about or talked about, this is the one that has generated the highest degree of outright derision. The moment the concern itself is viewed in a moral light, the feminist grievance becomes clear and straightforward, and the derision morally troublesome.

Consider the classic example, the use of "man" by itself and in compound words, to refer to mixed-gender groups. I will often adopt the practice in this book of referring to this purported generic sense of "man" as the prescriptive "man," following Donald MacKay's analogous use of the "prescriptive 'he'" (1983, 39); at other times, I will refer to this usage as the "pseudo-generic 'man.'" The traditionalist or the language purist will insist that one of the authentic meanings of "man," prescribed and enshrined by the dictionary, is the generic sense of "human being." Feminist research has established conclusively that "man" is not a truly generic term, regardless of what the lexicographers may prescribe.

The evidence that "man" is not a truly generic term abounds at both the theoretical and empirical levels. (See Eberhart 1976; Hamilton 1985; Hamilton 1988a; Hamilton 1988b; Harrison 1975; Harrison and Passero 1975; Henley 1989; Hyde 1984; Khosroshahi 1989; MacKay 1980a; MacKay 1980b; MacKay and Fulkerson 1979; Martyna 1978; Martyna 1983; Moulton, Robinson, and Elias 1978; Schneider and Hacker 1973; Shepelak, Ogden, and Tobin-Bennett

1984; Sniezek and Jazwinski 1986; Switzer 1990; Wilson 1978; Wilson and Ng 1988.) By theoretical evidence, I mean the logical inconsistency presupposed by expecting a single term to refer to human beings in general and to male individuals in particular. This inconsistency is discussed by Alma Graham (1975, 62) and Donald MacKay (1983, 44). The inconsistency is as follows: In one of its primary senses, the word "man" excludes women, and in another of its primary senses it includes women. It is hard to imagine how generations of lexicographers, scholars, and language teachers could have prescribed a generic sense of "man" in the face of this logical inconsistency and harder yet to imagine that generations of language users put up with such nonsense without linguistic rebellion. A few individuals, mainly feminists, have protested such prescription, but for the most part, their message has been greeted only by derision.

To get a better sense of the enormity of this hoax, try to imagine any other commonly used term performing a similarly inconsistent duty—for example, the term "book" to refer generally to all copyrighted documents (in which case it would include many video productions) and specifically to bound written documents (in which case it would exclude video productions). Try to imagine the term "blue" including "brown" according to one of its meanings and excluding it according to another, or "television" including "radio" according to one of its meanings and excluding it according to another. The emperor without clothes is a minor hoax, compared to the pseudo-generic "man."

The English language does offer us "day" and "night," which may appear to be a perfect counter-example of my claim. After all, according to one of its commonly understood meanings, "day" includes the night ("A week has seven days"), while according to another of its commonly understood meanings, "day" excludes the night ("Construction work is normally done during the day").

While admitting that these two commonly understood senses of "day" contain the same sort of contradiction as that emanating from the two commonly understood senses of "man," I argue that appealing to "day" as a counter-example is beset by two serious weaknesses. First, the contradiction inherent in "day" is less problematic than that in "man," because safeguards of clarification have been built into the language for "day"; second, the moral character of the contradiction differs radically for these two words. I shall discuss first the safeguard features in place for "day."

The contradictory senses of "day" have not been without problems in our use and understanding of the language; as a language-using community, we have acknowledged the problems inherent in these usages and have taken precautions to minimize the risk of misinterpretation. For example, we can eliminate the ambiguity totally by saying "day time" or "night time." In addition, when we talk about an hour of the day, we specify "a.m." or "p.m." (or use a twenty-four hour reference system) and hence eliminate any possible doubt as to whether our particular use includes or excludes the night. Unfortunately, there is no such convenient customary suffix as "a.m." or "p.m." available to be appended to "man" or "he" that would automatically eliminate all possible doubt as to whether the usage includes or excludes females.

The terms "day" and "man" differ even more dramatically when examined from moral grounds. Whether or not the hours of darkness are excluded from the day, while of great concern to people who write (and read) flight schedules, is normally of no moral import. Whether or not half the species is excluded when we use words that refer to the human race is clearly a moral issue in the sense in which the difficulty entailed by the contradictory senses of "day" is not.

For these reasons, it seems almost incomprehensible that sensible people would have demanded further evidence before abandoning the prescriptive "man"; in fact, however, not only did they demand further evidence, but when that evidence flooded in, they dismissed it as well. I am referring to the empirical evidence which thoroughly controverts the generic pretensions of the prescriptive "man." Dozens of empirical surveys indicate that as a matter of fact, regardless of what the dictionaries say, when people hear or read the term "man," they think "male." Several of these studies are discussed by Dale Spender (1980, 154-158.) Like the first whispered suggestion that the emperor was naked, this evidence was ridiculed, and the researchers who disseminated it dismissed as radical man-hating feminists without proper respect for the sanctity of the language.

How could this have happened? How could generations of people have been induced to swallow such an absurdity, with only a tiny handful of them choking on it? If it were simply a matter of words and nothing more, this is almost impossible to imagine. Suppose it were not just a matter of words, but a linguistic pattern, protecting and entrenching highly vested interests. Suppose this linguistic usage were tied to a deeply rooted sense about the rights of females and males, the worth of females and males, and the moral capacity of females and males. Suppose, to mention only three out of hundreds of possible instances, we believed with Aristotle that women were not fully human in the sense in which men were, or, with the Canadian Senate prior to 1929 that women were not persons, or, with the Roman Catholic Church that women were not fit to be priests. Here we seem to have a belief system capable of explaining the anomaly. Make no mistake. To preserve a contradictory sense of such a commonly used word as "man" requires a gargantuan linguistic campaign, not to mention gargantuan levels of self-deception on the part of language users. However, if females are perceived as not really counting, in other words, as trivial, then whether the term "man" includes them or not is largely irrelevant, and not an issue likely to arouse a great deal of concern. This hypothesis is directly confirmed by MacKay's research (1983, 45-46), which I shall discuss below.

Linguistic choices that exclude women and linguistic choices that trivialize women are overlapping and frequently interdependent segments on a spectrum. If language users adhere to a value scheme that trivializes women, then they will as a matter of course reject as silly *any form* of argument for the full inclusion of women in the language. The exclusion of women from the language is a trivial matter only if women are themselves perceived as trivial.

An equally powerful, if not stronger argument to that put forward against the prescriptive "man" can be advanced against the use of "he" and other forms of the pronoun to refer to mixed-gender groups. Again, I shall follow MacKay in referring to this use of "he" as the prescriptive "he" (1983, 39). Insofar as particular pronouns appear to be more deeply entrenched in the language than particular nouns, perhaps owing to their much higher frequency of occurrence, the prescriptive "he" promises to be more difficult to correct than the prescriptive "man." MacKay suggests that an educated American will experience one million repetitions of the prescriptive "he" in a lifetime and that this usage shares all the features of a

> highly effective propaganda technique: *repetition* (the frequency of prescriptive *he* implies repetition beyond all extant propaganda techniques), *early age of acquisition* (prior to age 6, according to Nilsen, 1977), *covertness* (use of prescriptive *he* is not usually intended as an open attempt to maintain or alter attitudes), *association with high prestige sources* (especially university textbooks), and *indirectness* (its message is presented indirectly as if it were a matter of common and well-established knowledge). (MacKay 1983, 47, author's emphasis)

The sex-specific import of "he" overshadows the generic import. Martyna claims that "in educational materials . . . the sex-specific *he* appears five to ten times for every single generic *he*" (1983, 32). In a survey of schoolchildren's books, Alma Graham analyzed one hundred thousand words of text, which contained 940 instances of "he," only thirty-two of which were clearly generic. Eight hundred and seventy-two were clearly male-specific (Graham 1975, 58). All major achievement tests, widely used in the school system to evaluate and compare students' aptitudes, show an overwhelming preponderance of male-to-female references—the ratio is as high as fourteen to one and is improved only a tiny bit when the prescriptive terms are taken into account, thus illustrating again that the vast bulk of "he" and "man" terms are used to refer specifically to males, not generically to human beings (Tittle, McCarthy, and Steckler 1974, 16-21, 76-78).

In spite of this, there is still widespread resistance to the introduction of an alternative to the prescriptive "he." Much (though not most) of the resistance comes from women. In a study specifically investigating whether females would perceive passages using the prescriptive "he" as less relevant to themselves personally and more difficult to understand than passages using the generic "they," MacKay (1980a) found that some did and some didn't, with a fascinating difference between the two groups.

Those who had revealed themselves (in a corresponding questionnaire) as sympathetic to the women's movement, and who perceived women and men to be different but equal, resisted the prescriptive "he," declaring written passages containing it to be less relevant to themselves personally and more difficult to understand. The other group of women, whose questionnaires indicated much less sympathy for the women's movement, together with an overall acceptance of and respect for male values and corresponding rejection and contempt for female values, embraced the prescriptive "he," declaring the passages that contained it to be more relevant to themselves personally and less difficult to understand than passages containing the generic "they." MacKay hypothesized that these women aspired to male values and "had little desire to identify with" (1983, 46) the class of women. They preferred to be "one of the boys," and hence resisted staunchly any linguistic moves that threatened to rob them of what they perceived to be the more prestigious male-identified terms.

Khosroshahi's research (1989), like that of MacKay, supports a weakened version of the Whorf hypothesis, stipulating merely a correlation between language and thought; neither MacKay's nor Khosroshahi's findings permit an extension to a causal hypothesis regarding the influence of language over thought (Khosroshahi 1989, 520). A fascinating wrinkle on even the weakened correlational thesis emerged from Khosroshahi's research, however. The participants in Khosroshahi's study were male and female university students, some of whose written language (their term papers) showed evidence of reform in terms of gender inclusivity and some of whose written language did not show evidence of such reform. The subjects were asked to describe images evoked by sex-indefinite paragraphs and this imagery was subsequently rated in terms of sex of the image. A clear correlation was shown to exist between the language and imagery of the unreformed female and male participants, whose written language choices and conceptual imagery both strongly favoured males, but with a much more dramatic favouring of males by the male participants (ibid., 517-519). A clear correlation also emerged between the language and imagery of the reformed female participants, but the tendency of members of this group reflected a predominance of female images rather than an egalitarian interpretation of the paragraphs (ibid., 519). No correlation whatsoever was found to exist between the gender inclusive written work of the "reformed" males and the overwhelming exclusion of females in their interpretations of the paragraphs. Khosroshahi hypothesizes as an explanation for the disparity between the reformed males and females that the language change of the women was rooted in a genuine attitude change which was subsequently internalized, whereas the attitude change of the men was superficial, motivated only by "concern about the impression they make on others" (ibid., 522).

Khosroshahi's work highlights the important observation that language changes are not always and not necessarily indicative of genuine attitude changes—they may be indicative of a social opportunism to look good and "get off the hook" for any deeper analysis. The sophisticated sexist can use superficial language changes to their own advantage. This emphasizes the importance of performing a moral analysis of language that delves below the surface and demands to know whether the language is, for example, honest. The opportunist who engages in a public show of fair language in order to make a good impression on others, while maintaining bigoted attitudes about people, fails the honesty criterion badly. Nevertheless, it may still be preferable for the bigot to make a show of fair language practices, rather than reverting to biased or exclusionary language practices. Ideally, there are strong reasons for urging that those in positions of influence, such as teachers, should not only be egalitarian in their outlook, but should also behave in egalitarian ways, including engaging in fair language practices. If we begin, however, with the reality of a teacher who in fact privately harbours sexist ideologies, there may well be more positive benefits for female students to be assigned textbooks and to participate in a classroom discourse that explicitly include females, than to be exposed to language that excludes females, even if the author and teacher in question privately harbour sexist views. MacKay's findings are consistent with this view.

MacKay argues further that the virtually ineradicable maleness of "he," by its association with "man," may have in part prevented "man" from ever reverting to the truly generic noun that it was between seven hundred and a thousand years ago (MacKay 1983, 50); at that time, "man" was free of the contradictory meanings now associated with it, for it referred only to human beings, including women, there being separate terms to refer to male human beings, excluding women, namely, "wer" and "carl" (Miller and Swift 1976, 25).

In spite of these serious objections to the prescriptive "man" and "he," malestream thought still by and large dismisses as trivial or ridiculous feminist concerns about the role of these two terms in controverting attempts to achieve sexually inclusive language. I believe such concerns will be less easily dismissed when they are perceived as having a basis in morality. To use "man" as though it referred to all human beings equally, when the research has so adamantly controverted this claim, is a powerful example of language that fails the democratic criterion. If we insist on ratifying the use of words that exclude large groups of human beings to *refer* to humanity, then we are simply thumbing our noses at any aspirations towards democratic language.

To choose, as a term referring to humanity, a word that leaves out over half the species is not a trivial matter. If it were trivial there would have been no objection to the substitution of a different term. Whenever men have found themselves left out of person-denoting nouns and pronouns (as in textbooks written for elementary school-teachers), the resistance to the use of these non-inclusive terms has been sufficient to bring about a replacement of the offending words

with a different set of non-inclusive terms, a male-identified set
(Miller and Swift 1976, 30). The emotional tenor of the objections to
abandoning the two major prescriptive terms, frequently approaching
hysteria, is a strong indication that people take their vocabulary
choices seriously, no matter how much they may deny the seriousness of language issues.

An identical claim to that made for the prescriptive "man" can
be made for various compound "man" words—e.g., "chairman,"
"mailman," "fireman," and "policeman," when used as though they
referred to female and male human beings equally. The verb "to
man," as in "to man the desk," "to man the course," or "to man the
operation," is similarly problematic. It will probably not surprise any
of us to learn that women are more likely to respond to job advertisements that are written in inclusive language than they are to job
advertisements containing the prescriptive "man" and the prescriptive "he" (Bem and Bem 1973, 13-16). The use of any of these terms
(and many more) in such a context flagrantly violates the principle of
democracy in language use. We can only ridicule campaigns to make
the language more democratic if we reject the democratic feature of
language as an ideal. This says something important about us, however; it says that we are comfortable with a language that is partisan
and exclusive. If the "we" in question happen to be members of the
favoured group, the group that is assured full, unquestioned inclusion,
then it is hard to say how the easy acceptance of these "rules" differs
from acceptance of apartheid policy by those whose privileges are sustained and entrenched by such racist ideologies. This analogy lends a
special poignancy to Alice Walker's (1982) claim that the term
"woman" also fails abysmally to achieve generic status, for it focuses
only on white women and consistently excludes First Nations
women, Black women, Asian women, and other women of Colour.

There is research which indicates that women have a clear sense
of being excluded by "he," "man," and "man" compounds. According
to Martyna, females use the prescriptive "he" less often than males,
and are more likely to use instead such inclusive pronouns as "they"
and "he or she" (1983, 31). Although females use the term "he" less
than males do, females are more likely to give it a generic interpretation when they do encounter it, whereas males are more likely to
interpret it in the exclusive sense of males only (ibid.). That females
are more reluctant than males to use the prescriptive "he" is not
surprising. One would expect that those who are never left out when

such words are used would be less sensitive to the words' limited extension than those who are generally left out.

Morally appropriate reform measures are for the most part self-evident, although this does not entail their being easily executed. Linguistic habits are among the most deeply engrained and probably among the most resistant to change. Nonetheless, moral analysis demonstrates that such change is mandatory, and recent history provides us with incontrovertible proof that change is possible. We have "human being" and "person" as substitutes for the prescriptive "man." We also have "letter carrier," "fire fighter," and "police officer," each of which is more descriptive of the occupation in question than the prescriptive "man" term which it replaces. "To staff" is a more accurate and meaningful verb than "to man."

The prescriptive "he" is more difficult, as there does not seem to be a single generic substitute which would be appropriate for all contexts. But there are several different terms available, each covering a fairly large context much more adequately than the prescriptive "he"—"they," "she or he," and "one" are all strong generic candidates. There is a great deal of interesting research on alternatives to the prescriptive "he." (See, for example, Baron 1981; Bodine 1975; Fisk 1985; Gastil 1990; Hyde, 1984; Khosroshahi 1989; MacKay 1983, 50-52; Schau and Scott 1984; Sniezek and Jazwinski 1986; Switzer 1990.) Current research provides strong evidence, however, that "they" is no longer a fully inclusive term, for it gives rise to a higher proportion of male than female images in people's minds when they hear the term. (See, for example, Sniezek and Jazwinski 1986.) Although it scores better than the prescriptive "he" in this regard (Switzer 1990), it is not as inclusive as the more linguistically cumbersome "she and he" (Hyde 1984; Khosroshahi 1989; Schau and Scott 1984). (For a much more detailed discussion of the empirical research on alternative generic terms, see Ayim and Goossens 1993.)

Each of the suggested substitutes for both the prescriptive "man" and "he" are more democratic choices insofar as they do not automatically exclude large groups of people. All are preferable for another reason as well, however—they are more accurate. In "manning a course," what we are actually doing is providing the staff to operate the course. What a "mailman" does is carry letters, and a "fireman" fights fires. Both females and males are human beings or people, and terms which suggest that females might be excluded are highly inaccurate. Inclusive word choice, in my analysis, serves to achieve not only more democratic ends, but clearer, more accurate descriptive language as well. In a similar vein Webb (1986) argues that non-sexist language is a requirement of communication. Accuracy and descriptiveness have always been hailed as criteria of good writing and speaking by language teachers. It is interesting to speculate on whether accuracy and descriptiveness might not also have a basis in morality. Are they related to my fourth criterion, honesty, for example? Would it make sense to construe more accurate language and more highly descriptive language as more honest language?

(2) Language that Trivializes Women: It is often difficult to differentiate between language that trivializes women and language that demeans women; many particular instances of vocabulary choice which are regarded as trivializing by some people will be regarded as demeaning by others. For example, when we refer to women as girls, do we trivialize them or demean them? What about "chick," "fox," "filly," "doll," and so on? Trivializing language significantly overlaps demeaning language. Part of the explanation for this may be that to trivialize someone simply constitutes a weak form of demeaning or insulting them. In other words, there are levels of insult, and words involving weaker levels of insult may be perceived as merely trivializing. Within this framework, referring to a woman as a "bit of fluff" may be seen to trivialize her, while referring her to an "old bag" or a "sow" may be seen to demean her.

But notice that if we accept the classification of these two examples as given, there appears to be an additional assumption at work—i.e., intelligence is not sufficiently central to a woman's worth that we can deeply insult her when we suggest that she is wanting in that quality, whereas her sexual attractiveness is sufficiently central. At the same time, we are all well aware that physical attractiveness is in fact a trivial feature, compared, for example, to intelligence, moral goodness, strength of character, etc., and thus the choice of terms which suggest that women are like bits of fluff may fall closer to the demeaning than to the trivializing end of the spectrum.

Ironically, then, the very basis on which we attempt to rescue "merely" trivializing terms from the charge of being demeaning, may itself be highly suspect; such vocabulary choices may be perceived as less than demeaning because we have bought into a prior value scheme—one which suggests that a woman's worth is to be calibrated on her sexual attractiveness and not on her intelligence or her strength of character—which is itself deeply insulting to women. In effect, those word choices which are often identified as trivializing are in fact deeply demeaning, insofar as they exclude women from the realm of fully rational, fully intelligent, fully moral human beings, thus illustrating the interdependence among the concepts of exclusion, trivialization, and insult.

The fact is that the majority of English language users would distinguish between trivializing and demeaning vocabulary choices to refer to women along the lines that I have drawn above. The explanation of this fact which I have provided also helps to explain why in many people's eyes, the application of terms such as "doll," "girl," or "chick" to a woman is complimentary rather than insulting. On the face of it, construing terms that liken women to artificial toys, children, or chickens is absurd. We need to understand that our historical tradition has excluded intelligence from the traits valued in women; Moely and Kreicker's analysis of "gentleman" and "lady" shows that while people perceive "gentleman" to connote someone of greater competence than a "man," conversely, they perceive "lady" to connote someone of lesser competence than a "woman" (1984, 351-352). While our historical tradition has excluded intelligence, it has focused almost exclusively on a notion of sexual attractiveness that is closely linked to the characteristics of youth and innocence in its portrayal of a valuable woman; thus it becomes clear why many people might honestly use "doll," "girl," and "chick" terms as attempts at genuine compliments and respond with hurt, confusion, and anger when charged with linguistic sexism. What they thought they were doing, after all, was saying that the woman possessed a feature highly valued in women, namely, sexual attractiveness.

Ironically, sexual attractiveness in a woman does not include the notion of sexual activity—quite the opposite is the case. A man may want to "enjoy" women that many men want—his own status will be augmented if he "gets" the woman whom many men desire; he is unlikely to desire a woman whom many men have "enjoyed," however. The English language reserves a special word of contempt for a man who is married to a woman who "goes" with even one other man—namely, "cuckold." Notice that there is no corresponding female word for "cuckold." The very fact that "girl," "doll," and "chick" are commonly perceived as complimentary terms tells us that in this society, it is sexually innocent, inexperienced, naive, and highly vulnerable women who are seen as sexually attractive. Dolls may be perfectly beautiful, but they don't fuck. Women who are very sexually active with multiple partners are "sluts" and "whores," and by no amount of stretching the imagination could these terms be construed as complimentary. To determine whether any particular vocabulary choice is morally offensive, one needs to go beyond the term itself, beyond the speaker's intention in using it, and consider the social context in which the word occurs.

We must not lose sight of the fact that the social context with which we are dealing is not only sexist, but also racist, classist, homophobic, ablist, and ageist. Our norms of sexual attractiveness themselves are based on a white society, a society in which "fair" often stands in as a synonym for attractive and "dark" for unattractive, a society in which some people of Colour alter the shape of their noses, eyes, and their lips, straighten their hair, even lighten their skin, in an attempt to approach the dominant caucasian norm of beauty. As Barbara McKellar claims, there is a wide-spread "assumption that European standards in beauty are the ones by which to judge all others" (1989, 73).

The terms that the English language provides for referring to women suggest that the choices of roles available to women are doubly or even triply binding. Those who opt into the "be attractive to men" role—the dolls and chicks—walk on a razor's edge; for while their goal is to make numerous men desire them, they must allow none (or at most, one) of those men to actually "attain" them. A woman who refuses to engage in the enterprise at all, a woman who spurns the role of the titillating chick, who refuses to dress, talk, or behave in ways calculated to attract men, is likely to be labelled "dyke" or "butch," to be harassed, and to be treated with contempt by large segments of the population regardless of her actual sexual preference; and for those who are lesbian or gay, Crumpacker and Vander Haegen tell us that "[f]ear of being labelled "queer," "dyke," or "faggot" influences behavior, causing students, for example, to alter friendships, refrain from participating in sports, and embrace stereotypical sex roles" (1990, 204).

Choosing to engage in the doll/chick enterprise also entails a risk, however. Those who walk on razors are unlikely to escape unscarred, and this particular choice has slashed the arteries of opportunity for many of those who engaged in it. If a woman tries and fails to achieve this role—and by definition, most women must fail because of the youth condition built into chick, doll, and girl images—then, like the seventy-year-old woman with the hair colour of a teenager, she is ridiculous. If she aspires to the role and succeeds in it, but succumbs to the sexual desires of the men who want her, she becomes a slut, harlot, or whore, no longer a desirable and attractive commodity.

The route to real success would appear to involve her successfully attaining the cute chick/little girl image while denying men sexual gratification, the desire for which our society links to her attractiveness. A closer examination of the role reveals serious pitfalls, however. For to the men who want her badly, she is a cockteaser, and the more attractive she is, the more vulnerable she will be to being perceived in this way. If she is sexually harassed or raped, she may suddenly find that she is the one blamed for her victimization, and that she joins those of her sisters already condemned as sluts and whores by the vast bulk of the populace. Ravishing women run the risk of being blamed when they are ravished.

In a social context in which girls as young as six have been labelled sexually precocious by judges and held largely responsible for their own sexual molestation by adult males, we begin to see the danger of the little girl or cute chick routine. In a social context in which a medical handbook dealing with pediatric emergencies informs us that "although it becomes increasingly evident that in many cases classified as rape the female is as willing a partner as the male, there obviously are certain instances in which a young girl may be attacked by an adult male" (Work 1968, 144), we should beware the apparent glitter of the cute chick and the little girl image. It is a route fraught with as much real danger as that of the dyke or the whore. For although the chick role is *defined* by what men approve of, such approval is precarious at best.

Notice that my language suggests there is an element of choice here—that a woman may "choose" to embrace the cute chick image if she so desires. This is simplistic and is itself not fully inclusive of all women's experiences. Some poor women, for example, are forced to turn to prostitution to earn a living and support children. The cute little girl image is not an option for them. Nor is it an option for a woman in a wheelchair, an elderly woman, or a physically large woman. In the words of Sara Lightfoot, "the strong black woman has never met the cultural ideal of a ·woman. Femininity, as defined by the stereotype, was an economic and social luxury she could not afford" (1980, 141). In fact, it is only a relatively small subset of women for whom this role is a possible choice.

I have claimed earlier that a speaker's good intentions are not sufficient to eliminate moral censure if the speaker uses sexist language. As Henley claims, even "well-meaning, nonsexist speakers may, simply by conventional usage, unwittingly use the language as conscious misogynists do: to trivialize, ignore, and demean females" (1989, 59). The relevance of the speaker's intentions to the attribution of moral praise or blame does need to be addressed, however. Intention, after all, is a critical component of moral judgment. A charge of murder, for example, cannot reasonably be made unless there is some basis for believing that the act was intentional; in the absence of such intention, a charge of manslaughter (sic) could be laid, but not murder. Notice, however, that while the intention to commit murder is a necessary condition for any reasonable judgment of murder, it is not a necessary condition for a judgment of moral culpability. The driver who kills a pedestrian while knowingly operating a motor vehicle with totally deficient brakes may not have desired or intended the pedestrian's death, and hence may not be a murderer; however, such a person is still held morally responsible for the consequences of such action, on the grounds that people should anticipate the possibility of serious consequences emanating from the operation of a vehicle with faulty brakes. The moral culpability, while not as extreme as in a case of murder, is definitely present.

The same claim can be made for language. Those who choose words with the explicit intention of excluding women in a humanity-wide context or those who choose words with the explicit intention of trivializing or demeaning women are more morally culpable than those who choose such language without explicitly intending these consequences. The non-intenders are still morally culpable, however. The evidence that the prescriptive "man" and "he" exclude women is incontrovertible, the evidence that terms like "chick," "girl," and "doll" trivialize women is easily graspable; these are things we can reasonably expect people of at least mediocre intellect to know and hence we are entitled to blame them morally when they choose the sorts of words that have the clear consequence of excluding, trivializing, or demeaning women.

(3) Language that Demeans Women: Much of the discussion of trivializing language applies directly to demeaning language. The selection of demeaning vocabulary items to refer to women will *clearly* be shown to be undesirable on a moral analysis, and many who eschew feminist critiques of language will nevertheless concur

that people ought not to use demeaning language. Many men and women who are totally comfortable with the prescriptive "man" and "he," and who use "girl" or "doll" as synonyms for "woman," will draw the line at "sow," "dog," "cow," "bitch," "cunt," "whore," and "old bag."

These terms violate the criterion of caring in such a blatant way that, by and large, even the critics join in condemning them. If caring language attempts to include others as full participants, then it is obvious that the use of animal or sexual metaphors to refer to women, suggesting as many of them do that women are appropriately relegated to the role of breeding animal or sexual object, undermines any attempt to establish a caring language.

In this society, we often "compliment" women by suggesting they are like men: "She thinks like a man," "She has a masculine intelligence," or "She's got a lot of balls," all suggest that the speaker thinks highly of the woman in question. We insult men, however, by suggesting that they are like women: "He's a real old maid," or "He's acting just like a woman," leave us with no doubt that the speaker has a very low opinion of the man in question. "What a fag!" insults not by suggesting that he is sexually active, but rather that he takes the position of a woman in sexual relationships.

There are *many* more demeaning insulting words for referring to females than there are for referring to males available to speakers of the English language (Miller and Swift 1976, 105-106; Nilsen 1977, 34-35; Schulz 1975, 71-72; Spender 1980, 16-19). There are nine times as many demeaning words with explicit sexual connotations for referring to women as there are for referring to men in the English language (Spender 1980, 15). This observation should provide us with a further index of just how much an ideal of caring has been violated by our ways of referring to women relative to our ways of referring to men. The research of Preston and Stanley, while it showed fewer sex differences than are normally hypothesized regarding the language of insults, did demonstrate that the deepest insult available for a woman in the eyes of both female and male speakers is an allegation of sexual promiscuity, whereas the deepest insult available for a man is an allegation of homosexuality (1987, 216-218).

Although there may only be one-tenth as many as those available for women, there are nevertheless many offensive words available to refer to men. These words offend in different kinds of ways than the vocabulary choices I have discussed offend women. While I shall not analyze the men-offending words in any detail, I do wish to examine one category of such words—what I call the plundering dick metaphors—for example, "ram," "stallion," "buck," "stud," "Don Juan," and "Casanova." Such terms are offensive to men who don't wish to be identified as an ever-conquering sex organ. Those males whose egos are bolstered by the sexual exploitation of women will of course not find such appellation offensive. Similarly, those women who aspire to the role of titillating the plundering dick will enjoy the "bunny/playgirl" family of terms and will question the response of those women who do find them offensive, perhaps attributing such a response to jealousy of "pretty" women or general hostility towards men.

Even though both sets of terms—anti-women and anti-men—are problematic, although not necessarily perceived as problematic by all their referents, there is an important difference between the two; the female set entails a form of contradiction that the male set does not. Bunnies, playgirls, chicks, and dolls arouse male sexual interest but they don't hop into bed with every Don Juan who fancies them; if they actually engage in the behaviour for which they are highly desired because of their attractiveness, then they will degenerate into sluts and whores and lose the attraction. This is not true of studs and stallions. It may (and I would argue *is*) morally gross to identify a man as a stud, just as I would argue that it is morally gross to identify a woman as a bunny. But as the term is used, a stud does not lose its charm insofar as it engages in widespread sexual behaviour; a bunny who so behaves does lose her appeal as a bunny. This does not tell us anything startlingly new. It reaffirms that there are double standards of behaviour available to women and to men, that the standards available to women frequently place them in serious double binds, and that the words with which we refer to women and men both reflect and promote this sexual discrepancy.

The choice of vocabulary for referring to women is not a trivial matter. Women are frequently totally excluded from words that purport to be synonyms for the human race; they are caught between "compliments" that impose inextricable double binds and the deepest insults that the language has to offer for women; they are stripped of their intelligence, their will, and their independence by words that liken them to playthings and dumb animals. The moral implications of the sheer abundance of such terms in the language is overwhelming.

Some people may make light of the negative impact of these terms, urging that their potency has disappeared with their metaphoric qualities, and that as dead metaphors these terms no longer have the power to shape the thoughts and feelings of those who use them. I shall conclude this chapter by quoting from Emily Martin who, although discussing different terms than those I have focused on, captures the point I wish to make very clearly. She says,

> Although the literary convention is to call such metaphors "dead," they are not so much dead as sleeping . . . and all the more powerful for it. Waking up such metaphors, by becoming aware of when we are projecting cultural imagery onto what we study will improve our ability to investigate. . . . Waking up such metaphors, by becoming aware of their implications, will rob them of their power to naturalize our social conventions about gender. (1991, 501)

Martin's depiction of sleeping metaphors not only provides me with a conclusion to this chapter, but also with a transition to the next, which examines violent metaphors in our language. To that I now turn.

Note

1 This chapter has been previously published in almost identical form in the following publication: Maryann Ayim, "The Moral Dimensions of Sexually Inclusive Language," in *A Reader in Feminist Ethics*, edited by Debra Shogun (Toronto: Canadian Scholars' Press, 1993), pp. 515-532.

Chapter Eight

Violence in Language[1]

Introduction

Both academic and ordinary discourse foster violent images, many of which emerge from metaphors. As metaphors are powerful devices for shaping thinking, the amazing prevalence of ordinary language and academic metaphors that involve domination, war, and violence is a serious matter. We live in a world saturated with violent talk. Even the medical metaphor for the body's response to disease is one of the battlefield, with fighter blood cells attacking the invading viruses.[2] Our everyday parlance describes a man who nicks himself shaving as "bleeding like a stuck pig"; a frantically busy person "runs around like a chicken with its head cut off"; an efficient person who accomplishes more than one thing at a time "kills two birds with one stone"; an employee who helps an organization over difficult problems is a "trouble-shooter"; an employer who must let workers go is a "hit-man," "an axe-man," or "a hired gun." Universities who manage to attract a big name to a faculty pull off an academic "coup." When

---

The notes to this chapter are on p. 173.

smaller-league faculty members consistently fail to "hit the mark," the dictates of reason may compel those in the bigger league to "shoot their ideas down."

Children's fairy tales and nursery rhymes teem with woodsmen who chop off the heads of wolves, old witches who are baked in ovens or otherwise unpleasantly disposed of, hateful stepmothers who reap their due, and tiny babies who plunge out of cradles suspended high in tree-tops. Our children are initiated as babies into this violent misogynist parlance by the traditional stories read to them. Somewhat later the children's television cartoons carry on. As they grow into early adolescence, the tradition continues with video games and even educational materials selected for use with computers, in which either the object or the reward of the game is to "shoot down" or "eat up" some enemy force. And needless to say, as they grow older yet, or even at adolescence, there is an endless supply of violent pornographic materials and a surfeit of violent shows available on television. Discourse in the Canadian parliament, now publicly broadcast, is almost a caricature of the confrontational style.

In the academy, violent metaphors are found in science, philosophy, and education, as well as in many other disciplines that are not discussed in this chapter. The metaphors are frequently bolstered by images of sexual domination, especially in science, where nature is often regarded as something female that the male scientist sets out to conquer and dominate. Within philosophy, argument is understood as a confrontation between one person who defends a position and another who attacks. Such metaphors also exist in education, where the acquisition of student competence is popularly described in terms of attack skills and learning is equated to mastery. I shall argue in this chapter that the centrality of these violent metaphors in both academic and ordinary discourse is problematic, and that if we were to alter our ways of thinking and switch to more cooperative, nurturant metaphors (such as those of needle work), there might be beneficial effects both for scholarship and for human relations.

We would be foolish to underestimate the power of metaphor, however. "In metaphor, a system of belief gets new life in a foreign land; it takes root among the alien corn" (Tourangeau 1982, 34). In this account, itself metaphorical, Tourangeau provides some indication of how metaphors work. Blown on the winds of change, like dandelion seeds, perhaps, they take tentative root "in a foreign land" (ibid.). Not all of them will survive. In a place too alien, the metaphor will, in Israel Scheffler's words, "languish and die" (1979, 129).

But of those that do survive, some will establish their roots deeply, and in so doing, will become central to the "process of creating new meaning" (Gerhart and Russell 1984, 98). They may actually take over the cornfield, changing the chemical composition of the soil. This soil will prove either hostile or conducive to the development of other new ideas, rendering the metaphors themselves central to the shape and growth of meaning. Hence the metaphors that survive and flourish will become "organizing element(s) in inquiry" (Fernandez 1977, 101); as such, they will come to exert powerful influence not only on the perception of what counts as a good solution to a problem but also on the logically prior perception of what constitutes a problem in the first place (Schön 1979, 255).

In this chapter I examine a powerful type of metaphor—one employed in academic discourse generally and especially prevalent in the language of science and philosophy. The following personal anecdote illustrates the nature of this genre of metaphor. A colleague of mine decided to include a component on a specific language in a computer science course that he teaches. Although he was relatively unfamiliar with the language himself, he deemed his students' exposure to it to be sufficiently worthwhile to merit its inclusion. The decision entailed concentrated work to familiarize himself with the language to the point of being able to teach it. After about two weeks, devoted almost exclusively to this task, he triumphantly declared that he had "beaten the language into submission."

It is important to emphasize that this colleague is by no means a violent, nasty, or even particularly aggressive person. As an academic, however, the image that occurred to him as a natural fit for his achievement in learning the computer language was one of violence. This picture of "beating into submission" captures all too aptly our standard perception of the nature of academic and intellectual success. Thus academic achievement is so closely calibrated with acquiring control over the subject matter that the notion of mastery is perceived as virtually synonymous with that of learning. The definition of the verb "to master" in the *Concise Oxford Dictionary* corroborates this perception. "Master" is defined as "overcome, defeat; reduce to subjection; acquire complete knowledge of (subject) or facility in using (instrument, etc.); rule as a master" (1976, 672).

This chapter will identify and analyze these types of metaphors as they occur in academic discourse; I shall look specifically at science, philosophy, and education as case studies. In scientific language, the metaphors of dominance, subjugation, manipulation, and control are many. In philosophical discourse, the most powerful metaphors connote not only dominance and subjugation, but also violence and outright warfare. Such metaphors can also be found in educational literature. Alternative metaphors, more closely aligned to nurturance than to subjugation, do exist for learning. I argue for the superiority of the nurturant metaphors and suggest that they should replace the violent metaphors so much in vogue in our academies of learning.

Science and the Pursuit of Truth—A Case Study in Manipulation and Control

As academics, we are participants in a tradition that values independence, objectivity, aggression, the clear separation of feelings from ideas, and the inability to express emotions—in short, we participate in a tradition that values maleness as it has been stereotypically identified. This is no surprise to any of us. Academia has been a male preserve, which literally forbade women entry for centuries. When its gates were opened to women, a strict condition was attached: to be an academic, a woman had to put aside her "feminine" nature—her subjectivity, her timidity, and her emotion (except for such "legitimate" emotions as anger and aggression). She had to learn to "think like a man," and to the degree that she achieved this feat, she would be accepted into the academic community.

The degree to which masculinity is perceived as a ticket of admission varies from one academic discipline to another, and has also varied over time. The "harder" disciplines, such as science and mathematics, exemplify the masculine stereotype most thoroughly. The "softer" disciplines, such as the fine arts, sociology, and education stray much further from these male-identified criteria of excellence.

In an intriguing paper entitled "Gender and Science," Evelyn Fox Keller provides us with some insight into the male nature of the scientific enterprise. She refers to the research of Anne Roe (Keller 1983, 201), whose personality inventories comparing scientists to other academics reveal that scientists fit the masculine stereotype most clearly. In her study devoted to the question of "what kinds of people do what

kinds of scientific research and why," Roe (1952, 1) reports that physicists and biologists in particular display a sense of "unease about
intimate personal relations . . . [and] are strongly inclined to keep
away from intense emotional situations as much as possible" (ibid.,
192). In a later work in which she presents a personality profile of
many occupations, including several associated with science, Roe
describes physicists and biologists as not valuing close personal relationships in their own lives and consequently not engaging in such
relationships. They do not even have strong emotional ties to their
parents, and there is a clear tendency towards "an open or covert attitude of derogation of their mothers [although] they almost universally
respect their fathers profoundly" (1956, 215). In general, these
researchers were uninterested in other people; their interest was
rather focused on "rational controls" (ibid., 217). They tended
towards "abstractions, and to formalized, objective thinking, with a
marked inhibition of any tendencies to project themselves into a situation. They empathize little, either with things or with other people,
and they have a rather passive emotional adaptation" (ibid., 218).
Interestingly, there were no significant sex differences among the
researchers studied, illustrating that the women who made it through
the gates of science did so by adopting the requisite male style (ibid.,
217). By contrast with biologists and physicists, nurse-counsellors
tended to be "extroverted, dominant, sensitive to the problems of others, well-adjusted, and practical in . . . problem-solving activities.
They give liking for and interest in people as their major reason for
selecting nursing as a profession" (ibid., 222).

It is interesting to speculate on how the history of science might
have differed, were it populated by sensitive, extroverted, well-
adjusted researchers, as opposed to people with little empathy, little
interest in other people, and clear derogatory attitudes towards their
mothers.

Nowhere has the notion of success been more closely identified
with mastery, control, and maleness than in the discipline of science.
To illustrate, I cite two voices from the scientific tradition—Francis
Bacon, whose work was among the most powerful in determining the
shape and direction of scientific thought, and Richard Feynman, a
contemporary scientist who achieved the ultimate hallmark of appro-
bation and honour among his peers in being selected as a Nobel prize
winner.

Although the identification of science with mastery predated
Bacon, it has probably been expressed most graphically in his writing.

In his *On the Dignity and Advancement of Learning*, he admonished the scientist "but to follow and as it were hound nature in her wanderings, and you will be able, when you like, to lead or drive her afterwards to the same place again" (1860, 296). The image of scientific knowledge emanating from the control and manipulation of nature arises clearly and directly from this passage. Another more indirect image is that of dualism, with definite boundaries between knower and the knowable, between the scientist and nature. The scientist comes to know nature by controlling it, manipulating it, or in Bacon's words, by leading it, driving it, or hounding it.

Another dualism basic to Bacon's picture of the scientific endeavour is that between male and female. The scientist is, of course, male and nature female. In a subsequent passage of the same work, Bacon fills out his metaphorical account of the scientific enterprise: "Neither ought a man to make scruple of entering and penetrating into those holes and corners, when the inquisition of truth is his sole object" (ibid.). This passage, with its clear allusion to sexual intercourse, metaphorically links scientific inquiry to male penetration of the female body. The earlier admonition to "hound," "lead," and "drive" nature suggests that where nature does not easily render herself to the scrutiny of the scientist, forcible entry or rape may be justified as a means to the acquisition of further knowledge. Nature, then, is characterized as knowable, passive, female, and rapable, and the scientist is active knower, male, and justified in committing rape in the name of science. (The analysis of this violent imagery is developed in more detail in the section of the chapter that focuses specifically on philosophy, but it is important to notice its presence in the language of science as well.)

Richard Feynman's identification of science with masculinity is equally graphic and equally worrisome from a moral point of view. In a public lecture in which he described the work that led to his Nobel prize, Feynman likened the process of formulating a scientific theory to falling in love. He said:

> That was the beginning, and the idea seemed so obvious to me and so elegant that I fell deeply in love with it. And, like falling in love with a woman, it is only possible if you do not know much about her, so you cannot see her faults. The faults will become apparent later, but after the love is strong enough to hold you to her. So, I was held to this theory, in spite of all difficulties, by my youthful enthusiasm. (Feynman 1966, 700)

He concluded his address by developing the metaphor further, describing the theory (and the woman) in its old age.

> So what happened to the old theory that I fell in love with as a youth? Well, I would say it's become an old lady, who has very little that's attractive left in her, and the young today will not have their hearts pound when they look at her anymore. But, we can say the best we can for any old woman, that she has been a very good mother and has given birth to some very good children. And, I thank the Swedish Academy of Sciences for complimenting one of them. Thank you. (Ibid., 708)

This characterization of the scientific undertaking is by no means original. It is evident in most of the contemporary feminist critiques of science and philosophy of science. Lloyd (1984, 10-17), Keller (1983, 187-205), and Harding (1986, 168-169, 237), for example, all provide vivid and abundant evidence for the metaphorical identification of scientific progress with conflict, mastery, manipulation, dominance, male sexuality, and even violent rape.

The metaphors of science have been among the most powerful in terms of shaping our thought, legitimating traditional scholarship, and virtually exerting the power of veto over radical innovations in the academic arena. As Harding says, "Neither God nor tradition is privileged with the same credibility as scientific rationality in modern cultures" (1986, 16). Harding claims, furthermore, that scientists' identification of the purpose of science with controlling, manipulating, and dominating nature has specifically benefited a select group of largely middle-class, white males (ibid.).

Hence, the nature of the metaphors found in scientific writing is very important indeed, and we cannot dismiss as trivial the characterization of science as domineering, manipulative, coercive, and inherently male that is provided by these metaphors. An interview conducted by the well-known American broadcaster Charles Kuralt with a sponge fisherman in Tarpon Springs, Florida, identifies beautifully the perceived nature of this relationship. In answer to Kuralt's question as to why he still continues to fish sponge for a living, Billiris replies:

> Because I don't believe anywhere in this country, or this world for that matter, you can find a more exciting life, because it is definitely a life of its own, it's excitement, it's adventure. Here it's different altogether. There's a gaiety, there's an anxiety, there's sorrow—you lose men or men are hurt, as they often are—and you exercise, I believe, every emotion that a man can possibly exercise, and these are all realistic, they're not false, there's no pretence, because it's a man's world. We live in a

man's world and think as men. . . . So, to work around a group of men
that think the same, act the same, feel the same, and still each man is
his own man in his own right, I think that's worth a little bit more than
the sign of a dollar bill. (1985, 212-213)

Although Billiris is describing his membership in the society of
sponge fishermen here, his account is also an apt description of membership in the bona fide scientific community. For this latter group,
too, has historically been an exclusive male preserve. Science is realistic because it gets to define and describe reality; it cannot be false
because it is the mandate of science to provide us with an account of
the truth. As a scientist one works "around a group of men that think
the same, act the same, feel the same" (ibid., 213). The homogeneity
of the members is ensured by strict admission criteria. In today's
world, the selection of new scientists is carefully monitored by the old
guard, who continue to make up the critical mass in selection committees of university departments, editorial boards for high-prestige
journals, and referees for the central grant-giving bodies. As Addelson
points out (1983, 178), those in positions of power in the scientific
world could well be in a position to silence all those critical of their
work by simply cutting off the resources necessary to it. The operant
language and metaphors characterizing the tradition within which
this powerful group operates will render meaningless and nonsensical
alternative modes of conceptualizing reality. This is not to say, of
course, that alternative modes of conceptualizing reality never occur,
but only to explain the incredible obstacles that a truly radical perception must overcome if it is to gain the tiniest plausibility in the scientific community.

Hand in hand with the vision of truth or reality given to us by
science is the notion of the method of science as being objective and
rational. Because science is not sidetracked by the emotional, its prod-
uct is not someone's mere subjective account of reality but an objective picture of the world as it really is. Interestingly, this meshes
smoothly with our earlier characterization of science as inherently
male. One of the standard sex-role stereotype questionnaires (Broverman et al. 1972, 63) identifies as masculine the following personality
traits: very objective, very dominant, very logical, not at all emotional, almost always hides emotions, very active, and easily able to
separate feeling from ideas. The counterparts of these traits, identified
as feminine on the questionnaire, are very subjective, very submissive, very illogical, very emotional, does not hide emotions at all, very
passive, and unable to separate feelings from ideas.

So the picture of science, which most of us hold, is one of an objective quest for the truth, untrammelled by the purely subjective and the emotional, and proceeding in a logical way towards its goal. We also have tended to see science as politically neutral, unfettered and untarnished by affiliation with particular political ideologies. We have somehow envisaged science, in its pursuit of knowledge, as pure and disconnected from the practical applications and consequences of that knowledge. This picture of science is related in obvious ways to our view of scientists as people relatively uninterested in other people, with little empathy, who tend toward "objective thinking with a marked inhibition of any tendencies to project themselves into a situation," and with "a rather passive emotional adaptation" (Roe 1956, 218). Whatever historical justification such a picture of science may have had, it is clear that such a view is no longer tenable. It is evident that scientific research is now selected for financial backing on the basis of its applicability to very specific practical goals and we can no longer afford to ignore the nature of the context within which science is allowed to operate (Harding 1986, 16).

The attainment of pure objectivity is simply not possible. Our scientific research will always be coloured by our ideals, our metaphysics, and our metaphors. This will be as true of a feminist approach to science as a traditional male-oriented approach. It is important that we not pretend we have done away with values and presuppositions, but that we make clear what these values and presuppositions are. The most worrisome assumptions are those that go undetected and hence unexamined.

As Harding argues, the alignment of science with maleness, domination, and control should be discountenanced not only because such a view is sexist, but also because it "makes bad science. It leads to false and oversimplified models of nature and inquiry that attribute power relations and hierarchical structure where none do or need exist" (ibid., 121). Hence feminist criticism will contribute not only to the achievement of higher moral standards in science through its emphasis on sexual egalitarianism, but it will also contribute to raising the standards of the scientific aspects of the research. In the advent of feminist criticism, science should become not only more just, but also more fully scientific.

Does philosophical discourse represent an improvement over its scientific cousin with regard to violent metaphors? The answer, I am afraid, is negative. I turn the focus of my discussion now to philosophy.

Violence in Academe—Philosophy as Paradigm

Philosophy's much-prized rational "man" has projected a single, consistent image throughout the history of philosophy—the image of violence. The philosophical literature abounds in metaphors of battle, confrontation, sword fights, arm wrestling, knifings, throwing, bullfights, torture, poisoning, and cold-blooded analyses of the resultant corpses. Out of a multitude of examples, consider the following four: "The weapon behind logical analysis, behind the appeal to reason, is nothing more serious than the sharp edge of inconsistency" (Scriven 1976, 34); "When you disagree with something, the logically appropriate response is to aim your critical arrows at that position itself" (Johnson and Blair 1977, 42); the battle metaphor appears even in the context of advice to the logic student about how to respond supportively in an argument: "Having done your best to attack the argument, you should now turn around and do your best to defend it" (Hitchcock 1983, 215); and the author of a book on the philosophy of social science states that his "aim was to attack a current conception of the relations between philosophy and the social sciences" (Winch 1958, 2). A much fuller exposition of the "argument is war" metaphor occurs in Lakoff and Johnson's *Metaphors We Live By* (1980).

In a similar vein, Sheila Ruth describes a philosophy conference as follows: "Someone reads a paper; he is quarry. The others, hunters, listen, waiting for a weak point, sniffing for blood. They attack; the quarry defends. Combat. So male. Is this the way to do philosophy? Is this the way to do any investigation?" (Ruth 1981, 48).

Philosophers teach students about arguments and provide for them what they believe are models of excellence. They expose the skeleton arguments of the historical giants, most of which they then proceed to tear apart. They are careful not to let students know with which world pictures their own sympathies lie, for it is supposedly not the particular metaphysical theories they want their students to acquire and to value but rather the philosophical manner of operation. Thus they teach how to lay bare an argument, how to identify the most critical premises and go for the heart of the discussion, how to move in for an attack. They want students to learn how to pinpoint and reject the merely extraneous and peripheral, so they will probably provide them with Ockham's Razor as a ready tool. (Ockham's Razor is a principle identified with William of Ockham, a medieval philosopher who advocated "shaving off" unnecessary metaphysical entities on the grounds that one should not multiply entities beyond necessity.)

Philosophers tend to value "sharper" students, whom they may openly praise for their "penetrating" insights. Occasionally they find students of "piercing" intelligence, one or two perhaps with minds like "steel traps." Philosophers regard such students as important: they require "tough-minded" opponents with whom they can "parry" in the classroom, so they can exhibit to the others what the "thrust" of philosophical argumentation is all about. This "battle of wits" is somewhat risky, however, and a "combatant" must take care always to "have the upper hand," to "win thumbs down," to "avoid being hoist by one's own petard." If you find yourself "pressed for time" at the end of a lecture, with your "back to the wall," or as it is occasionally even more colourfully expressed, "between a rock and a hard place," you may have to resort to "strong-arm tactics," to "barbed" comments, to "go for the jugular" to "cut an opponent's argument to pieces," or to "bring out the big guns or heavy artillery." If caught in the throes of a real dilemma, you may even have to "take the bull by the horns," or rebut the dilemma by advancing a "counter" dilemma (Ruby 1950, 295-297).

Philosophers justify such behaviour—for, by engaging in it, they are providing students with further grist for the mill of reason. They are giving them a view of the "cutting edge" of philosophical research. If necessary, this can be made clear in the next class session by performing a "post mortem" of the previous day's battle of ideas. It is interesting that much of this lexicon (for example, "piercing," "thrust," and "penetrating,") has overt sexual connotations not unconnected with the image of the violent duel; the fact that the word "vagina" originally referred to the sheath of a sword is another illustration of the linguistic link between violence and sexuality.

Philosophers insist that the strongest argument will be the one that provides a rebuttal to the archrival of its conclusion. In other words, as Janice Moulton points out, philosophical attention becomes focused on attempting to undermine the position of someone who holds the completely opposite point of view, with little time left over to "provide any positive reason for accepting a conclusion . . . or show how a conclusion is related to other ideas" (1983, 161).

Philosophers warn students about such fallacious reasoning as "poisoning the wells," *ad hominem* (an attack against the man), appeal to authority, and *ad baculum* (which literally translates as "appeal to the stick" or less formally as appeal to force—in other words, the use of covert threats as means of persuasion). Consider, as an example, the appeal to authority: Dropping an important name or appealing to a person's importance as evidence for the truth of a claim is frequently illicit and always suspect. The claims of authorities, like those of anyone else, philosophers say, must be supported by confirming evidence or compelling reasoning; it is to this evidence that we should turn, not to the status of the authority, when gauging the reasonableness of attaching belief to any particular claim.

At the same time that students are warned of the dangers of sliding into such shabby inference patterns as judging a statement's truth-value solely by virtue of the status of one of its proponents, classroom speech is liberally sprinkled with none too subtle reminders as to where the power of authority really rests. The words "obviously" and "clearly" occur with a frequency even higher than in ordinary discourse. I was partially rescued from this behaviour by a group of students in the first philosophy class I taught. These students taped several of my lectures and reported to me with great hilarity that the more confusing and the murkier the lecture became, the more I used the words "clearly" and "obviously." When what I said grew absolutely opaque, "clearly" and "obviously" constituted about 50 percent of the discourse. In the wake of this unflattering revelation, I began to claim that particular statements were "fairly obvious" and that certain states of affairs "seemed to me to be true." Now, after two-and-a-half additional decades in the educational forum, I am more inclined to speak of "things which seem to me to be fairly obvious."

The metaphors that both describe and prescribe the interactions of the typical philosophy classroom have not developed from pure coincidence. As Lakoff and Johnson claim, "People in power get to impose their metaphors" (1980, 87, 157), and so we operate with images of confrontation, duelling, and aggressiveness—in brief, the image of the battlefield is projected as the exemplary philosophy classroom. (For another interesting account of the adversary method as paradigm, see Janice Moulton [1980]; this adversary paradigm is further developed by Susan R. Peterson [1980].) So deeply is this notion embedded, that when I talk in class of developing a critical analysis of an argument's position that is largely supportive of the position in question, my students have great difficulty in understanding me. The notion of a critical analysis is so thoroughly welded into their minds as a purely negative and largely destructive response, that they view the terms "critical" and "supportive" as antithetical.

I believe it is time to stop focusing our attention exclusively on proving arguments that run counter to our own as wrong. We need to turn to the more integrating tasks of asking how these arguments mesh with different experience sets, different belief systems, different value codes, and even different reasoning styles; this point is also developed by Janice Moulton (1983, 161-162). The danger of the first focus (proving counterarguments wrong) is that while it enables us to isolate tiny chunks of reasoning, it also prevents us from moving beyond these isolated segments; the second focus will lead us to examine a much broader academic context. Whereas the first focus permits, and even encourages, a narrow, segmented approach, the second encourages an approach to philosophy that is more bound up in social consequences. The second approach will integrate philosophy into broader social issues such as sexism, racism, and the nuclear arms race—whereas the first will tend to encourage a focus on building stronger and stronger counterarguments against a rival's position without taking full account of the broader context. The segmentation of the first approach is often mistakenly confused with objectivity, while the second's concern with social issues may cause it to be dismissed as an abandonment of reason.

The rejection of the emotional and affective realms in the name of reason may be one facet of the rejection of femaleness in the realm of philosophy. This rejection comes as no surprise in a tradition in which prominent theorists have labelled the female sex as "being as it were a deformity" (Aristotle 1953, 461, Becker ref. 775a15-18) and "a sugary sliminess . . . the obscenity . . . of everything which gapes open" (Sartre 1957, 609, 613, cited in part by Finn 1982, 160). Ironically, in the same passage cited above, Aristotle admits that "in human beings, more males are born deformed than females" (ibid., 459, Becker ref. 775a4-7); this he attributes to the inherent *superiority* of the male embryo which, being "much hotter in its nature than the female . . . move[s] about more . . . and [hence] . . . get[s] broken more" (ibid., Becker ref. 775a5-12).

When such misogyny disappears entirely from the academic realm, a radical shift in philosophical parlance may occur. In the philosophy classroom of the future, perhaps words such as "seminal," now reserved to bestow the highest praise on an insight or an idea, will be supplemented with words like "ovarian" or "mammarian." There is much work to be done before we reach such a stage, however. Can we expect that education will provide a vehicle capable of contributing to such reform? The literature on philosophy of education does not provide us with much grounds for optimism, and I conclude my discussion of philosophy by turning briefly to this area.

Within philosophy of education, it is safe to say that the dominant paradigm is still that of forms of knowledge (Hirst 1974) to be mastered by the student, with the educator's task one of initiating the student into achieving this mastery. The paradigm is captured graphically by R.S. Peters, who says that children "start off in the position of the barbarian outside the gates. The problem is to get them inside the citadel of civilization. . . . That is why the educator has such an uphill task in which there are no short cuts" (Peters 1965, 107-108). The civilized world, as envisaged by Peters, is like the scientific world described at the beginning of the chapter—an exclusive preserve whose membership is strictly controlled by those already regarded as authorities. Although Peters nowhere advocates that women be kept outside the citadel gates, he does use the pronoun "he" throughout his paper, with a single exception. When discussing educators who adhere to the progressive or child-centred ideology, a view which he takes to be silly and mistaken, the feminine pronoun "she" appears for the first and only time in the article. Peters says, "He or, more likely, she, tends to believe that education consists in the development from within of potentialities rather than 'moulding' from without . . ." (ibid., 93-94). He then lists several people who have actually held this view, and not a single female name appears on his list.

I turn now to a discussion of education, asking whether that literature offers any ideas for a model of reform.

Education—A Vehicle for Reform?

Although violent, controlling, aggressive metaphors may be apparent in the realms of science and philosophy, by no means are they confined to these academic quarters. Small wonder that education should reflect this tradition, and that computer software games for teaching mathematics should be focused on the attack and destruction of alien space creatures, or that teachers' instruction manuals for reading should describe the phonetic and structural analysis that precedes the child's learning to spell as helping "to recognize and attack new words" and describe word recognition as encouraging "children . . . to attack new words" (Cross and Hulland 1975, xii). Reading specialists tell teachers that "using phonics is only one means for attacking unknown graphic representatives" (Petty, Petty, and Becking 1976,

328). They advise teachers to place particular emphasis on "determining whether the pupil is attacking unknown words" (ibid., 329).

Nevertheless, education gives us grounds for optimism. In the last ten years, the literature on reading has shifted radically away from mechanistic models, in which the violent metaphors particularly flourished. These models were in their prime until that time, and both works cited above fit this time frame. In fact, in a later edition of the *Experiences in Language* book cited earlier (Petty, Petty, and Salzer 1976), the authors appear to have expunged all occurrences of "attack" and its ilk. They speak in this later edition of the importance of "encouraging in the class a spirit of mutual pride and cooperation" (Petty et al. 1989, 294). The prominent contemporary theory in reading is whole language, and with this shift violent metaphors have largely disappeared. Interestingly, in the whole language approach, language is viewed as a social art, in which the context of student, teacher, text, and other students are integrated. The behaviouristic model that broke reading down into small separable sub-skills is shunned by the whole language approach.

The 1990s appear to be ushering in a return to the behaviouristic era in reading theory, however. Reader-centred, context-sensitive theory is thus not only a relative newcomer to the reading literature, but it is a fairly precarious one at that. While still by and large the preferred mode from the teachers' perspective, the whole language philosophy (Baskwill and Whitman 1988; Edelsky 1990; Goodman, Goodman, and Hood 1989; Schwartz and Pollishuke 1990; Weaver 1990) is under siege in North American elementary schools, with many powerful lobby groups exerting pressure on schools to return to the more teacher-centred, skills-oriented models focusing on phonics and spelling (see Adams 1990; Apple 1991; Giroux 1991; McKenna, Robinson, Miller 1990a, 1990b).

Guidelines currently specified by the Ontario Ministry of Education are remarkably free of controlling, violent, sexist language. The broad goals specified for intermediate and senior education are closely linked to dynamic learning, creative thinking, problem-solving skills, and personal responsibility in a social context (Ontario Ministry of Education 1984, 3). What little controlling language there is centres in the Ministry's guidelines for the primary division, which lists "master[ing] number facts an objective of arithmetic," "master[ing] a vocabulary that enables him or her to name, describe, reason, explain, and use qualitative words as he or she plays, observes, manipulates, creates, and experiments with stimulating material" as an objective of speaking, and "master[ing] a vocabulary of words, phrases, and expressions" as an objective of writing. For the junior division category, the only reference to mastery is in the reading guidelines, where "master[ing] the essential word recognition strategies" (Ontario Ministry of Education 1975, 6, 8, 10, 13) is listed as an objective. These are more than balanced, however, by the cooperative, interactive, and social objectives specified in the guidelines.

Although these changes in educational parlance provide some legitimate basis for hope that academia ultimately may abandon controlling, manipulative, and violent metaphors, our optimism may be dampened if we reflect on the current disillusionment at the university level with elementary and secondary school systems. Perhaps this disenchantment reflects a greater attachment by these "higher" institutions to the domination and violence metaphors. Furthermore, the language of greatest praise, when bestowed upon students of any age, still tends to be steeped in violent metaphors. For example, the twelve-year-old Alberta boy, Byung Kyu Chun, who placed first in the province in a grade eleven mathematics competition of students five years older than himself, was described in *The Edmonton Journal* as "a scholar of almost frightening skill" who is "getting his black belt in mathematics." The boy's father, Chong Suh Chun, was reported as claiming, "I'm teaching them [his son and daughter Su Jin Chun who placed first in the Alberta grade ten competition] mathematics like you teach martial arts" (McConnell 1992, A1).

So long as the institutions of "higher" learning continue to value mastery as a model of learning, so long as analytic thinking is emphasized in education, and so long as excellence in analytic thinking is found to be positively correlated to students' "(a) reluctance to be dependent on their family or friends, (b) striving for social recognition, and (c) concern with intellectual mastery" (Kagan, Moss, and Sigel 1963, 77), the shift in the elementary and secondary school lexicon away from mastery, control, manipulation, and violence gives us little cause to hope for any easy or immediate change within educational circles.

I conclude by examining a manual prepared for use in the university classroom that advocates a cooperative model of learning as opposed to the standard model in which the professor delivers the text or the form of knowledge to the student. In his *Learning Thru Discussion* (1962, 33, 38), William Hill sketches what the objectives of such a classroom would be and offers practical suggestions for the realization of such objectives. In a classroom built around discussion, some of the specific skills to be developed are giving and asking for reactions, giving examples, clarifying, synthesizing, standard setting, sponsoring, encouraging, and group tension relieving. Aggressing, blocking, competing, status seeking, and dominating are deemed by Hill to be absolutely non-functional classroom behaviour, and only when they are excised does he believe real learning will occur. Ironically, in his introduction to this book, Herbert Thelen seems to have missed Hill's point. In a passage whose language is utterly incongruous with the spirit of Hill's advice, Thelen describes Hill as showing "the variety of ways in which the material can be pinched, punched, squeezed, kicked, and, ultimately, mastered" (1962, 9).

A classroom focused on the development of such skills as sponsoring, encouraging, and group tension relieving would teach students how to learn through cooperation rather than competition, a capacity of which our world, whose leaders confront one another with ever larger supplies of deadly technology and aggression, is in dire and immediate need. Nor would such an approach be acritical. Hill specifically includes standard setting as one of the important skills to be developed. There is every reason to believe that in a context in which students were not constantly "under attack," they could afford to be more critical and more open about the deficiencies of their own ideas.

The model of supportive interaction rather than self-aggrandizing confrontation is one that is developed systematically in the pragmatic philosophy of C.S. Peirce. Peirce sees scientific progress as attainable only through the cooperative efforts of a community of scientists. He says that "One generation collects premises in order that a distant generation may discover what they mean. . . . One [scientist] contributes this, another that. Another company, standing upon the shoulders of the first, strike a little higher" (Peirce 1931-1958, 7.87).

For Peirce, if learning or getting closer to the truth is truly the goal of scientific inquiry, it follows that the scientific method must be rooted in the scientific community rather than individual scientists. Discovering a law of nature, for example, is simply too big a task for any individual scientist to accomplish alone. Only through building on the work done by former generations of scientists in which many investigators have made some contribution, will individual scientists be able to use the scientific method to bring us closer to the truth.

It is important to be aware that critical appraisal is an integral part of Peirce's approach to scientific inquiry. Scientists must subject their own ideas to the severest kinds of tests before advocating their acceptance in the scientific forum. Scientists who perceive the acquisition of knowledge rather than their own self-aggrandizement as the goal of scientific inquiry will be eager to subject their ideas to such a critical appraisal. Thus, on Peirce's analyses, an individualistic focus *will get in the way of* honest and extensive critical appraisal, whereas a community focus will foster even higher levels of critical appraisal.

Interactional cooperation offers a better means of acquiring knowledge than does adversarial exchange. It may well be the case that women can provide the models for this interactional exchange. As discussed earlier in this book, empirical studies of gender-specific language patterns show that in mixed-sex conversations such constructive interactions are consistently present in women's speech and consistently absent in men's. (See, for example, Benton 1973; Brenner and Vinacke 1983; Fishman 1977, 1983; Gleason and Greif 1983; Shakeshaft 1987; Zeldin, Small, and Savin-Williams 1982; Zimmerman and West 1975.) As women have traditionally been tutored in the battlefield metaphor by men, perhaps women will become the tutors within the context of this new metaphor. A quilting bee provides an explicit example of a particular cooperative community where the excellence of any one quilter's contribution is not undercut or negated by the excellence of another quilter's work. Contrast this with the duelling metaphor, in which achievement of success entails that others come out losers. The quilting metaphor, which commits us to no such problematic stance, is generalizable in a way in which the duelling metaphor is not.

Jane Roland Martin (1981) provides an insightful analysis of the inadequacy of traditional models of academic excellence. These models provide a picture of the ideal that is not fully human. They focus on the rational and cognitive aspects of human development, to the exclusion of the affective and the emotional. They have, furthermore, brought us to the brink of peril in terms of objectification of nature, depletion of natural resources, and hostility of people against people that threatens us with extinction. A superior model would be a nurturant cooperative one, one that puts humanity in its proper place—as part of the natural world and very much dependent on it. Caring, compassion, and nurturance should be as integral to our truly educated person as objectivity, scientific rigour, and rationality itself. I urge that our classrooms could only be improved by adopting this wider notion of education that Martin depicts. Reason itself will be better served if we abandon the metaphor of the battlefield for the more humane and more human metaphor of the cooperative community.

Having discussed the nature and impact of violent imagery in academic and ordinary discourse, it is appropriate now to turn to Chapter Nine, in which I address the very current topic of political correctness, focusing on the race and gender dimensions of this literature.

Notes

1 Various parts of this chapter have been previously published in highly similar form in the three following publications: Maryann Ayim, "Dominance and Violence in Scientific Discourse: A Portrait of the Scientist as a Young Man," in *Rights, Justice, and Community*, edited by Creighton Peden and John K. Roth (Lewiston, NY: Edwin Mellen Press, 1992), pp. 9-23; Maryann Ayim, "Violence and Domination as Metaphors in Academic Discourse," in *Selected Issues in Logic and Communication*, edited by Trudy Govier (Belmont, CA: Wadsworth, 1988), pp. 184-195; and Maryann Ayim, "Warning: Philosophical Discussion, Violence at Work," *Resources for Feminist Research/ Documentation sur la Recherche Feministe*, 16, 3 (September 1987), 23-24.

2 I am grateful to Colm O'Sullivan for this example.

Chapter Nine

Political Correctness: Some Linguistic Issues Regarding Race and Gender

M ost of this chapter will be devoted to a discussion and analysis of the currently popular concept of political correctness. Before initiating this discussion, however, I will address the topic of racism in communication in a more general way, and then turn to the issue of the politics of language and identity.

Racial Bias in Communication[1]

"Really, dear," said Nigel, "you're not suggesting that Celia's below the age of consent or anything like that, are you? She's free, white and twenty-one."

"That," said Mr Chandra Lal, "is a *most* offensive remark."

"No, no, Mr Chandra Lal," said Patricia. "It's just a—a kind of idiom. It doesn't mean anything."

"I do not understand," said Mr Akimbombo. "If a thing does not mean anything, why should it be said?"

Elizabeth Johnson said suddenly, raising her voice a little:

"Things are sometimes said that do not seem to mean anything but they may mean a good deal." (Christie 1955, 57, author's emphasis)

The notes to this chapter are on pp. 201-202.

In this first part of the chapter, I will explore particular aspects of racist communication which, in Elizabeth Johnson's words, may "not seem to mean anything but . . . [which] may mean a good deal" (ibid.). The impact and even the presence of these aspects of racist language will be more obvious in some cases than in others; but what is obvious will itself vary according to person, time, and place. In the small farming community in northern Ontario in which I grew up, the phrase uttered by Nigel, "free, white, and twenty-one," was used unthinkingly by children and teenagers as a synonym for "entitled."

In most communities in this country today, there now exists a wide range of overt and easily identifiable racist terms—"nigger," "gook," "jap," "chink," "chief," "fresh off the reserve," and "honky" being examples of some of the most offensive. We are now perfectly aware that the use of these terms is fraught with meaning, a meaning that imparts more information about the user than about the referent.

Other words referring to skin colour, which appear to be neutral (i.e., non-discriminatory) and even factually based, are interesting to examine. The colour terms "white," "black," "yellow," and "red" are examples. All are either false or highly inaccurate, and one wonders why, given the huge repertoire of colour words available, a more accurate selection of terms was not made. "White" and "black" are particularly interesting, their genesis owing less to observable differences in skin colour than to a climate of mutual hostility and distrust, a climate in which difference and opposition were prized by both groups. "Black" and "white" are not simply at opposite ends of the spectrum—they are literally *off* the spectrum.

There are other words whose racist import is evident only within the context of the discussion. "Boy," referring to a Black adult male, is one of these. In a fascinating and still timely article dealing with stereotypic language, Robert Baker (1975) develops the argument that a metaphorical rather than a literal use of the term "boy" is being employed here. He then depicts in graphic unflattering detail the assumptions that are at work in the heads of people who use the term "boy" metaphorically to capture their notion of a Black adult male (ibid.).

In general, the English language makes "white" a positive term and "black" a negative term. We insult and demean people by darkening them—consider "the black sheep of the family," "to be in one's black book," and "a black mark on one's character," as opposed to "a little white lie," "so and so's little fair-haired boy," and "to whitewash an unsavoury event." One of the meanings of the word "fair" in the English language is beautiful or attractive. Textbooks, from elementary school through to university, are filled with racist bias. Exclusion plays a major role. Native peoples, for example, have often been left out of accounts of North American history. Where they are included, they are often portrayed as violent, heathen savages, with battles won by the European settlers referred to as "victories," while battles won by the Native peoples are referred to as "massacres." Exclusion is a factor not only in curriculum materials but also in pedagogical considerations; Lisa Delpit outlines the ways in which whole language, the currently popular reader-centred, context-sensitive approach to the teaching of reading in North America that was discussed in the previous chapter, totally excludes any consideration of Black and working-class children, who learn better from more teacher-centred models, which focus on specific skills such as phonics and spelling (1988).

In an English as a second language textbook (Anderson 1986, 93), the sample sentence, "What is Ethel doing right now?" was provided as an example of the present continuous tense. A diagram, displayed near the sample sentence, depicted a Native woman scrubbing a toilet bowl. We need to understand that textbooks teach more than grammar, more than math, more than science—they teach as well an ideology, a value scheme, a particular slant on what is knowledge, what is worth learning, who the authorities and the professionals are, who is excluded from the privilege of defining knowledge, along with the permissible forms for the dissemination of that version of knowledge.

A more subtle example of racist communication that means more than it appears to is the assumption that when the Caucasian sector has been represented or had its say, we've covered the whole territory. Those of us who teach courses on North American history and leave out or merely mention in passing the aboriginal peoples, those of us who teach courses on women's literature and limit our syllabi to the writing of white women, and those of us who teach psychology courses exclusively from the perspective of the white male, are all guilty of harbouring this assumption. (For a more extended discussion of this and related issues, see Martha Ayim 1992.)

As scholars, we tend to operate with the assumption that Caucasian is the norm, and what is non-Caucasian is a deviation that requires a specific colour modifier. For example, when discussing people whose racial membership is Caucasian, we feel no need to make note of that fact. For other racial groups, this is dramatically not the case. "Florence Kennedy, the Black American activist," has a "natural" sound to it, whereas, "Maryann Ayim, the white philosopher of education," sounds awkward and highly "unnatural." We specify non-white in contexts in which it would never occur to us to specify non-Black.

The literature on gender development provides an example of the illicit generalization from white to whole. Phoenix argues that "the reality of racism" (1987, 50) is such that Black and white children can reasonably be expected to have very different sets of experiences, and hence any generalization from the experiences of white children to all children is bound to be problematic. She makes a similar claim regarding the fallacious generalization from middle-class to working-class children (ibid., 59). When Black families are included in the researchers' data banks, it is often as instances of perceived deviance and abnormality—for example, the teenage Black mother and the absent Black father (ibid., 50-61). The scholarship on intelligence provides a notorious example of the tendency to demean Black people, interpreting success among Black and white students as features of rote learning and intelligence, respectively (Sayers 1987, 28).

I shall conclude this section of the chapter by listing three measures for helping to grapple with racist communication that I have learned from my students and that colleagues have reported to me as learning from their students. First, racist jokes (like sexist jokes) are not funny; they are sad. If they make people laugh, this is sadder yet. Classrooms in an educational institution should not be a place in which racist (or sexist) jokes flourish, or even survive.

Second, within the classroom, diverse points of view from *all* students should be actively solicited, and special attention should be devoted to providing an atmosphere in which students who represent racial and ethnic minorities feel sufficiently confident and respected within the context of the classroom to contribute to the discussion of such important social issues as racism. If only the mainstream perspective is ever articulated, then the education of all students is diminished. The sharing of diverse perspectives and the fostering of real learning require, however, a context of mutual respect. Students who are obvious members of racial minority groups should not be singled out on the spot by the teacher in class and asked to represent that group or to respond to such social and ethical issues as racism. This tactic will not contribute to the provision of an open forum for honest and profitable discussion of sensitive issues.

Third, we should ensure that the message about racial groups that classrooms promote is not totally negative. The coverage of Black people on the bulletin boards of an elementary classroom in Toronto, for example, was limited to a depiction of the starving populace of Ethiopia (Augustine 1990). No matter how laudable the teacher's intentions were in raising awareness among the students about mass starvation and the unjust distribution of privilege, this message may be a very harmful one, particularly to young Black students at an impressionable age. This bleak picture, although there is no doubt that it needs to be painted, should be supplemented with positive and joyful images as well.

If we all strove to achieve communication free of the limitations of racism, then perhaps, to parallel the words of the Agatha Christie character Elizabeth Johnson, what we say will not only mean a good deal, but will have a good meaning as well.

The Politics of Language and Identity[2]

In her heart-rending novel *Beloved* (1988), Toni Morrison tells us that the power of naming has been usurped by the oppressor; the toll of this usurpation on Black people is poignantly explored in her novel. In this section of the chapter, I will develop in more detail than has occurred in earlier chapters, some of the racial issues involved in the politics of naming, identifying, and silencing. As a woman, I feel easy about discussing these issues from the point of view of gender; as a white woman, and hence a member of the oppressing race, I feel less easy about discussing them from the point of view of race. However, to omit the discussion entirely, or relegate it to a footnote, would be even less defensible than writing, as a white woman, an account of racism in language.

As a woman with a feminist perspective on the politics of naming, identifying, and silencing, it seems clear to me (as I have argued in Chapter Seven) that the most commonly used word in the English language to refer to human beings, "man," is a word that basically excludes females, or at best, includes us only by extension or as a special case. The exclusive nature of "man" and "he" has been established by arguments and evidence that are incontrovertible, yet both terms continue to be widely used in popular, legal, and educational documents as though they were truly inclusive, egalitarian words.

This is neither accidental nor trivial. If it were accidental, we would not have had a British Act of Parliament (in 1850) declaring "he" to be generic. The passing of an act of parliament is one thing that could not possibly be construed as either accidental or apolitical. Nor is it trivial. The fact that a word widely used to refer to human beings leaves out over half of the world's population speaks volumes about the ideology of those who have held the political power to name.

Those in political control, while they have wielded the power to name in one hand, have wielded the licence to silence and censor in the other. African slaves, like the fertile women in Margaret Atwood's chilling futuristic novel, *The Handmaid's Tale* (1985), were forbidden access to the written word by law; they were robbed of their own names and renamed by their oppressors; they were also forbidden speech with one another, and in the case of the African slaves, were forbidden to speak in their own languages. Together with the power of naming goes the power of silencing, and racist oppressors have exercised that power with a heavy hand.

I have argued in the earlier chapters of this book that the male dominance theory of language, in spite of being spurned by many contemporary researchers, has much to recommend it; the same claim could be made for a Caucasian dominance theory of language. Some researchers have made precisely this claim. Smitherman-Donaldson and van Dijk (1988, 17), for example, provide such an analysis of the relationship between race bias and language. They describe racism as a form of power of the dominant over non-dominant groups, and point out that this power may be "direct and immediately physical, as with military or police action or imprisonment" (ibid.). Frequently it is indirect, "as with social policies that adversely affect minority life" (ibid.). The authors claim that the dominant group's retention of power depends on the perceived legitimation of such power—at this point, socializing institutions like the school and the mass media play a very important role. They say:

> Language and discourse are vital in this reproducing of racial oppression and control of blacks and other minorities. . . . They are linked with opinions and attitudes, and these also need expression, verbalization, and persuasive formulation in a variety of communicative contexts and in various types of talk and text. We find them in everyday storytelling as well as in news reports, in corporate meetings as well as in job interviews, in comics, in racial graffiti, in classroom talk and textbooks, in television comedies, in novels, and in many, many other forms of communication and language use. In other words, the expression, enactment, and legitimation of racism in society takes place also, and sometimes predominantly, at a symbolic level. (Ibid.)

As Greenberg, Kirkland, and Pyszczynski claim, people are threatened by those not similar to themselves because "dissimilar others threaten the consensual validation we require to maintain faith in the way we construe the world" (1988, 77). Thus it becomes important to both silence those who "threaten the consensual validation" (ibid.) and to legitimate this act of silencing through such powerful socializing institutions as the schools.

Ironically, at the same time as oppressed racial groups (and women generally) are excluded from, trivialized by, and demeaned by the language, racist treatment of these groups is sometimes "justified" in terms of group members' so-called lack of facility with the language. It is important to note the North American tendency to equate literacy with fluency in English; this equivalence appears to be a standard political assumption in North America, reflected in the literature on literacy itself. Facility in English *does not* necessarily translate into jobs and success for members of oppressed groups, however. Discussing how this issue affects the lives of South Asian immigrants to Britain, Jupp, Roberts, and Cook-Gumperz show that the standard language-deficit interpretation is simply false.

> If communicative problems only arose from a 'language deficit,' increased ability in English would be matched by increased communicative and social power. However, many South Asian speakers of English with extensive lexical and grammatical knowledge do not succeed communicatively in speech events of key significance to them. (1982, 234)

The authors add that these South Asian workers are further disadvantaged because British employers are "introducing more formal recruitment procedures which also depend on linguistic evaluation" (ibid., 237). They say,

> The three factors of class position, ethnicity, and speaking practices create a social identity for ethnic minority group workers which cannot be characterized as mere cultural difference, because the interactive effect of this position feeds into its own evaluation and tends continually to reproduce it. (Ibid., 244)

The authors add that perceived competence in communication in English depends not only on language acquisition but also on language socialization (ibid.). Furthermore, because the deficit model is standardly assumed, i.e., because it is assumed that doors are closed to immigrants on the basis of their deficient language rather than on the basis of racism in the society, it will not occur to the oppressors

that they have the responsibility to make changes "to the communicative environment with which the second language speaker has to
cope" (ibid.).

It is difficult to deny that the educational system commits many
sins against oppressed groups—the sins of excluding, trivializing,
demeaning, silencing, and then blaming the victims, for example.
Because of the racism in society, however, access to the educational
system becomes an important commodity for members of these
groups, for without such access they are bound to face even higher
levels of job discrimination. Against this racist context, it is small
wonder that, contrary to the popular perception, North American
Black women are more educated than North American white women
on some measures. The research of Giele and Gilfus reveals these
little-known facts:

> The 1982 Life Patterns Study is based on life histories of 2,902 alum-
> nae who graduated from three colleges between 1934 and 1979. This
> survey allows comparisons by *race* (2131 white, 663 black, and 108
> others) and by *college* since it includes a coed college in the Midwest
> (n = 941) a Seven Sisters college in the Northeast (n = 1,223), and a
> black women's college in the South (n = 663). (Giele and Gilfus 1990,
> 180, authors' emphasis)

> The 382 black women in our study who were over thirty-five reported
> higher overall educational and occupational attainments than did the
> 1,633 white women of comparable age. The black alumnae of the
> classes of 1934-1969 spent more adult years in school and in the labour
> force, were less likely to marry, and bore fewer children. (Ibid., 183, 185)

The authors go on to point out that the Black women aged
thirty-five and over in their study were more likely to have achieved
some post-college education than the white women of the same age,
and that the Black women were also more likely to have earned a
Master's degree, although the white women surveyed were more
likely to have earned a Ph.D. (ibid., 185).

For many members of oppressed groups, the outrage of being
silenced is often coupled with a fear of speaking out; this fear of
speaking out is, for many Black, Native, and Asian people, a real fear,
grounded in an accurate perception of the consequences of speaking
out. *The Chilly Climate for Women* video (March 1991) as well as the
accompanying facilitator's manual (Joyce 1991) documents the occurrence of some of these phenomena in the university and the college
setting. People of Colour have not only been robbed of the right to

name themselves, but have been robbed also of the right to discuss, bring into the open, and express outrage against this appropriation of their rights. White people, and this may be particularly true of Canadians, shrink from thinking of themselves as oppressors. Many people of Colour refuse to protest against this discrimination because they understand that by protesting, they will be labelled in yet another way—as troublemakers and whiners. I personally know many Black people who have decided it was too risky to talk about these issues, so they tell white people that there is no racial discrimination in this country. And some white people actually believe this.

As Florence Howe claims, education is ultimately a highly political act (1984, 282-283). It is the kind of political act that determines who has access to prestigious well-paid jobs and who is excluded from the ranks of privilege. We are naive if we believe that education is neutral; we are naive if we believe that language is neutral; both are steeped in political ideology, as well as racism, sexism, classism, and heterosexism.

We are even more naive if we believe that there will be no fall-out when we try to turn this around. Where the Niagara River changes direction, it creates a whirlpool—a dangerous whirlpool. Attempts to change the direction of education and of language will create whirlpools of angry resistance; make no mistake, many of us who struggle to change the direction will be sucked into that whirlpool, for those who hold the reins of power have enormous vested interests in maintaining the status quo. At the very moment at which I write these words, a petition is being circulated at my university to protest against anti-racist legislation and communication guidelines in the name of freedom of expression. Those who try to change the course of these established trends run enormous risks, but the risk of silent compliance is greater. To be silent about and compliant towards racism and sexism and all other forms of immoral discrimination is to drown our souls in a stagnant swamp of prejudice. Any promise of safety here is given in bad faith. Far better to leap into the whirlpool and do our damnedest to keep afloat!

Political Correctness—Some Preliminary Remarks[3]

The debate surrounding political correctness is hampered by misunderstandings so fundamental that one must consider whether it is fuelled by a passion to achieve understanding and truth or a desire to make mischief. "Mischief," however, like "political correctness," is a mischievous term, for it makes light of serious concerns in ways that are inappropriate. The debate itself promotes this "making light," for one of its deepest misunderstandings is the reduction of serious moral considerations to matters of mere etiquette. It is thus easy to understand why the term "political correctness" suited many of the people writing about this issue—one can dismiss demands for political correctness, unlike moral or ethical correctness, as interfering, irrational, or hysterical. In this milieu, the imposition of labels and categories will be more highly fraught with difficulty than usual; nonetheless, it is necessary to introduce some labels to render the discussion intelligible. Hence, with some misgivings, I identify the two major positions on political correctness as the neo-conservative position and the reform position. One of my misgivings is that the term "neo-conservative" does not capture what may be seen as the liberal ideology inherent in the work of people like D'Souza and Bloom. The classical liberal aspects of their thinking include an emphasis on the notions of freedom of expression and liberal education, as well as a reliance on the work of John Stuart Mill to justify their position. My second misgiving is with the term "reform." In urging the outlawing of certain forms of expression, the reform position necessarily advocates repression, or even censorship of certain kinds of communication, and hence adopts a stance more usually associated with conservatism than reform. I shall argue, nevertheless, that in certain contexts, repression or even censorship of certain forms of expression is not only consistent with reform, but may be genuinely necessary to it. In spite of these shortcomings, I shall use both terms throughout the remainder of the chapter as a means of distinguishing the two prominent positions on this issue.

Advocates of the neo-conservative position reduce genuinely ethical considerations to merely political ones. D'Souza, for example, refers to universities' attempts to outlaw racist, sexist, and stereotypic language as "racial etiquette" (1991, 140), "social etiquette" (ibid., 156), and as "a kind of liberal or political etiquette" (D'Souza and MacNeil 1992, 36). Racist, sexist, and homophobic speech is reduced to "insensitive speech" (D'Souza 1991, 141), "unpopular forms of expression" (ibid., 142), or "offences against the sensitivities of blacks, feminists, and homosexuals" (ibid., 146). The trivializing of such speech as merely insensitive or unpopular is consistent with D'Souza's outrage that "some schools go so far as to outlaw racially or sexually 'stigmatizing' remarks—even 'misdirected laughter' and 'exclusion from conversation'—which are said to make learning for minorities impossible" (1991, 238).

In a similar vein to D'Souza, Hentoff equates hurt to "hurt feelings" (1992, 17), as though all those who oppose racist and sexist slurs, for example, are prima donnas who feel irrational hurt in the presence of such language, and that minority students who feel hurt when confronted with stereotyped expectations or outright racism would be well advised to grow thicker skins so that they can live in the real world. "Increasingly, at colleges and universities, students are being taught to see themselves as fragile" (ibid.), Hentoff laments. What D'Souza and Hentoff are claiming, essentially, is that racist language may be rude, but even rude language must be protected by a right to freedom of expression. On the other side of this issue is Van de Wetering, who states that it is not simple etiquette that forbids us to use racist slurs, "but a long and dreadful history of rock-pelting, derision, and segregation. . . . Nomenclature, in short, is not devoid of significant history and education" (1991, 100).

In this chapter, I will argue for Van de Wetering's perspective on this issue. In other words, I will argue that racist and sexist language descend to lower depths than mere rudeness and that they may involve severe harm far in excess of the hurt feelings of the emotionally fragile (although hurt feelings should not be dismissed as trivial either). No attempt will be made to develop any particular inclusive or fair language policy in this chapter; my task is the more formal and in many senses more trivial one of exploring the assumptions made by several contemporary thinkers who would a priori outlaw such policies. I will argue that the trivializing of sexist and racist language as mere bad manners is rooted in three erroneous assumptions: First, all speech is lumped together in terms of its right to protection; hence speech that interferes with other people's freedom of expression, such as sexist or racist speech, receives no special analysis or censure. Second, all harms (and hence avenues to overcome such harm) are perceived as specific and individual, with no cognizance of their historical and contextual grounding, resulting in the inability to understand the impact of systemic harms and the necessity of systemic solutions to some sorts of harm. Third, while reform measures and policies, such as guidelines for non-racist language and affirmative action in hiring, are perceived as highly political and hence suspect in an academic institution, the status quo is perceived as apolitical and hence suited to institutions of "higher learning." If my responses to these assumptions appear simplistic, I urge that this is a consequence of the simplicity of the assumptions themselves.

Following a discussion of these three mistaken assumptions, I shall examine the links made by several of the participants in this debate between the tradition of a liberal education and their rejection of political correctness. I shall argue in this regard that these writers ignore at least two major philosophical justifications of the educational curriculum, focusing on one specific theory of curriculum justification, and that their rendition of even this theory involves oversimplification and misrepresentation.

Three Mistaken Assumptions of the Neo-conservative Position

(1) The first mistaken assumption is that all speech is to be lumped together in terms of its right to protection; hence speech that interferes with other people's freedom of expression, such as sexist or racist speech, is to receive no special analysis or censure. In other words, all forms of expression, whether racist slur, scientific formula, or radical social criticism, are treated alike as being equally deserving of protection; hence attempts to eradicate any of these forms of expression also score equally on a villainy scale, with feminist attempts to institute inclusive language guidelines being perceived as McCarthyism. There is no apparent cognizance of the fact that some forms of expression, in and of themselves, erode freedom of expression. As Van de Wetering points out,

> Political correctness has, today, become confused with issues of censorship and totalitarianism. . . . PC, starting first as a satire of the excesses of the language of affirmative action and multiculturalism, became later, in the hands of frightened scholars and laymen, a convenient label for curricular changes which seemed threatening to the traditional and established structure of the white, masculine-dominated educational system.
>
> Simple humane rules of decent conduct thus become targets for tests of free speech, under the mocking aegis of politically correct. (1991, 101)

"Perhaps the most important lesson universities can teach their students is to think and search for truth in freedom," (D'Souza and MacNeil 1992, 46) says D'Souza, but without elucidating further on freedom for whom. "Offensive, erroneous, and obnoxious speech is the price of freedom" (ibid., 47), he continues, again avoiding the question of freedom for whom. Consider the following example of offensive speech between a female and male grade ten student, which was documented in a Canadian study on sexual harassment in the high school:

> I was talking to this guy who sits beside me in class. He ended up call-ing me a bonehead and I said you're the one that's a boner and he said, you'd better not say that or I'll stick my dick up your ass so far you won't even be able to breathe, and then he started laughing. (O'Connor 1992, 16)

Whose freedom is assured, and whose freedom is curtailed, by pro-tecting this speech? Unfortunately, the neo-conservative theorists never provide an answer to this question; while lamenting the suffer-ing of those who "trespass on prevailing orthodoxies" (D'Souza and MacNeil 1992, 45), and of "whites [who] are the real victims now" (D'Souza 1991, 132), there is no evidence of concern for the suffering of those who struggle to eradicate social inequities. Not only are whites victimized by restraints on their speaking in sexist and racist ways, according to D'Souza, but they are also falsely accused, for it is the restraints themselves that produce such speech:

> Campus browbeating and balkanization come to public attention by way of the public outcomes they produce—the racial joke and the racial incident. Both represent white exasperation with perceived unfairness, double standards, and suppression of independent thought on the American campus. (Ibid., 239)

Why this represents white exasperation rather than white bigotry is not made clear. These harsh "censorship codes" do not lead to greater sensitivity, only to a tighter regulation of "outward expression" (ibid., 241). This remark only makes sense if racism is being looked at *solely* from the perspective of those not victimized by it—for there is no doubt that the victim of racism is better off if the bigot ceases to utter racist slurs in public, even if still thinking them in private.

Bloom laments an atmosphere in which people hold back from making claims for which they fear being branded sexist or racist as an atmosphere that makes "detached, dispassionate study impossible" (1987, 355); D'Souza worries that charges of racism and sexism are directed toward white males, whereas Black women are immune to being branded by such charges (1991, 130). No concern is expressed for an atmosphere so poisoned against women generally or women and men of Colour, for example, that they are denied access to "detached, dispassionate study." In this regard, it is instructive to examine the different reasons for which Black and white people approved of the education of Black females. For Black women, according to Ihle, education was frequently viewed "as a means of protection [of Black women] from white men" (1990, 75). Ihle claims that an education offered a Black woman the possible opportunity of employment outside domestic service positions, where she was at high risk of being sexually abused by white men. Black families understood this risk to their daughters so well that many of them gave preference to their daughters over their sons for post-elementary education, if they could not afford to send all their children to secondary and post-secondary school (ibid., 74). White curriculum designers, when they did argue for the importance of education for Black girls and women, often did so for deeply racist reasons. For example, white educators, stereotyping Black women as sexually promiscuous, urged the importance of moral education for Black females if they were to be the saviours of the Black family.

It is worth reiterating an observation made earlier, namely, that advocates of the neo-conservative position reduce genuinely ethical considerations to merely political ones. Occasionally reform measures are likened, not to political etiquette, but to religious fervour. This confusion is abetted by the use of terms that equate the social reformer to the religious zealot, such as "prevailing orthodoxies" rather than "reform measures to achieve egalitarianism."

A similar move is made by Christina Sommers in her critique of radical socialist feminism and her defence of liberal feminism, in which she likens the claims of non-liberal feminists to the religious convictions of Zoroaster (1991, 141-158). Allan Bloom takes this move one step further when he speaks of "the radical orthodoxy" (1987, 355) of reformers who seek to remove racist and sexist bias from the classroom, where scholars who trespass against this orthodoxy are treated as "the equivalents of atheist or communist in other days with other prevailing prejudices" (1987, 355). The attempt to alleviate racist and sexist bias, not the bias itself, has been cast in the role of prejudice.

D'Souza appeals to Mill for justification of the view that there should be no constraints on expression; D'Souza speaks of "John Stuart Mill's argument, in On Liberty, that even offensive speech served the purpose of illustrating error" (D'Souza 1991, 153). D'Souza neglects to mention that according to Mill's analysis in On Liberty, any behaviour that injures other people is appropriately subject to "moral reprobation, and, in grave cases" (Mill 1972, 135), to "moral retribution and punishment" (ibid.). Mill includes among those actions injurious to other people "unfair or ungenerous use of advantages over them" (ibid.). It is important to notice that he deems as immoral and "fit subjects of disapprobation" (ibid.), not only direct actions that injure others, but also "the dispositions which lead to them" (ibid.). Among these dispositions, he includes:

> the love of domineering over others; the desire to engross more than one's share of advantages . . . ; the pride which derives gratification from the abasement of others; the egotism which thinks self and its concerns more important than everything else, and decides all doubtful questions in its own favour. (Ibid.)

Mill's discussion raises a host of fascinating questions: What is to distinguish the imposition of a Eurocentric curriculum on all students from an "unfair or ungenerous use of advantages over them" (ibid.)? Does resistance to any affirmative action based on race or gender reflect a "desire to engross more than one's share of advantages" (ibid.)? Is insistence on the centrality of the "classics," as traditionally perceived, an instance of "the love of domineering over others" (ibid.)? Are the neo-conservative theorists' constant references to the underachievement of Black students an indication of "the pride which derives gratification from the abasement of others" (ibid.)? Does Bloom's (1987) and D'Souza's (1991) persistent use of male language that excludes females illustrate an "egotism which thinks self and its concerns more important than everything else, and decides all doubtful questions in its own favour" (Mill 1972, 135)?

Having raised these questions, which any serious appeal to Mill suggests, it is interesting to ask what presuppositions bolster the neo-conservative theorists' minimization of the seriousness of such language. I believe there are two possible answers to this question, both of which receive support from the neo-conservative position. The first presupposition is that the university milieu represents a true meritocracy, or at least it did until affirmative action came along. There is evidence that the neo-conservative theorists uphold this first presupposition. For today's students, "considerations of sex, colour, religion, family, money, nationality, play no role in their reactions," Bloom (1987, 88) assures us. This meritocracy is done up in a Rushton (1995) colour scheme where White and Yellow represent achievement and worth, but Black doesn't quite cut it.

We are also told that white students harbour no racist attitudes towards Black students (ibid., 92). Not surprisingly Bloom also believes that sex is no longer a significant factor in the university setting (ibid., 107). For Bloom then, students—at least white students—are both gender-blind and colour-blind. There is a not-so-subtle suggestion that Black students fail to share the typical white student's indifference to skin colour, however. We are told that Black students maintain a kind of separatism from the rest of the university population via Black studies courses (ibid., 92-93). Not only is Black studies a form of separatism, it is also, according to Bloom, an academic cop-out, a desperate attempt to placate Black students who are not achieving up to par in the regular curriculum (1987, 94-96). The same point is made by D'Souza (1991, 247). D'Souza quotes with approval a Michigan undergraduate, who says that "Black Power says you don't need to do well in university. . . . You don't need to improve your SAT scores. You are special as you are" (1991, 129). D'Souza argues that pressure for a "minority-oriented" (1991, 247) curriculum emanated from the failure of minority students to succeed in "the core curriculum of Western classics" (ibid.). Neither white nor Asian students require any watering down of the regular curriculum, presumably because they are sufficiently competent to manage it in its pure form (Bloom 1987, 96-97).

The glue holding all these colour claims together is the assumption of the intellectual purity of the university. "The real community of man [sic] . . . is the community of those who seek the truth" (ibid., 381), Bloom assures us. In the same vein, Schmidt, Jr. insists that "the most important lesson universities can teach their students is to think and search for truth in freedom" (1991, 46). According to D'Souza, the "fundamental purpose . . . [of the university is] the disinterested pursuit of truth" (1991, 120) and the university is defined by "liberty of mind" (1991, 142). The questions of "Which community?" and "Freedom for whom?" and "Disinterested according to whom?" are not raised by Bloom, Schmidt, Jr., or D'Souza.

I have discussed what I regard as the first presupposition of this minimization of the seriousness of such language, namely, that the university campus is a meritocracy, and any belittlement of Black students that exists is a function of the absence of Black merit, not a function of the presence of white bias. I believe there is a second presupposition at work here, namely, the existence of a strong distinction between speech and behaviour, with the result that behaviour, but not speech, is seen as reasonably subject to restrictions. This presupposition makes it easy to slide into the "sticks and stones can break my bones, but words will never hurt me" position, which sees only restrictions on speech or expression as harmful, never the speech or expression itself, which can at worst be mere bad taste capable of hurting feelings perhaps, but not of doing any real harm. If speech is totally unlike other forms of behaviour, it is possible to make a special argument for absolute freedom of expression; without this presupposition, it is difficult to make sense of the neo-conservative position on this issue.

(2) The second mistaken assumption of the neo-conservative position is that harm is strictly an individual matter; there is no understanding of systemic harms with the result that relevance of context is consistently ignored. In particular, the context of social/political power is ignored in any analysis that perceives the social system as a pure meritocracy to which all individuals have equal access and from which each individual has an equal chance of gain. As June Jordan points out, "There is difference and there is power. And who holds the power shall decide the meaning of difference" (1992, 18).

While much of the discussion on political correctness from the neo-conservative perspective assumes that the situation is somehow context-free, in fact the context must be taken into account. There can be no a priori assumptions about the amount of harm done by racist speech, for example, because the harm will be in part determined by one's race, class, and gender membership. This mistaken ignoring of the context has led to other related errors in the neo-conservative position, namely, a rejection of affirmative action as unfair and a favouring of gender-blind and colour-blind approaches to social policy. I will address each of these points in turn. D'Souza, for example, states that affirmative action in faculty hiring and student admission policies represents a denial rather than an affirmation of equality of opportunity (D'Souza and MacNeil 1992, 30). Such a position on affirmative action only makes sense if one assumes that the world is a true meritocracy, and that social goods are already being dispensed to individuals strictly on the basis of their individual qualities, with no race or gender bias, for example, interfering with people's access to these goods. As Scott points out, however, in a less than utopian "society where individuals are not equals to begin with, a policy of neutrality can only protect the already privileged group(s)" (1992, 7). So long as we live in a world in which social, political, and economic structures bar certain groups of people from attaining full equality, it is reasonable to endorse affirmative action measures to counter such systemic bias. Seen in this way, affirmative action, far from undermining equality of opportunity, is rather a necessary condition to achieving it.

The notions of truth and freedom are given pride of place in much of the neo-conservative discussion of political correctness with the understanding that they will naturally emerge from an open debate among the many differing parties. This claim will receive a more detailed discussion later in the chapter when I turn specifically to curriculum considerations, but I must point out at this time its assumption that each individual "discussant" has an equal opportunity to participate in the discussion, to be heard, and to influence the outcome of the discussion; the reality, unfortunately, is quite different, for systemic race, sex, and class bias preclude equal participation of all in the debate, without even raising the question as to whether debate is the best mechanism for generating truth and freedom. So long as racist, sexist, and homophobic slurs, for example, are not merely tolerated, but passionately protected in the name of freedom of expression, people of Colour, women of all colours, and gay and lesbian people will continue to be gagged in the very forum that prides itself on fostering freedom of expression. To understand how this gagging phenomenon operates, we need to be aware of the impact of discriminatory discourse on people. In Chapter One I outlined some of the forms of harm believed to ensue from racist language. These included the "perpetuation of violence and degradation of the very classes of human beings who are least equipped to respond" (Matsuda 1993, 35), "feelings of humiliation, isolation, and self-hatred" (Delgado 1993, 91), as well as stress, inhibited anger, and even shortened life expectancy (ibid., 92). Gay bashing is a common enough social phenomenon that it requires no great feat of the imagination to perceive gay men experiencing stress and inhibited anger in the presence of homophobic discourse. The same argument applies to other oppressed groups as well.

I claimed earlier that the mistaken ignoring of the context has led to two related errors in the neo-conservative position, namely, a rejection of affirmative action as unfair and a favouring of gender-blind and colour-blind approaches to social policy. I turn now to a discussion of gender and colour-blindness. D'Souza specifically promotes colour-blindness as a mechanism for generating racial equality (D'Souza and MacNeil 1992, 38). Like the neo-conservative position on affirmative action, the policy to ignore race (or gender) in the allocation of social goods only makes sense on the assumption that it has already been ignored in the broader system. It is inconsistent to both acknowledge that race has indeed been paid attention to (via racism) in our social organization and to urge that it should be ignored in our dealings with people within that organization. If race, for example, had been irrelevant to the formation of social structures, then refusing to give it any credence in making social policy decisions could be a sensible decision. It is hard to argue, living on a continent that participated in the slave trade, among other atrocities, that race has been irrelevant to the formation of our social structures. It does not follow, however, that such an argument has not been made. Bloom, for example, states with what I consider unbelievable naivete, that

> Contrary to fashionable opinion, universities are melting pots, no matter what may be true of the rest of society. Ethnicity is no more important a fact than tall or short, black-haired or blond. What these young people have in common infinitely outweighs what separates them. The quest for traditions and rituals proves my point and may teach something about the price paid for this homogenization. The lack of prejudice is a result of students' failing to see differences and of the gradual eradication of differences. When students talk about one another, one almost never hears them saying things that divide others into groups or kinds. They always speak about the individual. The sensitivity to national character, sometimes known as stereotyping, has disappeared. (1987, 90-91)

Hand in hand with the view discussed earlier—that students harbour no ethnic or racial prejudice against other students and that stereotyping has disappeared from the university campus—goes the view that the university is a meritocracy in which Black students are not as good as white students.

The basis for Bloom's belief that the university is a meritocracy can perhaps be traced to his claim that "reason cannot accommodate the claims of any kind of power whatever, and democratic society cannot accept any principle of achievement other than merit" (1987, 96). If we presume that reason and democracy reign supreme on the university campus, then perhaps we can at least understand Bloom's belief. It is not surprising that Bloom also rules sex out as a factor of any importance in the university. The numerous studies that attest to the importance of sex in classroom dynamics notwithstanding (see, for example, Cline and Spender 1987; French and French 1984a, 1984b; Spender 1981; Spender 1982; Spender 1984), Bloom confidently states that "Academically, students are comfortably unisexual;

they revert to dual sexuality only for the sex act. Sex no longer has any political agenda in universities except among homosexuals, who are not yet quite satisfied with their situation" (1987, 107); Bloom fails utterly to see the political parameters of non-inclusive language, sexual harassment, date rape, and heterosexual privilege. Bloom notwithstanding, where people's opportunities, aspirations, self-concepts, even their language, have been shaped according to race, it makes no sense to drop cognizance of race out of the formula governing allocation of social goods. In other words, at this juncture of our racist history, it is too late to ignore race. Of course, if the case can be made for specific contexts that have evolved free of any considerations of race, then an argument can be made for policies of colour-blindness within that context, on the grounds that where colour really does not make a difference, ignoring it is a sensible option.

If we close our eyes to colour, we also close our eyes to the systemic structures of racism; a colour-sensitive rather than a colour-blind approach is required to allow us to take account of racism as a structural impediment to equality. (See Wasserstrom 1979, Martin 1981, and Houston 1985 for a detailed development of these concepts.) In other words, it is important to remember that in rejecting skin colour as a possible basis for dealing with people, we also ignore what a history of racist imperialism has meant for people of Colour.

(3) The third mistaken assumption of the neo-conservative position is that while reform measures and policies, such as guidelines for non-racist language and affirmative action in hiring, are highly political and hence suspect in an academic institution, the status quo is apolitical and hence suited to institutions of "higher learning." Schmidt, Jr. captures this assumption when he states that society is denouncing those who "use their academic positions to indoctrinate students in bizarre ideologies" (1991, 45). But we need to ask who gets to decide what is bizarre. If a feminist view is perceived as bizarre, how should we perceive a male chauvinist view? It seems self-evident that if feminism, for example, represents a political stance, so too does patriarchy. I am not assuming that views are to be slotted into either "feminist" or "patriarchal positions," with nothing in between. I am suggesting, however, that many of the traditional university courses, which raised few hackles, were deeply committed to conservative ideologies and policies. They were not at all value-free, but only thought to be because the values they endorsed were so deeply entrenched in the social framework that people failed to see them. Neither is feminism value-free, but, as it wears its values on its

sleeve, so to speak, it is seldom misperceived in this way. Certainly there are possible "compromises" between feminist and patriarchal positions (although if by "feminist" we mean "fair with respect to gender," any such compromises are morally suspect), but these compromises too will entail the endorsement of ideologies and policies. There is no such thing as a "neutral" course which remains objectively removed from commitment to any ideology or policy. Conservatism is as deeply based in ideology as any of the more radical stances are. It is true that supporting hiring quotas involves taking a side on a much politicized issue, but not supporting hiring quotas is as deeply political as supporting them.

D'Souza maintains that special interest courses endorse separatism and segregation rather than integration, on which liberal education should be focused (D'Souza and MacNeil 1992, 30). Again, however, we must ask why courses that offer, for example, a feminist interpretation of events are any more conducive to separatism and segregation than more traditional courses that offer a patriarchal interpretation of events. Furthermore, what makes a feminist course a special interest course, whereas a traditionally male-oriented course is considered generally applicable to all students? And why should Black Studies entail separatism and segregation? Why shouldn't Black Studies, rather, be included in everyone's curriculum, so that all students attain a broader, deeper, and more critical understanding of their history? As Van de Wetering states, "Multiculturalism is . . . an acknowledgement, not an invention, of who we are" (1991, 102).

As we have seen in our earlier discussion, proponents of the neo-conservative position claim that merit ought to be the only factor taken into consideration in student admissions and faculty hirings, with no apparent realization that people's concepts of merit vary widely, and the particular concept of merit selected as a student admissions criterion, for example, will be consistent with the political views of its proponents. A few years ago my faculty made a decision to consider work experience, in addition to academic records, in selecting student applicants for admission. This was not a decision to move away from merit as the sole criterion of admission, but a decision to broaden the concept of merit so as to include both academic grades and work experience.

Not everyone agreed with this particular expansion of the concept of merit, of course, and not everyone who supported it did so on academic grounds; some argued, for example, that we needed to include experience in our admissions policy because there was intense pressure from the school boards to do so, and to ignore this pressure would be to risk these boards' refusal to hire our students. It is also important to point out that not all supporters of the grades-only admissions policy based their support in academic considerations. An efficiency argument for this policy was voiced by some faculty members, who claimed that decisions based strictly on grades could be made quickly and easily, with significant saving of faculty and staff time; some voiced a legalistic addendum to this efficiency argument—justification of student rejections based simply on grades would be a straightforward matter, unlike justification of student rejections based on their work experience, which could be very messy and involve the faculty in appeals and lawsuits that they might well lose.

There is significant overlap between this third assumption (that only reform measures, unlike the status quo, are political in a problematic way), and issues surrounding the multicultural curriculum; I turn now to a discussion of the multicultural curriculum.

Curriculum Justification, Liberal Education, and Political Correctness—Some Misunderstandings

Of the three standard theories of curriculum justification, namely, the transmission of knowledge theory, the student-centred theory, and the social reform theory (see Milburn 1977, 192-198, for a succinct discussion of these three theories), it is strictly the transmission of knowledge theory that is presupposed by what I have characterized as the neo-conservative approach to political correctness. The neo-conservative theorists assume, without discussion, that transmission of knowledge is what our schools—at least our universities—ought to be about. While one might argue that the second of these three theories, the student-centred theory which focuses on the self-actualization and development, both affective and intellectual, of the students themselves, is more suited to a justification of a primary rather than a tertiary curriculum, the neo-conservative theorists have not advanced any such argument. The most D'Souza offers is a snide dismissal of a student-centred curriculum. In a chapter section entitled "Profiles in Cowardice," D'Souza quotes disparagingly a critic of Bloom who claimed that "the purpose of liberal education was to 'address the need for students to develop both a private self and a public self, and to find a way to have those selves converse with each other'" (1991, 246). Nor have the neo-conservative theorists put forward any argument against the third theory, that of social reform, which is far less easily dismissed as an underlying rationale for the university curriculum. The neo-conservative theorists simply *assume* that the function of the university curriculum is the transmission of knowledge to its students. (See, for example, Bloom 1987, 341.) These theorists are so single(narrow?)-minded about the overall purpose of education that their position gives the impression of backlash against alternative accounts. Howard makes a somewhat similar point when he refers to these theorists as "altogether intolerant of a different view of educational purpose" (1991, 757).

Equally worrisome, the neo-conservative theorists also assume without question that the traditional male Eurocentric curriculum constitutes precisely the knowledge that the universities should transmit to their students. Throughout the entirety of their books, for example, both Bloom (1987) and D'Souza (1991) use language that excludes females. Undoubtedly, these authors would view any admonition to use neutral (i.e., "they") or specifically inclusive (i.e., "she or he") pronouns as an infringement upon their freedom of expression; they probably also believe, in spite of overwhelming empirical evidence to the contrary (Eberhart 1976; Graham 1975; Hamilton 1985; Hamilton 1988a; Hamilton 1988b; Harrison 1975; Harrison and Passero 1975; Henley 1989; Hyde 1984; MacKay 1980a; MacKay 1980b; MacKay 1983; MacKay and Fulkerson 1979; Martyna 1978; Martyna 1983; Moulton, Robinson, and Elias 1978; Schneider and Hacker 1973; Shepelak, Ogden, and Tobin-Bennett 1984; Sniezek and Jazwinski 1986; Switzer 1990; Tittle, McCarthy, and Steckler 1974; Wilson 1978; Wilson and Ng 1988) that females are in fact fully included in their pseudo-generic terms "he" and "man."

Bloom also speaks of "the moral unity of learning" and "the goodness of science" (1987, 356), adding that "our way of life is utterly dependent on the natural scientists, and they have more than fulfilled their every promise" (ibid.). Challenges occur only at the margin according to Bloom, in the raising of such issues as the application of science to the production of nuclear weapons, but these are merely peripheral, for in science "in general . . . all is well" (ibid.). Even the professional schools are lacking insofar as they fail to emphasize a liberal education, according to Bloom (ibid., 370).

The neo-conservative theorists never address the social and political implications of the whole process of defining knowledge. They ignore totally June Jordan's questions: "And who shall decide what these many peoples of America shall know or not know? And what does that question underscore besides the political nature of knowledge?" (1992, 23). According to Bloom,

> The real community of man . . . is the community of those who seek the truth. . . . But in fact this includes only a few, the true friends, as Plato was to Aristotle at the very moment they were disagreeing about the nature of the good. Their common concern for the good linked them; their disagreement about it proved they needed one another to understand it . . . this, according to Plato, is the only real friendship, the only real common good. It is here that the contact people so desperately seek is to be found. The other kinds of relatedness are only imperfect reflections of this one trying to be self-subsisting, gaining their only justification from their ultimate relation to this one. (1987, 381)

Bloom neglects to point out that one possible reason why this "real community of man . . . includes only a few" (ibid.) is that the many were performing the forms of supportive labour required for even a few to indulge in careers devoted to "disagreeing about the nature of the good" (ibid.). While a host of well-known, little-known, and totally unknown intellectuals have spent their lives enmeshed in such disagreement, countless others, whether through choice or not, have spent their lives raising children, growing crops, preparing food, tending the sick, and disposing of garbage. It is these other lives that have made it possible for a privileged few to attain the leisure to seek and disagree about the nature of the truth.

The oddness of identifying as "the common good" (ibid.) something that "includes only a few" (ibid.) apparently does not occur to Bloom; nor does he anywhere indicate that the identification of the common good with the search for and disagreement about truth rather than, for example, good health or adequate food for all, is a value judgment, and a contentious one at that.

Equally worrisome is Bloom's failure to challenge the primacy of the impersonal relationship among "truth-seekers," which he attributes to Plato. Why does this relationship have primacy over the parent-child relationship? Who is it exactly "who so desperately seek" (ibid.) this contact rather than other forms of relationships? Would it be unfair to answer, "Perhaps those incapable of what is more usually perceived as an intimate or a caring relationship"? (For an extended discussion of this perspective, see Ayim 1992a, 9-11; Keller 1983, 187-205; Roe 1952, 1956; Shakeshaft 1987.) It is interesting to speculate on whether scientific, philosophic, and educational traditions would have been radically different had the relevant scholars chosen their areas of research because of a "liking for and interest in people" (Shakeshaft 1987, 173) rather than the politically headier passion for seeking "the truth . . . [and] the nature of the good" (Bloom 1987, 381).

At any rate, the neo-conservative theorists have assumed without question the rightful place of the traditional male Eurocentric perspective in the centre of the university curriculum. It is therefore not surprising that alternative perspectives, such as those found in a multicultural curriculum, receive little sympathy. Draper, for example, claims that "For a generation now, we have been living in this country with a conservative ascendency. Multiculturalism, despite its radical pretensions, has strongly promoted that ascendancy. It is a part of the problem, not a part of the solution" (1992, 17).

D'Souza correctly urges that the multicultural curriculum should be, and often is not, studied critically (D'Souza and MacNeil 1992, 31). The same point is made by Kolenda (1991, 40). I am in agreement with this important point—if multiculturalism is to be part of the university curriculum (or the secondary or even elementary curriculum, for that matter), then it must be studied within a critical context. However, the same admonition applies to the traditional mainstream curriculum, from which any form of critical analysis has often been abysmally absent. For example, the sexist and racist outrages of Canadian history were never made apparent to me and never discussed in formal schooling which stretched from elementary school through to university. Critics are eager to point out that young girls standardly undergo genital mutilation in certain African countries—D'Souza, for example, generalizing to all of Africa, advises us that "authentic African virtues such as spiritual depth and freedom from materialism must be balanced against human sacrifice, tribal warfare, executions, female circumcision, infanticide, and primitive medicine" (1991, 121). Such critics seldom mention that clitorectomies have been commonly performed in the past on females in Canadian psychiatric institutions as a way to deal with insanity (with *female* insanity, that is), that "helpful" family doctors performed this operation on female children (at least as late as 1925 this surgery was performed in Hamilton, Ontario) as a "corrective" measure for masturbation, that the tribal warfare in Ireland is as long-lasting as any in Africa, and that political executions in Bosnia can match those of any African nation.

Two of the arguments employed by the neo-conservative theorists against "censorship regulations outlawing racially and sexually offensive speech" (D'Souza 1992, 30) are that such regulations will erode not only free speech, but academic standards as well. D'Souza, for example, refers to "a recent Michigan gag rule prohibiting racially stigmatizing speech against minorities" (1991, 129). For all D'Souza's passionate argumentation that the university must be the locus of a disinterested search for the truth, this kind of language is far from disinterested. Those who are inclined to use racially stigmatizing speech are described as being gagged by anti-racist speech legislation; there is no sense, in D'Souza's discussion, that Black or Native people, for example, are gagged by racist language in the senses that I outlined earlier in the chapter. As discussed above, it is imperative that we ask whose freedom of speech is being considered. As for the preservation of academic standards, it is far from apparent that sexually and racially offensive language stand as paradigms of academic rigour. In fact, although the neo-conservative theorists appeal to a historical notion of liberal education as a justification for many of their educational ideas, their justification of racist and sexist language violates one of the most prominent contemporary accounts of liberal education—namely, that of R.S. Peters.

In his spelling out of the criteria for the educational ideal, Peters stipulates that "something of value should be passed on" (1965, 92). For education to have occurred, "some change for the better" (ibid., 91) must have occurred in the student's state of mind. Although Peters does not raise this point, I suggest that the transmission of racist or sexist ideologies violates this requirement, hence providing a strong *educational* reason for justifying a curriculum that promotes an egalitarian ideology. In addition, Peters maintains that the educational ideal rules out any procedures of transmission in which the students' engagement in the educational enterprise lacks voluntariness or wittingness (ibid., 96). While Peters was concerned to rule out conditioning and indoctrination as true forms of education, I believe this requirement also eliminates from the educational realm classrooms where the students unwittingly participate in, for example, a white supremacist ideology. Of course, the unwitting participation of students in a Black supremacist ideology would equally be disqualified as education, but in our present historical context, the likelihood of unwitting participation in a Black supremacist ideology seems far more remote. The same point can be made about sex. Classrooms where students unwittingly participate in a male or female supremacist ideology would fail one of R.S. Peters' educational requirements. At the present moment, it is hard to imagine the unwitting participation of students in a female supremacist ideology—the empirical research discussed earlier makes it clear that when females who constitute one half the student number receive even one third of the teacher's attention, male students are perceived as being cheated of their fair share of the teacher's attention (Cline and Spender 1987; French and French 1984a, 1984b; Spender 1982).

Conclusion

One of the deepest misunderstandings to emerge from the debate on political correctness is the reduction of serious moral considerations to matters of mere etiquette. D'Souza (1991) and Hentoff (1992) claim, as we have seen, that racist and sexist language may be rude, but even rude language must be protected by a right to freedom of expression. I have argued against the equation of racist, sexist language with rudeness, urging instead, as Van de Wetering (1991) does, that racism can be neither understood nor corrected in a vacuum, but must be seen in its full (and dreadful) historical context. Against such a context, racist and sexist language are not simply rude, but are morally and educationally problematic. Were racist and sexist language as trivial as the neo-conservative theorists would have us believe, it would be difficult to understand both their resistance to reform and the thousands of pages of print that they have produced to shield those who engage in such language.

Issues of racism and sexism in language are not simply matters of *political correctness*; they are, however, deeply political, and like the concepts of intelligence and knowledge, will go a long way towards determining the allocation of privilege, dignity, and even human worth. Those who have traditionally defined such concepts have wielded an enormous power, for we all have a stake in which particular definitions gain acceptance as correct. If we want, like Peirce, to insist that scholarship "not block the way of inquiry" (Peirce 1931-1958, 1.135) on such important issues, we must begin not by reducing them to matters of etiquette, but by acknowledging their profound impact on all of us.

Notes

1 Much of this part of the chapter appears in Maryann Ayim, "Racial Bias in Communication," *Western News*, 26, 19 (May 24, 1990), 14.
2 Much of this part of the chapter appears in Maryann Ayim, "The Politics of Language and Identity," in *Remedies for Racism and Sexism in Colleges*

and Universities; Conference Proceedings, Fanshawe College, London, ON, 1992, pp. 63-70.

3 Much of this part of the chapter appears in Maryann Ayim, "Political Correctness: The Debate Continues," in *The Gender Problem in Philosophy of Education: Theory, Pedagogy, & Politics*, by Ann Diller, Barbara Houston, Kathryn Pauly Morgan, and Maryann Ayim (Boulder, CO: WestviewPress, 1996), pp. 199-214. Reprinted by permission of WestviewPress.

Chapter Ten

Educational Reform: Impediments and Expectations[1]

Introduction

Females have been and continue to be judged by standards that are doubly and triply binding. In the first section of this chapter, I will explore the ways in which generic differentiation and contextual skewing operate to ensure that privilege remains largely a male preserve from which women are systematically excluded; these facets undermine attempts of educational institutions to rectify the inequities discussed in earlier chapters. On a more optimistic note, I will next examine the possibility of a radical restructuring for which a model exists in some of the literature on women in educational administration. I will then, in a concluding section, integrate the discussion of the preceding chapters within a moral context.

The first facet referred to above I shall label "generic differentiation," following Jane Martin (1981). By this term, I mean that the very same character traits are evaluated in opposite ways, depending on the sex of the person who exhibits the trait. Females are often

---

The notes to this chapter are on p. 226.

expected to conform to male styles and if they achieve these standards are then judged as less competent than males for exhibiting precisely the same behaviour; furthermore, they are frequently perceived
as cold, impersonal, and uncaring, in other words as inadequate
women. The second facet, discussed briefly in Chapter Five, I have
labelled "contextual skewing." By this I mean that we tend to judge
the system with which we have grown familiar as "normal" or even
"fair," and deviations from that system as "abnormal" or "unfair."
However, the common context against which all of us operate is
highly sexist (as well as racist, classist, and heterosexist); hence even
minimal gains made by women (or First Nations people, or Black
people, or working-class people, or gay men, or lesbian women) in
terms of representation in management positions, for example, are
often viewed as instances of reverse discrimination against (straight
white middle-class) men and judged to be acts of gross political inter-
ference with a meritocratic system. Ironically, the sexist practices that
excluded or at least ensured the underrepresentation of women and
other groups in particular occupational categories are perceived as
being somehow "objective," and untainted by political considerations.

It has been my experience that people often wish to terminate
this discussion and revert to the status quo by pointing out that
someone they know had a woman "boss" who was inadequate and
impossible to work for. I am not suggesting that there are no bad
female managers and no good male managers. Of course there are.
Nor is it to say that no particular men are unfairly penalized by
affirmative action policies which have as their goal the augmentation
of proportions of women in particular job categories. Some men do
occasionally fall into this category, and if they are men who have not
themselves personally contributed to the exclusion and marginaliza-
tion of women, the unfairness is even more unpalatable. I want to
emphasize the terms "some" and "occasionally," however, for having
personally participated in university hiring committees for over two
decades, I have *never* served on a committee that judged a male candidate to be of equal or higher calibre than a female candidate, but
offered the position to the female as an affirmative action gesture.
The *only* female candidates who have been offered positions at my
university as an outcome of the hiring committees on which I have
worked have been offered those positions *because* the committee
judged them to be the *best* of the applicants. Frequently, however, I
have learned through the grapevine that male candidates who lost the

competition to a female complained loudly that their rejection was an instance of reverse discrimination.

It's important to understand that the barriers placed in the way of women are of a different order than instances of discrimination against individual men. Particular women may of course be discriminated against for some of the same reasons as particular men are— for instance, if hiring committee members do not approve of their style of dress or their politics. But what I wish to explore in this chapter is a different form of discrimination against women, one that is systemic and structural rather than individual and personal, that is locked into the very definitions that control how we may talk about things, and that enjoys the sanction of a social political context which is based on a devaluation of the female and hence guarantees that women are locked securely in place at the bottom of the hierarchy. In other words, the features of genderic differentiation and contextual skewing systematically bolster a myth of male meritocracy, according to which any underrepresentation of women can be accounted for on the grounds that they are underqualified, underskilled, and in general incompetent relative to men.

Genderic Differentiation

The evidence for differential gender judgments of behaviour is overwhelming, informing both our professional and our personal lives. In fact, it is so integral a part of the way we perceive ourselves and other people that we often fail to notice it. Like a speck on the end of one's nose, it is *too* close to be seen in any acritical way of looking at things. Once seen, however, it is next to impossible to be unaware of it again. Many of us are familiar with the genderically differentiated judgments entailed by the statements "He's straightforward; she's pushy;" "He's a social drinker; she's a lush;" "He speaks his mind; she's mouthy." Of course it is not only women who are penalized by the application of opposite gender standards to behaviour. "She's gentle; he's a wimp," captures the sense in which men are penalized for behaving in ways that would be considered praiseworthy if engaged in by women. The particular problem for women emerges from the fact that it is precisely the sorts of behaviour that have been traditionally linked to competence in the public (as opposed to the private) sphere that are perceived negatively for women, hence barring them *by logic alone* from being accepted on an equal basis with men in the public forum.

To illustrate the debilitating impact of generic differentiation on the achievement of and judgments about women, let me provide a few examples that emerge from the literature. As early as 1975, Thorne and Henley (27-28) document many illustrations of generic differentiation arising from the linguistics literature. Among others, they discuss the following instances—the amount of talking done by men is *positively* correlated to their perceived amount of influence, whereas the amount of talking done by women is *negatively* correlated to their perceived amount of influence; while male verbal fluency creates a good impression, female verbal fluency creates a bad impression. In an anthology published eight years later by Thorne, Kramarae, and Henley (1983, 13-14), the discussion of opposing perceptions of identical female and male speech is augmented. Whereas women's use of qualifying phrases was used as evidence of their poor decision making in small groups, men whose speech contained many qualifying phrases were not judged in this way; women professors, unlike their male counterparts, were judged by their students to be less competent, although more likeable, the greater the amount of student participation they elicited in their classes. For some indication of how early generic differentiation emerges in our interpretations of behaviour, the authors discuss a study published in 1976 in which an infant's crying was identified as anger when the participants believed that the infant was a boy, but identified as fear when they believed the infant was a girl. Yet other examples of generic differentiation emerging from the literature, many of which were cited earlier in Chapter Four, are the greater hostility directed towards female than male leaders (Kahn 1984, 274-275), the fact that both females and males disagree more with female leaders than with male leaders (Alderton and Jurma 1980, 59), "that when a male and a female say the same thing, more attention will be paid to what the male says than to what the female says," (Gruber and Gaebelein 1979, 307), and that male executives will be listened to by their staff more closely than their female counterparts (Booth-Butterfield 1984, 40-41). The problems of being heard and taken seriously are even greater for Black women (Doughty 1980, 170; Ihle 1990; Pollard 1990). Pollard also points out that Black women experience significant difficulty finding interpersonal support in the form of mentors while they occupy the roles of student and worker—faculty, staff, or administration—in institutions of higher learning or research and development institutions (1990, 263-264). Arnold Kahn's research indicates that men perceive a weaker man's helping a more powerful person in gender-specific ways: in helping a powerful woman, a weaker man is perceived to ensure his powerlessness, but in helping a powerful man, he is perceived to have raised his own "power and status" (1984, 243).

As I pointed out earlier in Chapter Four, perceptions of expertise are also generically differentiated. Males tend to be credited with more expertise than females, whether or not they actually have more expertise. As summarized in Chapter Four, Goldberg's research established that both female and male readers perceived an article believed to have been written by a male to be more authoritative and knowledgeable than the same article believed to have been written by a female (1974, 40-42). Another study referred to in Chapter Four, conducted by Dale Spender, also illustrates the phenomenon of generic differentiation. Because Spender's observations are highly relevant to this discussion, I shall reiterate them. The classroom in question was situated in a faculty of education with students who were both aware of the problem of sexism (1984, 134) and claimed that they were concerned to eradicate it from their own behaviour as educators (ibid., 134, 136). All Spender's students were given and asked to evaluate a report card; the report cards were identical, except that half had the name "Jane Smith" and the other half the name "John Smith" at the top (ibid., 134). The students' responses to Jane and John were dramatically different. They believed Jane would probably drop out of school, that she would make a good secretary or receptionist, and that she would need to be closely managed (ibid., 135); John, on the other hand, was perceived as able to do anything he wanted, not understood by his teachers, and capable of managing people (ibid., 136).

Not only are females credited with less expertise than males but they are also resented more than male experts, and thus may be tempted to disguise their expertise. Leet-Pellegrini's analysis of expertise and gender, also discussed in Chapter Four, indicated that when female experts were paired with male non-experts, the females exhibited submissive assenting behaviour and no dominant behaviour. The expert women, "in the presence of non-expert men, responded with *even more supportive, collaborative work than usual* (1980, 103, my emphasis); furthermore, women experts assented more with male partners . . . than with female partners" (ibid., 102). Charol Shakeshaft's work indicated that when working with male subordinates, females "try to look less authoritarian, less in charge, and less threatening in an effort to be effective" (1987, 204). Hence "women administrators often downplay their power, intelligence, and skill . . . [making] themselves more tentative and less threatening" (ibid.).

Exploring similar avenues, Kramarae claims that

> Although women do not necessarily encounter hostility in all public
> speaking situations, women's public speech is especially restricted
> when women wish to address mixed-sex or male adult audiences, and
> when women attempt to speak on issues and in places considered
> important to men. St. Paul's declaration that women should be silent in
> public places is not quoted when a woman addresses a large gathering
> of the women's auxiliary church group in the church basement, on the
> topic of collecting money to aid hungry children. But St. Paul is often
> cited when a woman tries to talk from the pulpit. (1981, xiv)

What these examples show in the most dramatic way possible is
that the world in *not* an open forum providing equal opportunity for
the participation of all, with praise and prizes being awarded to the
most meritorious. Women are disadvantaged in this competition by
sexist traditions that demand of them the bulk of childcare and
household labour, and by a disinclination on many women's part to
engage in highly competitive activities in which there are by definition many losers and few winners. More insidiously, however, *the
logic of genderic differentiation* guarantees that even those women
who do excel in "playing the game by the rules" will be deemed to
have failed. The rules that define the public realm, the marketplace,
or the business world are not universal mandates created by deity
however; to the contrary, they have been created by men and they
reflect one very particular paradigm: a paradigm defined in terms of
hierarchy, competition, and authoritarianism. The implications of a
different paradigm defined in terms of democracy, cooperation, and
consultation will be discussed later in this chapter. The point I wish
to make at this time is simply that the so-called open marketplace of
competition in which the superior person emerges as the victor has
not been open to women; it has in fact been closed *by definition* to
women as a function of the feature of genderic differentiation, which
automatically negates the perceived worth of any woman who
achieves the male-valued standard.

Contextual Skewing

Contextual skewing is a powerful repressive phenomenon, creating
the illusion that the status quo has been fairly arrived at through
open competition, while ignoring the sexist, racist, and classist forces
that have been defining factors in the usurping and allocating of
power. To say that it will be a challenge to make our classrooms bias

free in the face of this political historical setting is to speak euphem-
istically. We may well ask how it will be possible for us to establish a
fair environment in which education can flourish, given that it is the
oppressors who by and large get to define what is fair; when we work
to clarify the form that racism and sexism take in the classroom, we
must not lose sight of this. This is clearly connected to the issue of
political correctness discussed in Chapter Nine, in which universities
are eager to point out the victimization of white males. While the status quo has been granted a kind of political asylum, threats to the status quo have received a quite different treatment, and have been seen
as blatantly political attempts to undermine those who have fairly
earned their positions in a competition equally open to all. Notice
that I am making two separate claims here—first, that the everyday
world is overwhelmingly biased in favour of males, and second, that
attempts to redress this imbalance are consistently undermined by a
labelling of the reform as itself discriminatory and unfair. I will draw
heavily on the educational literature in the examples I provide of each
of these facets of contextual skewing.

The overwhelming sexism of the school setting is particularly
powerful support for my claim, given the educational rhetoric surrounding the school's mandate to provide equal opportunity for all.
That the typical classroom *heavily* favours male students cannot be
doubted by anyone who has seriously examined the literature on perceived classroom dynamics. French and French, in their research on
British primary school classrooms discussed briefly in Chapter Two,
describe one particular lesson, "which comprised 66 pupil turns at
interactions, [and] 50 of these were produced by boys who numbered
less than half the class" (1984a, 61). They add that "a good many of
these turns were not 'spontaneously' allocated to boy pupils by the
teacher, but achieved through interactional techniques designed to
gain the teacher's attention" (ibid.).

Barrie Thorne, in her research on two American elementary
schools, notes that

> On the playground, boys control as much as ten times more space than
> girls, when one adds up the area of large playing fields and compares it
> with the much smaller areas where girls predominate. Girls, who play
> closer to the building, are more often watched over and protected by the
> adult aides. (1986, 176)

She also notes that

> Boys invade all-female games and scenes of play much more than girls invade boys. This, and boys' greater control of space, correspond with other findings about the organization of gender and inequality, in our society: compared with men and boys, women and girls take up less space, and their space, and talk, are more often violated and inter-rupted. . . . (Ibid.)

She also observes that the boys who most associated with the girls, either by joining them in their games or sitting closest to them during the lunch period, were the most devalued of the boys. The boys indi-cated that they devalued other boys by referring to them as "girls." In Thorne's words, "Gender is sometimes used as a metaphor for male hierarchies; the inferior status of boys at the bottom is conveyed by calling them 'girls'" (ibid.).

Some research (discussed earlier in Chapter Six) indicates that even at a preschool age, girls hesitate to ask for an adult's help in per-forming a task, whereas boys will nonchalantly ask for the help (Pel-legrini 1982, 213). This same pattern, also discussed in Chapter Six, continues with school-aged children, with boys making more direct requests than girls (Haas 1981, 925, 932-933). There are dozens of such studies, dealing not only with interactional dynamics, but extending as well into analyses of curriculum materials in the typical school. (See Graham's [1975] classic treatment of this topic, as well as more contemporary accounts: Cooper 1987; Campbell 1985.)

Nevertheless, it is important that I mention at this point a paper that challenges several of the specific studies referred to above as well as the overall conclusions reached by these researchers. Dart and Clarke (1988), in their analysis of 24 grade eight science classes involving 3 teachers and 113 students, did not find any significant gender differences in any of the categories of student-teacher interac-tion that they examined. They did find gender differences, which in all categories but one supported the prevalent research findings, of pro-male bias among teachers, but as mentioned above, these differ-ences were not statistically significant. We need to emphasize that even though Dart and Clarke's study did not turn up any *statistically significant* gender differences in the categories they examined, their results (with a single exception to be discussed in a moment) consist-ently supported a thesis of pro-male bias among the teachers. So even though short of statistical significance, their findings contribute to the general *weight of evidence* for the pro-male bias theory. A more detailed discussion of two of their claims will be useful at this time.

First, their critique of much of the research they challenge is primarily based on the fact that this research is qualitative rather than quantitative. Hence they criticize French and French (1984b) for analyzing only a single lesson (Dart and Clarke 1988, 43) and Spender (1982) for reporting her findings "in an anecdotal fashion" (Dart and Clarke 1988, 42). I do not disagree with their commentary about the work of either French and French (1984b) or Spender (1982); I would say, however, that the analysis of a *single* lesson would be highly unusual and that the work of Sadker and Sadker (1985) and Shakeshaft (1987), for example, on whose analyses of classroom dynamics and administrative style I have relied heavily, involve much broader data than that collected from one lesson. Even single lessons that do not achieve statistical significance may add to the general weight of evidence supporting a theory of sexist bias, however, in precisely the same way as Dart and Clarke's own study has done. But a great deal of the feminist research that argues for this theory, and nearly all of the research on which I have relied heavily, goes well beyond the single lesson mode. Zimmerman and West's early work (1975) on cross-sex interruption patterns, for example, was based on an analysis of transcripts of eleven interactions in which forty-eight interruptions occurred, forty six (or 96 percent) of which comprised males interrupting females. The achievement of statistical significance is not a problem with this data. Although their later work reflects a development of their views on interruption and although the data are not quite so dramatic, showing 75 percent or twenty-one out of twenty-eight cross-sex interruptions that comprise males interrupting females (West and Zimmerman 1983, 107), it remains nevertheless statistically persuasive. Fishman's (1983) work on conversational interaction, on which I have also relied heavily for my empirical data, analyzes fifty-two hours of tape-recorded conversation between three heterosexual couples; the analysis revealed that the women attempted, forty-seven different times, to initiate topics of conversation with the males, who rejected twenty-eight of these attempts and offered the appropriate linguistic cooperation for only seventeen of the women's attempts to get a conversation going. The men, on the other hand, attempted twenty-nine times to initiate a topic of conversation, and twenty-eight of these attempts succeeded because their female partners engaged in the requisite linguistic labour (1983, 91-92, 96-97). These data too easily achieve statistical significance. It is clear that a generalization from three couples to the general populace on the basis of this single study is not recommended, any more than a generalization from Dart and Clarke's three teachers to the teaching profession as a whole is recommended. Nevertheless, both Fishman's study (1983), which does achieve statistical significance for its specific subjects, and Dart and Clarke's (1988), which does not, both contribute to the general weight of evidence for a theory of pro-male bias. Sachs' findings of a *much* higher proportion of softened or mitigated utterances in girls' rather than boys' pretend play (Sachs 1987, 182-183) are not credited with generalizability by her, but are offered only as a description of the language of the children in her study (ibid., 182); nevertheless, given that sixteen minutes of play of twenty paired boys and twenty-six paired girls were analyzed (ibid., 178-179), the likelihood of her findings arising purely from chance is remote. Gleason's work, on which I have also relied fairly heavily, involved analyzing the parent-child discourse of twenty-four different families (1987, 193), a far cry from the "single lesson" bemoaned by Dart and Clarke. It is not my purpose here to analyze and defend every study I have cited. I do want to establish that the work on which I have relied the most heavily is not, however, subject to the sort of criticism that Dart and Clarke have raised.

Much of the preceding commentary is not a criticism of Dart and Clarke, who never claimed that the conclusions of the studies I have just cited were wrested from a single lesson. It is a caution against generalizing from one study carried out within a feminist framework to other such studies. Furthermore, the analysis of a single lesson may be very heuristic in suggesting avenues for future studies that cover a wider terrain, and in some cases, provide statistically significant quantification of the data. Anecdotal reports, while similarly lacking in statistical force, may provide great insight from the author, precisely because they *are anecdotal*. Reliance on a single lesson and an anecdotal reporting procedure are devastating flaws only if we presume that the research paradigm is strictly quantitative. Spender's work, although decidedly *not* quantitative, is nevertheless of enormous importance, because she provides a conceptual analysis of the *symbolic structure* of language, a task equally as important as the collection of empirical data. I don't want to belittle the importance of quantitative research; it is a respectable form of scholarly inquiry and when done well, may be very useful in explaining empirical data. Like all forms of research it has its limits, however, and I think it would be wrong-headed to mandate quantitative research as the only acceptable model.[2] Yet, on the basis of Dart and Clarke's reasons for dismissing the findings of French and French (1984b) and Spender (1982), that seems to me to be precisely what they are doing.

I mentioned above that Dart and Clarke claimed that their results, with a single exception, consistently supported a thesis of pro-male bias among the teachers. I wish now to focus the discussion on this second claim. In my opinion, the single category that demonstrates a pro-female bias on their analysis may be more intelligently interpreted in precisely the opposite way. The category in question is that girls initiate more interactions with teachers than boys do (ibid., 46). The authors claim that their findings here (even though not statistically significant!) contradict the work of other authors showing "that boys are more likely than girls to ask questions, volunteer information and make heavier demands on the teacher's time" (ibid.). In my opinion, a much more detailed analysis of the *sorts* of initiations of interactions with teachers engaged in by the girls is required to make sense of this interpretation. For example, how many of the girls' initiating attempts failed and how many succeeded? Were their attempts to initiate an interaction with a teacher frequently ignored, requiring them to try two or three times in order to get a response? If so, then this finding illustrates a pro-male, not a pro-female, classroom bias. Since Dart and Clarke do not specify in any way what form these initiations took, it is impossible to know what their finding does indicate. It is consistent with other research, however, to speculate that the girls needed to make more initiation efforts than the boys in order to achieve any interaction at all.

Fishman's research (1977, 1983), for example, shows that in mixed-sex conversations, women's attempts to introduce topics are *much more* likely to be ignored by men than vice versa. Hence if women want to get any of their topics on the discussion table at all, they are forced to initiate discussion much more often than men are. Consistent with this, in their conversations with men, women are also forced (like children in their conversations with adults) to use a disproportionate number of attention-getters—phrases like "Do you know what?" "This is really interesting!" etc.—in an attempt to focus attention on what they are saying (ibid.). Did any of the girls' initiation efforts reported by Dart and Clarke fall into the attention-getting category? This too would be useful information.

I listed earlier two separate claims connected to the phenomenon of contextual skewing and stated that I would provide examples of empirical research supporting both claims. So far, I have dealt only with the first of these claims—namely, that the everyday world is overwhelmingly biased in favour of males; I turn now to the second claim—that attempts to redress this imbalance are consistently undermined by a labelling of the reform as itself discriminatory and unfair.

The research supporting this second claim is even more intriguing. Dale Spender's work although already discussed in Chapter Two, illustrates this feature of contextual skewing so clearly that I shall review her findings here. The study in question involved soliciting teachers' and students' impressions of the gender dynamics of their classrooms. Teachers and students alike felt that the girls had done more of the talking and received more of the teachers' attention, badly short-changing the boys. However, when the classroom interactions of such teachers were videotaped, it was "often found that over two thirds of their time was spent with the boys who comprised less than half the class" (1982, 54). In other words, even though the boys received much more than their fair share of time and attention, they were *perceived* as being discriminated against. The research of Myra Sadker and David Sadker (1985, 54) reveals that in analyzing videotapes of classroom situations in which the boys outtalked the girls at a ratio of three to one, administrators and teachers alike *perceived* that the girls had done the bulk of the talking. They all interpreted the interactions as skewed towards the girls, and were unable to see the male bias until the researchers explicitly pointed it out to them.

Furthermore, male students perceive themselves as being short-changed when they cease to get their traditional share of the teacher's time and attention. Male students who are still favoured over female students, but favoured less dramatically than they are accustomed to, become obstreperous in class, requiring teachers to devote the bulk of their attention to them in order to maintain control in the classroom (Cline and Spender 1987, 58; Spender 1982, 54, 56-58).

Reforms that attempt to make the curriculum more inclusive frequently receive similar protests of outrage. Anyone who has tried to augment the meagre coverage of women in any discipline will understand Dale Spender's observation that "While almost the entire curriculum is about men, the inclusion of a few women can be perceived as political and subversive" (1982, 100). The reformer along with the reform is likely to be viewed as subversive, accounting at least in part for vilifying the feminist. Unger discusses research in which college students were given thirty photographs of women, were told that half of these women were feminists, and were asked to identify the feminists from the photographs; both male and female students systematically selected the women they perceived to be least attractive as the feminists (1979, 71). In the face of the joint impact of generic differentiation and contextual skewing, it is amazing that there has been any gender reform whatsoever. I turn now to the next section of this chapter, in which I examine some of the current feminist literature on educational administration for a clarification of one reform model. This section illustrates clearly the ways in which this administrative model captures three of the four moral criteria of language stipulated in Chapter Five—in particular, the criteria of being caring, cooperative, and democratic.

Women and Educational Administration: A Management Paradigm?

In terms of the underrepresentation of women, educational administration is no different than any other management area. (See Rees' [1990] gender breakdown of teachers and administrators in the Canadian school system.) What is different about educational administration, however, is that many of the female administrators have abandoned the male paradigm based on authority and hierarchy, replacing it with a scheme based on consultation and democracy. I will outline some of Charol Shakeshaft's observations about the style of women educational administrators and then discuss a point of logical difference between the traditional male and female styles. (Related findings are documented in the research of Gips 1989; Helgesen 1990; Lee 1993; Pearson 1981; Rosener 1990; Sagor 1992; Sergiovanni 1992; Shantz 1993.)

According to Shakeshaft (as mentioned earlier in Chapter Four), female administrators are more democratic and participatory than male administrators in their approach to issues (1987, 187). Some of the specific claims made by Shakeshaft regarding these different administrative styles are as follows: Female administrators are "more willing to submerge displays of personal power in an effort to get others to participate in the decision-making process" (ibid., 187), and they are more democratic and participatory than male administrators in their approach to issues (ibid.). Women in educational administration tend to spend their day differently than men. Women superintendents spend more time visiting classrooms and teachers, whereas male superintendents spend more time walking in the halls with head custodians and principals (ibid., 171); women principals "interact with male teachers much more than male principals interact with female teachers" (ibid.), although both women and men principals interact more with members of their own gender (ibid.); female principals and superintendents also spend more time with students than their male colleagues do, and they "are more likely to assist beginning teachers with instructional problems and direct them in their initial teaching experiences" (ibid., 172) than their male colleagues. Furthermore, women administrators "give more attention to the importance of individual differences among students" (ibid., 173), show more concern about students' academic achievement, and exhibit more knowledge of the curriculum (ibid.).

Women are also attracted to administration for quite different reasons than men, according to Shakeshaft; whereas women want "to be of service to people, to use professional skills for creative management, and to work with highly qualified and motivated people" (ibid.), men typically "want to meet important people and to have high prestige in the public eye" (ibid.). Women administrators also favour "more people-oriented projects than . . . the men [and] women community leaders were more often supportive of affirmative action for minority people and health and safety issues than men" (ibid., 174).

In addition, according to Shakeshaft, "women are more likely to use strategies that include long-range planning and evaluative data in making decisions and thus have been rated as better planners" (ibid., 188) than men. Female administrators are more flexible and more informal than male administrators (ibid., 173), they are "more concerned with delinquency-prone pupils" (ibid.), they are more likely to use power to empower others (ibid., 206), they are more collegial in their decision making (ibid., 188), and they are more adept at conflict resolution (ibid., 188-189) than male administrators are. As this list of features might lead us to expect, the behaviour and style of female administrators are more likely to result in more orderly schools and to promote high morale and commitment among staff members than the typical male administrative style (ibid., 200). I find it hard to disagree with Shakeshaft's claim that the female leadership style is more conducive to what most of us think of as good schools (ibid., 199). Furthermore, with its emphasis on consultation, participation, and democratic procedures, this style of management could provide us with an opportunity to put a true meritocracy into place. The traditional male style of management, built upon hierarchy and dominance, *presupposes* the exclusion of most participants in the educational system from decision-making positions.

These differences in style are reflected in the speech of children as young as four years old, according to Jean Berko Gleason (1987, 198) and in the games of children even younger, according to Jacqueline Sachs (1987). Sachs' research (also cited earlier in Chapter Four) with very young children playing a game of doctor showed that the boys would tell their partners which role to take and the boy giving this order would try to grab the high-status role of doctor for himself. The girls, on the other hand, asked their partners which role they wanted, appeared as interested in playing the patient, mother, or baby role as the doctor role (1987, 180), and frequently suggested that they could both be doctors or both be patients (1987, 181), something that never happened with any of the male pairs. Given the hierarchical arrangement of boys' play, it is easy to understand why they perceived two doctors in the game to be inconceivable; if the game provides participants with more egalitarian roles and more cooperative relationships to one another, then the possibility of augmenting the number of doctors arises naturally. The boys showed a distinct preference for giving orders and consequently issued many direct imperatives (1987, 183), while the girls exhibited a preference for a much more cooperative style, issuing very few direct imperatives, but many utterances that invited the participation of the other player.

Conclusion

Peirce claims that the external world's most important realities "have the mode of being of what the nominalists call 'mere' words . . . The nominalist is right in saying that they are substantially of the nature of words; but his 'mere' reveals a complete misunderstanding of what our everyday world consists of" (8.191). My position on words, as developed in this book, has been deeply pragmatic in the sense outlined by Peirce. In terms of both the dynamics and the content of talk, I have urged the importance of taking words very seriously indeed. I have argued in fact, that our words, as our *other forms of behaviour*, should be judged according to moral criteria. It is hard to imagine paying language any more serious heed than this. I have emphasized the phrase "other forms of behaviour" because it is relevant to the thesis of this book that language does not occur in a vacuum. Rather, it occurs entrenched in a context with social and political dimensions. The context against which I have written this book is permeated by sexist and racist norms; these norms are expressed in the work world where women receive less pay than men for doing work of equal value, in many institutionalized religions where women are barred from the most prominent roles, in higher education where women and people of Colour generally are eligible to receive degrees, but must endure a "chilly climate" to do so, in coeducational facilities where female students and students of Colour generally receive far less teacher attention and time than white males, in intimate hetero-sexual relationships where women are often subjected to violent abuse by their male partners, in families where statistics provide ever-increasing reasons for horror at the levels of incestuous abuse suffered by female children at the hands of older male relatives. I could with little difficulty expand this context against which language occurs into a much lengthier list of sexist and racist ills of society. Although such an exercise wouldn't be irrelevant, neither is it required, for the examples that I have already provided amply demonstrate my mean-ing when I speak of the prevalence of sexist and racist norms in soci-ety.

It is important to my thesis to understand that language use occurs within this context. In fact, stronger than this, language pat-terns reflect and corroborate these broader social patterns, thus exac-erbating the problem. If we lose sight of the links that bind language to other social institutions and other social phenomena, then we may fail to understand the capacity of certain sorts of language to harm people. This in turn may interfere with any understanding of the importance of carrying out a moral analysis of language. Because the male patterns of taking up most of the conversational time, interrupt-ing female speakers, demanding most of the teacher attention in the classroom, etc., while contributing little to the caring labour that sus-tains conversations, because these patterns are widespread, replicated in other social practices, and glorified, this renders a moral analysis of language imperative. We must analyze the interplay between talking and doing before it is possible to carry out a realistic assessment of the harm done by bad talk; MacKinnon provides a particularly helpful account of this. She says,

> Words and images are how people are placed in hierarchies, how social stratification is made to seem inevitable and right, how feelings of infe-riority and superiority are engendered, and how indifference to violence against those on the bottom is rationalized and normalized. (1993, 31)

In this book, I have discussed both conversational patterns (Chapters One to Six) and speech content (Chapters Seven to Nine). Just as it is important to understand the links between language and other social phenomena, as I have argued above, so it is important not to lose sight of the links between conversational patterns and speech content. The empirical research I have summarized in previous chapters indicates that those who take most of the talking time in mixed-sex conversations—males—also determine and monitor the *topic* of the conversation. This constitutes an important link between speech patterns and speech content. Those who are linguistically interrupted, ignored, and denied equal time will also have less opportunity to challenge and expose the falsehoods embedded in discriminatory discourse.

Practical work needs to be done on how our knowledge of this linguistic research can be applied to real-life crises engendered by society's endorsement of aggression. I have argued in Chapter One that tolerance and even celebration of mock and real violence in male behaviour is one of the cornerstones of these crises. This aggression and violence can be found in male linguistic behaviour as well as other forms of behaviour. It is evident in children's games, adult games, wife abuse and other forms of social violence, and even in academic discourse. I have suggested in Chapter Two that the general rejection of the male dominance theory by researchers may be in large part because it fits *so well* with a moral accounting of gender and language—a moral accounting which I have noticed that researchers are decidedly disinclined to do. Deborah Tannen (1990), for example, presents a dramatically depoliticized account of language, in which gender differences have nothing to do with power differentials, domination, and abuse of power, but have everything to do with the failure of males and females to understand what each other means. In the literature on men's linguistic interactions with young children, language that is not adapted to the linguistic level of the child, that is filled with interruptions, commands, and even threats, that is rude and inconsiderate, language that is best described as dysfunctional, is praised as "cognitively and linguistically more challenging than the mother[s]" (Gleason and Greif 1983, 148), as having "a positive effect on children" (ibid., 149), and as serving "special functions in their children's cognitive and linguistic development" (ibid.).

The reluctance of researchers to blame men for their behaviour is reflected in a general social reluctance to assign blame, particularly to men and boys. That there is less reluctance to assign blame to females is evident, I believe, in the widespread phenomenon of "mother-blaming." Nevertheless, there is a distasteful feel to blaming people, as well as being blamed, and this undoubtedly accounts at least in part for the reluctance of language researchers to find fault with male speech patterns typically directed to young children. We know, of course, that dominance *does not justify* power differentials, although it does *explain* them. Because we know this, we are likely to hold accountable people who behave in obnoxious ways and resort to a theory of male dominance as their justification. Thus one clear way to avoid holding them accountable is to eschew any theory of male dominance. This may account for the greater popularity of the sex roles socialization theory of gender and language over the male dominance theory of gender and language.

Although the sex roles theory, as I have discussed in Chapter Three, is compatible with a male dominance perspective, in which males are socialized into dominant aggressive behaviour and females into submissive affiliative behaviour, the sex roles theory also sees both males and females as limited and victimized by the prevailing sex roles ideology. There is little doubt, however, that sex roles socialization *does* occur, that it has an impact on language as well as other forms of behaviour, and that it is incredibly harmful. Sex roles socialization is seen by some as desirable because it promotes complementarity of male and female roles; I see the so-called complementarity, however, as not only false but dangerous. For when males are socialized to be aggressive and females to be affiliative, males to be rough and females to be gentle, the harmful toll of the male sex role is masked by the socialized sex role labour of females. In conversations, for example, the damaging impact of males not participating in topics of conversation introduced by females does not translate into a breakdown of conversations altogether; because women respond to male conversational forays with supportive behaviour, male-initiated conversations most frequently succeed, with the result that the destructive potential of the male styles for the maintenance of conversations has never been systematically assessed. The so-called complementarity of content of sex roles, with males and females being socialized into very different, almost opposite norms, not only underwrites a society based on differential privileges and obligations, in other words, a male dominant society, but underwrites as well a heterosexist society in which "legitimate" sexual intimacy and desire is predicated on this notion of "opposites" both attracting and in some sense completing each other.

The appropriate registers theory of gender and language, as I have argued in Chapter Four, is similarly compatible with both a male dominance theory (for the dominant group will get to define what is "appropriate") and a sex roles socialization theory (for common sense dictates that one's sex role socialization is likely to be a determining factor in the roles that one aspires to perform as well as the roles that society will encourage people to perform). As I have also argued in Chapter Four, the appropriate registers theory of gender and language is equally as guilty as the male dominance and the sex roles socialization theories in letting us off the moral hook too easily. To link gender differences in parental language with children to child-care roles while omitting any historical-political analysis of the gendered content of those roles is like attempting to explain certain behaviour patterns of American Black people as springing from service-oriented roles, while ignoring the institution of slavery. Men and women may, as Tannen suggests (1990), talk at cross-purposes to one another, but this does not entail that such talk should lie outside the boundaries of moral appraisal. The appropriate registers theory relies heavily on the notion of individual choices and individual contexts, and *inappropriately* glosses over what Kramarae refers to as the power of the "social structure" (1981, 140) in controlling and manipulating those choices. All three theories of gender and language—male dominance, sex roles socialization, and appropriate registers—quite the opposite of ruling out a moral analysis of language—require just such an analysis to be performed if one is to develop guidelines for good talk.

Earlier in this chapter, I discussed some of the criticisms of the empirical literature that I have cited in Chapters Two, Three, Four, and Six. I also attempted at that point to "rescue" some of the literature, arguing that it *did* meet requisite research standards. The moral claims made in this book are, however, *independent* of the empirical literature, whatever its standards may be. In other words, we *ought* to be maintaining democratic, honest, cooperative, and caring standards in our talk with one another *regardless* of whether women's or men's speech better attains these standards at this time and regardless of whether male dominance, sex roles socialization, appropriate registers, or any other account explains the relative superiority of one genders' talk over the other. The empirical work is, in an obvious sense, morally trivial; what it does account for, however, is the otherwise surprising absence of any substantial moral analysis of this whole area of behaviour—namely, our talk. As I have argued earlier, the need for a moral analysis is not apparent if the linguistic labour of females is masking the fact that there are any problems. If female labour keeps conversations operating smoothly even over the rough patches of male interruption and dominance, then the incidence of interruption and dominance may be rendered invisible. According to an old adage, "If it ain't broken, don't fix it!" If conversations survive because of female labour, it may appear that there's nothing to fix, and hence the necessity of moral appraisal may not be readily apparent. If one shares anything at all of the views of Wittgenstein that "The limits of my language mean the limits of my world" (1961, 115) or Charles Sanders Peirce that "My language is the sum total of myself" (1931-1958, 5.314), then disavowing the importance of moral standards to discourse is rendered incomprehensible.

Moral standards are appropriately exacted of the content as well as the style of talk. The vocabulary pertaining to girls and women in the English language is a grim reminder of how low those standards have slipped. As I have argued in Chapter Seven, the words available to speakers of English as substitutes for the word "woman" span a gamut from exclusion, through trivializing, to outrightly demeaning. Many have argued that the issue of linguistic exclusion is trivial, often poking fun at discussion surrounding the pseudo-generic terms "man" and "he." One can only regard the exclusion of women as a trivial issue, however, if one regards women themselves as trivial. The empirical literature makes it adamantly clear that the terms "man" and "he" *do not* fully include females in the way that they fully include males. Thus, to continue to use these terms as synonyms for humanity or to refer to any person regardless of their sex, is to violate the criterion of democratic language use in the most flagrant possible way. In any attempt to evaluate the significance of our ways of talking about women, it is important to look at the context in which such talk occurs. If we understand that historical tradition has excluded independence and intelligence from the traits valued in women, then the impact of such trivializing "synonyms" for "woman" as "doll," "girl," "chick," and "baby" becomes more apparent. The historical context will also help us to understand the racist, classist, heterosexist, ageist, and ablist parameters of the terminology frequently employed to refer to women. As for the overtly demeaning words, such as "sow," "cunt," "whore," and "slut," there is little doubt in anyone's mind that such terms are undesirable on a moral analysis; thus many of those who reject feminist analyses of language will nevertheless frown, for moral reasons, on the use of such terms. As I argued in Chapter Seven, these terms violate the moral criterion of caring so blatantly that even the critics join in condemning them. Peirce said that "A symbol, once in being, spreads among the peoples. In use and in experience, its meaning grows" (1931-1958, 2.302); if

Peirce is right, we have every reason to be alarmed at the symbols available in the English language for referring to women. Words purporting to be synonyms for "the human race" often totally exclude women. Women are caught between "compliments," which impose intolerable double binds and the deepest insults available for women. Women are likened to dumb animals and toys, are stripped of their intelligence, their will, and their independence. Even a sprinkling of such terms in the language would raise moral questions; the sheer abundance of such terms renders the need for moral analysis overwhelming.

If the nouns and pronouns used as substitute terms for "woman" in the English language are discouraging in terms of their symbolic import, so too are the dominant metaphors of academia. I have argued in Chapter Eight that within science and philosophy, violent and often misogynist images pervade the discourse and are used to capture the ideals of excellence pursued by scholars. In philosophy, the vocabulary surrounding arguments is particularly dramatic in terms of its sword fighting, arm wrestling, and bullfighting metaphors. Classical scientific accounts liken (and justify) the pursuit of scientific truth, where such truth is difficult to access, to raping a woman. Exposure to violent and misogynist imagery begins almost at birth through the classical nursery rhymes and fairy tales, continues with children's cartoon programming on television, is promoted through video games, many of which are featured in educational settings where the goal is to "eat up" or destroy an alien force, and emerges in full-blown horror in pornographic magazines, movies and videos. As Fernandez claims, metaphors are powerful "organizing elements" (1977, 101) of our experience; we would be naive to underestimate their importance, especially in terms of their heuristic potential in the academic disciplines. The operant metaphors determine (not absolutely, but strongly) both the scholarly problem worth pursuing and the acceptable solution. Not all metaphors survive—some, in the words of Israel Scheffler, will "languish and die" (1979, 129), but those that do survive will help to organize, construct, and evaluate our notions of reality. The metaphors so popular in the academy as indicators of excellence—the battlefield metaphors— have much in common with the play structure of little boys documented by Sachs (1987) which I discussed in Chapter Four: in both cases, logic places strict limits on the number of winners. If both boys in the dyad want to be the doctor and the rules of the game permit but a single doctor, then logic guarantees that one boy is doomed to disappointment. The metaphors of arm wrestling, sword fighting, and other battlefield scenes permit winners only on the assumption that there are losers as well. The little girls studied by Sachs changed the rules of the game, however, permitting both girls to be doctors if they so desired; they restructured the game so that everyone could play the role of their choice. There is no reason why the operant metaphors of the academy should not mirror this radical reconstruction invented by the girls. A quilting bee metaphor, as I have argued in Chapter Eight, does not require that some participants lose in order for others to achieve excellence—to the contrary, the stronger and more talented each individual quilter, the higher the quality of the overall quilt will be. It is time that the academy was structured less by competitive metaphors where winning entails losing and it is time that it was structured more by cooperative metaphors, such as the quilting bee, where winning singly entails winning jointly.

I have argued from the very beginning of this book the necessity of examining language within its social political context in order to understand the·importance of performing a moral evaluation of talk. One of the major shortcomings of the neo-conservative writers on political correctness is that they fail utterly to take the context into account, focusing on each instance of racist, sexist, or homophobic discourse in the university as though it occurred in a vacuum. Thus I argue in Chapter Nine that important moral issues of equity and fairness are camouflaged by the very language of the political correctness debate, which reduces these concerns to mere matters of etiquette, insensitive expression, or unpopular speech; furthermore, the debate is framed by the neo-conservatives in such a way as to suggest that while the positions of feminist and race theorist scholars advocating reform in the university is highly political, their own position—a conservative maintenance of the status quo—is apolitical. In Chapter Nine, I have argued that both these positions represent political stances and must be recognized as such.

Many scholars have attempted to trivialize the significance of language, including those who advocate a position of conservative laissez-faire surrounding the use of racist or sexist speech, reducing the serious moral connotations of such language to political correctness. This stance is very ironical, because the very thing they are attempting to trivialize—namely, racist and sexist language—is the same thing they are struggling to protect their right to engage in. Like poststructuralists, the neo-conservatives are caught in the contradiction of both regarding language as eminently important (and hence struggling fiercely to protect their right to continue to talk as they see fit, without limits imposed by concerns of gender and race fairness) and dismissing the relevance of value judgments to linguistic behaviour, thus reducing it to merely ways of speaking.

When language, including both speech patterns and vocabulary choices, is evaluated from within a moral framework, it becomes clear that certain ways of speaking are harmful and ought to be discouraged, whereas other ways of speaking augment the overall social good, and hence ought to be encouraged. I have argued that, although not without exception, many of the sorts of language styles that promote moral ends may be identified in the typical speaking patterns of girls and women; girls and women have received no credit for the ways in which their language focused on caring, however. Furthermore, in terms of gender, the linguistic caring has all been unidirectional, from females to males. Sex roles have promoted the expectation that females would do this caring, interactive linguistic labour, and like housework, it was only noticed when left undone.

We desperately need to develop strategies for teaching and rewarding caring language styles together with strategies for transforming language styles to other life styles. The literature on gender and educational administration suggests that this task just might be doable. As the literature discussed in the earlier part of this chapter has indicated, the speech and other behaviour patterns of the female administrators studied, achieved with flying colours the criteria of being cooperative and democratic. These administrators abandoned the male paradigm of authority and hierarchy as *the* model of excellence, replacing it with a new paradigm rooted in strategies of consultation and sharing. The road to empowerment for the female administrators lay through *empowering others*, and *better schools* appear to have emerged from this new style of management, thus illustrating that excellence does not depend on cut-throat competitive approaches, but may in fact be better achieved through highly cooperative endeavour. Reenter the quilting bee metaphor! A concern and willingness to include others in the decision-making process could well form the basis of a working meritocracy, a meritocracy that invites everyone to participate and that struggles to create an environment sufficiently comfortable that people will take the invitation seriously, a meritocracy that refuses to participate in sexual stereotyping which systematically devalues the achievements of some social groups, a meritocracy that refuses to glorify the sexist and racist underpinnings of society, in short, a meritocracy to which we could aspire with moral pride. In the same way, a concern and willingness to choose our language according to standards embodying caring, cooperative, democratic, and honest language will entail better talk in a moral sense—talk that will enable us to respect and learn from the contributions of the other participants and also augment our own selves in the process.

Notes

1 Much of this chapter appears in highly similar form in Maryann Ayim, "Women in Management: Double Jeopardy Explored," in *Women in Management—Business Practice and Research: Scaling the Great Divide; Proceedings of the Annual Conference of the Administrative Sciences Association of Canada—Women in Management Division*, edited by Lou Hammond-Ketilson, 14, no. 11 (North York: Ontario Administrative Sciences Association of Canada, 1993), pp. 82-91.
2 For an excellent account of various research models, see *Forms of Curriculum Inquiry*, edited by Edmund C. Short (1991).

Bibliography

Abbey, Antonia, and Christian Melby. 1986. "The Effects of Nonverbal Cues on Gender Differences in Perceptions of Sexual Intent." *Sex Roles: A Journal of Research*, 15, nos. 5-6, 283-298.

Abrahams, Roger D. 1972. "The Training of the Man of Words in Talking Sweet." *Language in Society*, 1, 15-30.

_____. 1975. "Negotiating Respect: Patterns of Presentation among Black Women." *Journal of American Folklore*, 88, nos. 347-350, 58-80.

Ackerman, Bruce. 1989. "Why Dialogue?" *The Journal of Philosophy*, 86, no. 1, 5-22.

Adams, Karen L., and Norma C. Ware. 1979. "Sexism and the English Language: The Linguistic Implications of Being a Woman." In *Woman: A Feminist Perspective*, edited by Jo Freeman, pp. 487-504. 2d ed. Palo Alto, CA: Mayfield Publishing.

Adams, Marilyn Jager. 1990. *Beginning to Read: Thinking and Learning about Print. A Summary*, prepared by Steven A. Stahl, Jean Osborn, and Fran Lehr. Urbana-Champaign, IL: Center for the Study of Reading; The Reading Research and Education Center; University of Illinois.

Addelson, Kathryn Pyne. 1983. "The Man of Professional Wisdom." In *Discovering Reality: Feminist Perspectives on Epistemology, Metaphysics, Methodology, and Philosophy of Science*, edited by Sandra Harding and Merrill B. Hintikka, pp. 165-186. Dordrecht, Holland: D. Reidel Publishing.

Ahmed, Paul I., Aliza Kolker, and George V. Coelho. 1979. "Toward a New Definition of Health: An Overview." In *Toward a New Definition of Health: Psychosocial Dimensions*, edited by Paul I. Ahmed and George V. Coelho, with the assistance of Aliza Kolker, pp. 1-22. Current Topics in Mental Health. New York: Plenum.

Alderton, Steven M., and William E. Jurma. 1980 (Fall). "Genderless/Gender-Related Task Leader Communication and Group Satisfaction: A Test of Two Hypotheses." *The Southern Speech Communication Journal*, 46, 48-60.

Allen, Barry. 1993. "Demonology, Styles of Reasoning, and Truth." *International Journal of Moral and Social Studies*, 8, no. 2, 95-122.

Amidjaja, Imat R., and W. Edgar Vinacke. 1965. "Achievement, Nurturance, and Competition in Male and Female Triads." *Journal of Personality and Social Psychology*, 2, no. 3, 447-451.

Anderson, Audrey. 1986. *Developing a Northern Curriculum*. Canada: With the Assistance of the Department of the Secretary of State of Canada, Multiculturalism and the Ontario Ministry of Citizenship and Culture, Newcomer Services Branch.

Andersson, Lars, and Peter Trudgill. 1990. *Bad Language*. Oxford, UK: Basil Blackwell.

Apple, Michael. 1991. "Teacher, Politics, and Whole Language Instruction." In *The Whole Language Catalogue*, edited by Ken Goodman, Lois Bird, and Yetta Goodman, p. 416. Santa Rosa, CA: American School Publishers.

Aries, Elizabeth. 1987. "Gender and Communication." In *Sex and Gender*, edited by Philip Shaver and Clyde Hendrick, pp. 149-176. Review of Personality and Social Psychology, 7. Beverly Hills: Sage Publications.

Aristotle. 1953. *Generation of Animals*. Book 4, chap. 6. Edited by T.E. Page et al. Translated by A.L. Peck. London: William Heinemann.

Atwood, Margaret. 1985. *The Handmaid's Tale*. Toronto: McClelland and Stewart.

Augustine, Jean. 1990 (January 26). "Towards Empowerment and Equity: Race and Gender Issues in the Classroom." Public Address to the Faculty of Education, The University of Western Ontario, London, ON.

Ayim, Martha. 1992 (April). "My Experiences as a Black Woman in Philosophy." *University of Toronto Philosophy Newsletter*, pp. 2-3. Also presented at the "Diversifying the Philosophy Curriculum" Conference, University of Toronto, February 29, 1992.

Ayim, Maryann. 1983. "The Implications of Sexually Stereotypic Language as Seen through Peirce's Theory of Signs." *Transactions of the Charles S. Peirce Society*, 19, no. 2, 183-197.

————. 1987a. "Warning: Philosophical Discussion, Violence at Work." *Resources for Feminist Research/Documentation sur la Recherche Feministe*, 16, no. 3, 23-24.

————. 1987b. "Wet Sponges and Band-aids: A Gender Analysis of Speech Patterns." In *Proceedings of the Seventh Annual Meeting of the Semi-*

otic Society of America, edited by John Deely and Jonathan Evans, pp. 29-43. New York: University Press of America.

———. 1988. "Violence and Domination as Metaphors in Academic Discourse." In Selected Issues in Logic and Communication, edited by Trudy Govier, pp. 184-195. Belmont, CA: Wadsworth Publishing.

———. 1990. "Racial Bias in Communication." Western News, 26, no. 19, 14.

———. 1992a. "Dominance and Violence in Scientific Discourse: A Portrait of the Scientist as a Young Man." In Rights, Justice, and Community, edited by Creighton Peden and John K. Roth, pp. 9-23. Lewiston, NY: Edwin Mellen Press.

———. 1992b. "The Politics of Language and Identity." In Remedies for Racism and Sexism in Colleges and Universities; Conference Proceedings, pp. 63-70. Fanshawe College, London, ON.

———. 1993a. "The Moral Dimensions of Sexually Inclusive Language." In A Reader in Feminist Ethics, edited by Debra Shogun, pp. 515-532. Toronto: Canadian Scholars' Press.

———. 1993b. "Women in Management: Double Jeopardy Explored." In Women in Management—Business Practice and Research: Scaling the Great Divide; Proceedings of the Annual Conference of the Administrative Sciences Association of Canada—Women in Management Division, 14, no. 11, edited by Lou Hammond-Ketilson, pp. 82-91. North York, ON: Administrative Sciences Association of Canada.

———. 1996. "Political Correctness: The Debate Continues." In The Gender Problem in Philosophy of Education: Theory, Pedagogy, & Politics, by Ann Diller, Barbara Houston, Kathryn Pauly Morgan, and Maryann Ayim, pp. 199-214. Boulder, CO: Westview.

Ayim, Maryann, and Diane Goossens. 1993. "Issues in Gender and Language: An Annotated Bibliography." Resources for Feminist Research/ Documentation sur la Recherche Feministe, 22, nos. 1-2, 3-35.

Bacon, Francis. 1860. The Works of Francis Bacon. Vol. 4. Edited by James Spedding, Robert Leslie Ellis, and Douglas Denon Heath. London: Longman.

Baker, Robert. 1975. " 'Pricks' and 'Chicks': A Plea for 'Persons.' " In Philosophy and Sex, edited by R. Baker and F. Ellison, pp. 45-64. Buffalo, NY: Prometheus.

Baron, Dennis E. 1981. "The Epicene Pronoun: The Word That Failed." American Speech, 56, 83-97.

Barron, Nancy. 1971. "Sex-Typed Language: The Production of Grammatical Cases." Acta Sociologica, 14, nos. 1-2, 24-42.

Baskwill, J., and P. Whitman. 1988. Evaluation: Whole Language, Whole Child. Richmond Hill: Scholastic—TAB Publications.

Beasley, Mary. 1983. "Women in Educational Leadership." In Changing Focus: The Participation of Women in Educational Management in Aus-

tralia, edited by Shirley Randell, pp. 13-16. Carleton, Victoria: The Australian College of Education.

Bem, Sandra L., and Daryl J. Bem. 1973. "Does Sex-Biased Job Advertising 'Aid and Abet' Sex Discrimination?" *Journal of Applied Social Psychology*, 3, no. 1, 6-18.

Benton, Alan A. 1973. "Reactions to Demands to Win from an Opposite Sex Opponent." *Journal of Personality*, 41, no. 3, 430-442.

Berger, Joseph, Bernard P. Cohen, and Morris Zelditch, Jr. 1972. "Status Characteristics and Social Interaction." *American Sociological Review*, 37, no. 3, 241-255.

Bettelheim, Bruno. 1984. "Fathers Shouldn't Try to Be Mothers." In *Feminist Frameworks: Alternative Theoretical Accounts of the Relations between Women and Men*, edited by Alison M. Jaggar and Paula S. Rothenberg, pp. 306-311. 2d ed. New York: McGraw-Hill.

Bloom, Allan. 1987. *The Closing of the American Mind: How Higher Education Has Failed Democracy and Impoverished the Souls of Today's Students*. New York: Simon and Schuster.

Bodine, Ann. 1975. "Androcentrism in Prescriptive Grammar." *Language in Society*, 4, 129-146.

Booth-Butterfield, Melanie. 1984. "She Hears . . . He Hears: What They Hear and Why." *Personnel Journal*, 63, no. 5, 36-42.

Brenner, Otto C., and W. Edgar Vinacke. 1979. "Accommodative and Exploitative Behavior of Male versus Female Managers versus Nonmanagers as Measured by the Test of Strategy." *Social Psychology Quarterly*, 42, no. 3, 289-293.

Broverman, I., S. Vogel, D. Broverman, F. Clarkson, and P. Rosenkrantz. 1972. "Sex-role Stereotypes: A Current Appraisal." *Journal of Social Issues*, 28, no. 2, 59-78.

Bublitz, Wolfram. 1988. *Supportive Fellow-Speakers and Cooperative Conversations: Discourse Topics and Topical Actions, Participant Roles and 'Recipient Action' in a Particular Type of Everyday Conversation*. Amsterdam: John Benjamins.

Campbell, Synne. 1985. "Training the Managers: Thoughts from Where I Am Now." Special Issue: *Men and Women in Organisations, Management Education and Development*, 16, no. 2, 99-103.

Carroll, Lewis. [Charles Lutwidge Dodgson]. 1991. "Resident Women Students." From "A Miscellany." In *The Complete Illustrated Lewis Carroll*, with an introduction by Alexander Woollcott and illustrations by John Tenniel, 1068-1070. Ware, Hertfordshire, UK: Wordsworth.

Christie, Agatha. 1955. *Hickory Dickory Dock*. Glasgow: William Collins Sons.

Christie, Richard, and Florence Geiss. 1968. "Some Consequences of Taking Machiavelli Seriously." In *Handbook of Personality Theory and Research*, edited by Edgar F. Borgatta and William W. Lambert, pp. 959-973. Chicago: Rand McNally.

Cline, Sally, and Dale Spender. 1987. *Reflecting Men at Twice Their Natural Size*. London: Andre Deutsch.

The Concise Oxford Dictionary. 1976. Edited by J.B. Sykes. 6th ed., rev.

Cooper, Pamela J. 1987 (November). "In or Out of the Pumpkin Shell? Sex Role Differentiation in Classroom Interaction." Paper presented at the Annual Meeting of the Speech Communication Association, Boston, MA.

Corsaro, William A., and Thomas A. Rizzo. 1990. "Disputes in the Peer Culture of American and Italian Nursery-school Children." In *Conflict Talk: Sociolinguistic Investigations of Arguments in Conversations*, edited by Allen D. Grimshaw, pp. 21-66. Cambridge: Cambridge University Press.

Crosby, Faye, and Linda Nyquist. 1977. "The Female Register: An Empirical Study of Lakoff's Hypotheses." *Language in Society*, 6, 313-322.

Cross, Marion E., and Jan Hulland. 1975. *Teacher's Guidebook for Starting Points in Reading (C), First Book: With Notes on Starting Points in Language (C), Book 2*. Toronto: Ginn and Company.

Crumpacker, Laurie, and Eleanor M. Vander Haegen. 1990. "Valuing Diversity: Teaching about Sexual Preference in a Radical/Conserving Curriculum." In *Changing Education: Women as Radicals and Conservators*, edited by Joyce Antler and Sari Knopp Biklen, pp. 201-215. Albany, NY: State University of New York Press.

Dart, Barry C., and John A. Clarke. 1988. "Sexism in Schools: A New Look." *Educational Review*, 40, no. 1, 41-49.

Delgado, Richard. 1993. "Words That Wound: A Tort Action for Racial Insults, Epithets, and Name Calling." In *Words That Wound: Critical Race Theory, Assaultive Speech, and the First Amendment*, edited by Mari J. Matsuda, Charles R. Lawrence III, Richard Delgado, and Kimberlè Williams Crenshaw, pp. 89-110. Boulder, CO: Westview.

Delpit, Lisa D. 1988. "The Silenced Dialogue: Power and Pedagogy in Educating Other People's Children." *Harvard Educational Review*, 58, no. 3, 280-298.

Doughty, Rosie. 1980. "The Black Female Administrator: Woman in a Double Bind." In *Women and Educational Leadership*, edited by Sari Knopp Bilken and Marilyn B. Brannigan, pp. 165-174. Lexington, MA: Lexington Books, D.C. Heath.

Draper, Roger. 1992. "Writers and Writing: P.C. Pipe Dreams." *The New Leader*, 75, no. 5, 16-17.

D'Souza, Dinesh. 1991. *Illiberal Education: The Politics of Race and Sex on Campus*. New York: The Free Press.

D'Souza, Dinesh, and Robert MacNeil. 1992. "The Big Chill? Interview with Dinesh D'Souza." In *Debating P.C: The Controversy over Political Correctness on College Campuses*, edited by Paul Berman, pp. 29-39. New York: Laurel, Dell.

Dubois, Betty Lou, and Isabel Crouch. 1975. "The Question of Tag Questions in Women's Speech: They Don't Really Use More of Them, Do They?" *Language in Society*, 4, no. 3, 289-294.

Eakins, Barbara Westbrook, and Rollin Gene Eakins. 1978. *Sex Differences in Human Communication*. Boston: Houghton Mifflin Company.

Eberhart, Ozella Mae Yowell. 1976. "Elementary Students' Understanding of Certain Masculine and Neutral Generic Nouns." *Dissertation Abstracts International*, 37, 4113A-4114A.

Edelsky, Carole. 1990. "Whose Agenda Is this Anyway? A Response to McKenna, Robinson, and Miller." *Educational Researcher*, 19, no. 8, 7-11.

Engle, Marianne. 1980. "Family Influences on the Language Development of Children." *Women's Studies International Quarterly: A Multidisciplinary Journal for the Rapid Publication of Research Communications and Review Articles in Women's Studies*, 3, nos. 2-3, 259-266.

Erickson, Bonnie, E. Allan Lind, Bruce C. Johnson, and William M. O'Barr. 1978. "Speech Style and Impression Formation in a Court Setting: The Effects of 'Powerful' and 'Powerless' Speech." *Journal of Experimental Social Psychology*, 14, no. 3, 266-279.

Expline, Ralph V., John Thibaut, Carole B. Hickey, and Peter Gumpert. 1970. "Visual Interaction in Relation to Machiavellianism and an Unethical Act." In *Studies in Machiavellianism*, edited by Richard Christie and Florence L. Geiss, pp. 53-75. New York: Academic Press.

Fairweather, Hugh. 1976. "Sex Differences in Cognition." *Cognition: International Journal of Cognitive Psychology*, 4, no. 3, 231-280.

Fernandez, James. 1977. "The Performance of Ritual Metaphors." In *The Social Use of Metaphor: Essays on the Anthropology of Rhetoric*, edited by J. David Sapir and J. Christopher Crocker, pp. 100-131. Pennsylvania: The University of Pennsylvania Press.

Feynman, Richard. 1966. "The Development of the Space-Time of Quantum Electrodynamics." *Science*, 153, no. 3737, 699-708.

Finn, Geraldine. 1982. "On the Oppression of Women in Philosophy—Or, Whatever Happened to Objectivity?" In *Feminism in Canada: From Pressure to Politics*, edited by Angela R. Miles and Geraldine Finn, pp. 145-173. Montreal: Black Rose.

Fisher, Sue, and Stephen B. Groce. 1990. "Accounting Practices in Medical Interviews." *Language in Society*, 19, no. 2, 225-250.

Fishman, Pamela M. 1977 (May). "Interactional Shitwork." *Heresies: A Feminist Publication on Arts and Politics*, 2, 99-101.

———. 1980. "Conversational Insecurity." In *Language: Social Psychological Perspectives: Selected Papers from the First International Conference on Social Psychology and Language Held at the University of Bristol, England, July 1979*, edited by Howard Giles, W. Peter Robinson, and Philip M. Smith, pp. 127-132. Oxford: Pergamon.

_____. 1983. "Interaction: The Work Women Do." In *Language, Gender and Society*, edited by Barrie Thorne, Cheris Kramarae, and Nancy Henley, pp. 89-101. Rowley, MA: Newbury House.

Fisk, William R. 1985. "Responses to 'Neutral' Pronoun Presentations and the Development of Sex-biased Responding." *Developmental Psychology*, 21, no. 3, 481-485.

Fowler, Gene D., and Lawrence B. Rosenfeld. 1979. "Sex Differences and Democratic Leadership Behavior." *The Southern Speech Communication Journal*, 45, no. 1, 69-78.

Fox, Thomas. 1990. *The Social Uses of Writing: Politics and Pedagogy*. Norwood, NJ: Ablex Publishing.

French, Jane, and Peter French. 1984a. "Sociolinguistics and Gender Divisions." In *World Yearbook of Education 1984: Women and Education*, edited by Sandra Acker (Guest Editor), Jacquetta Megarry (Series Editor), Stanley Nisbet (Associate Editor), and Eric Hoyle (Consultant Editor), pp. 52-63. New York: Kogan Page; London: Nichols.

_____. 1984b. "Gender Imbalances in the Primary Classroom: An Interactional Account." *Educational Research*, 26, no. 2, 127-136.

Gall, Meredith D., Amos K. Hobby, and Kenneth H. Craik. 1969. "Non-Linguistic Factors in Oral Language Productivity." *Perceptual and Motor Skills*, 29, 871-874.

Garfinkel, Harold. 1967. "Passing and the Managed Achievement of Sex Status in an 'Intersexed' Person: Part 1." In *Studies in Ethnomethodology*, by Harold Garfinkel in collaboration with Robert J. Stoller, pp. 116-185. Englewood Cliffs, NJ: Prentice-Hall.

Gastil, John. 1990. "Generic Pronouns and Sexist Language: The Oxymoronic Character of Masculine Generics." *Sex Roles: A Journal of Research*, 23, nos. 11-12, 629-643.

Gerhart, Mary, and Allan Melvin Russell. 1984. *Metaphoric Process: The Creation of Scientific and Religious Understanding*, foreword by Paul Ricoeur. Fort Worth: Texas Christian University Press.

Giele, Janet Z., and Mary Gilfus. 1990. "Race and College Differences in Life Patterns of Educated Women, 1934-1982." In *Changing Education: Women as Radicals and Conservators*, edited by Joyce Antler and Sari Knopp Biklen, pp. 179-197. Albany, NY: State University of New York Press.

Gilligan, Carol. 1982. *In a Different Voice: Psychological Theory and Women's Development*. Cambridge, MA: Harvard University Press.

Gips, Crystal J. 1989 (November 17-21). "Women's Ways: A Model for Leadership in Democratic Schools." Paper presented at the Annual Meeting of the National Council of States on Inservice Education, San Antonio, TX.

Giroux, Henry. 1991. "Literacy, Cultural Diversity, and Public Life." In *The Whole Language Catalogue*, edited by Ken Goodman, Lois Bird, and Yetta Goodman, p. 417. Santa Rosa, CA: American School Publishers.

Gleason, Jean Berko. 1987. "Sex Differences in Parent-child Interaction." In *Language, Gender and Sex in Comparative Perspective*, edited by Susan U. Philips, Susan Steele, and Christine Tanz, pp. 189-199. Cambridge: Cambridge University Press.

Gleason, Jean Berko, and Esther Blank Greif. 1983. "Men's Speech to Young Children." In *Language, Gender and Society*, edited by Barrie Thorne, Cheris Kramarae, and Nancy Henley, pp. 140-150. Rowley, MA: Newbury House.

Goldberg, Philip. 1974. "Are Women Prejudiced against Women?" In *And Jill Came Tumbling After: Sexism in American Education*, edited by Judith Stacey, Susan Bereaud, and Joan Daniels, pp. 37-42. New York: Dell.

Goldberg, Steven. 1977. "The Inevitability of Patriarchy." In *Sex Equality*, edited by Jane English, pp. 196-204. Englewood Cliffs, NJ: Prentice-Hall.

Goodman, K.S., Y. Goodman, and W.J. Hood. 1989. *The Whole Language Evaluation Book*. Portsmouth, NH: Heinemann.

Goodman, Robert F., and Aaron Ben-Ze'ev, eds. 1994. *Good Gossip*. Lawrence, KS: University Press of Kansas.

Goodwin, Marjorie Harness, and Charles Goodwin. 1987. "Children's Arguing." In *Language, Gender and Sex in Comparative Perspective*, edited by Susan U. Philips, Susan Steele, and Christine Tanz, pp. 200-248. Cambridge: Cambridge University Press.

Govier, Trudy, ed. 1988. *Selected Issues in Logic and Communication*. Belmont, CA: Wadsworth.

Graddol, David, and Joan Swann. 1989. *Gender Voices*. Oxford, UK: Basil Blackwell.

Graham, Alma. 1975. "The Making of a Nonsexist Dictionary." In *Language and Sex: Difference and Dominance*, edited by Barrie Thorne and Nancy Henley, pp. 57-63. Series in Sociolinguistics. Rowley, MA: Newbury House.

Greenberg, Jeff, S.L. Kirkland, and Tom Pyszczynski. 1988. "Some Theoretical Notions and Preliminary Research Concerning Derogatory Ethnic Labels." In *Discourse and Discrimination*, edited by Geneva Smitherman-Donaldson and Teun A. van Dijk, pp. 74-92. Detroit: Wayne State University Press.

Greif, Esther Blank. 1980. "Sex Differences in Parent-Child Conversations." *Women's Studies International Quarterly*, 3, 253-258.

Grice, Paul. 1975. "Logic and Conversation." In *Speech Acts*, edited by Peter Cole and Jerry L. Morgan, pp. 41-58. Syntax and Semantics, 3. New York: Academic Press.

———. 1981. "Presupposition and Conversational Implicature." In *Radical Pragmatics*, edited by Peter Cole, pp. 183-198. New York: Academic Press.

Gruber, Kenneth J., and Jacquelyn Gaebelein. 1979. "Sex Differences in Listening Comprehension." In *Sex Roles: A Journal of Research*, 5, no. 3, 299-310.

Haas, Adelaide. 1981. "Partner Influences on Sex-Associated Spoken Language of Children." *Sex Roles: A Journal of Research*, 7, no. 9, 925-935.

Habermas, Jürgen. 1970. "Towards a Theory of Communicative Competence." *Inquiry*, 13, 360-375.

Halberstadt, Amy G., Cynthia W. Hayes, and Kathleen M. Pike. 1988. "Gender and Gender Role Differences in Smiling and Communication Consistency." *Sex Roles: A Journal of Research*, 19, nos. 9-10, 589-604.

Hall, Judith A. 1979. "Gender, Gender Roles, and Nonverbal Communication Skills." In *Skill in Nonverbal Communication: Individual Differences*, edited by Robert Rosenthal, pp. 32-67. Cambridge, MA: Oelgeschlager, Gunn, and Hain.

————. 1984. *Nonverbal Sex Differences: Communication Accuracy and Expressive Style*. Baltimore and London: The Johns Hopkins University Press.

————. 1987. "On Explaining Gender Differences: The Case of Nonverbal Communication." In *Sex and Gender*, edited by Philip Shaver and Clyde Hendrick, pp. 177-200. Review of Personality and Social Psychology, 7. Beverly Hills: Sage Publications.

Hall, Roberta M., with Bernice R. Sandler. 1982. "The Classroom Climate: A Chilly One for Women?" Project on the Status and Education of Women, Association of American Colleges, 1818 R Street, NW, Washington, DC 20009.

Hamilton, Mykol Cecilia. 1985. "Linguistic Relativity and Sex Bias in Language: Effects of the Masculine 'Generic' on the Imagery of the Writer and the Perceptual Discrimination of the Reader." *Dissertation Abstracts International*, 46, 1381B.

————. 1988a. "Masculine Generic Terms and Misperception of AIDS Risk." *Journal of Applied Social Psychology*, 18, no. 14, 1222-1240.

————. 1988b. "Using Masculine Generics: Does Generic *He* Increase Male Bias in the User's Imagery?" *Sex Roles: A Journal of Research*, 19, nos. 11-12, 785-799.

Harding, Sandra. 1986. *The Science Question in Feminism*. Ithaca: Cornell University Press.

Harding, Sandra, and Merrill B. Hintikka, eds. 1983. *Discovering Reality: Feminist Perspectives on Epistemology, Metaphysics, Methodology, and Philosophy of Science*. Dordrecht, Holland: D. Reidel Publishing.

Hare, R.M. 1973. "Language and Moral Education." In *New Essays in the Philosophy of Education*, edited by Glenn Langford and D.J. O'Connor, pp. 149-166. London and Boston: Routledge & Kegan Paul.

Harrigan, Jinni A., and Karen S. Lucic. 1988. "Attitudes about Gender Bias in Language: A Reevaluation." *Sex Roles: A Journal of Research*, 19, nos. 3-4, 129-140.

Harris, Lauren J. 1977. "Sex Differences in the Growth and Use of Language." In *Women: A Psychological Perspective*, edited by Elaine Donelson and Jeanne E. Gullahorn, pp. 79-94. New York: John Wiley.

Harrison, Linda. 1975. "Cro-Magnon Woman—In Eclipse." *Science Teacher*, 42, no. 4, 8-11.

Harrison Linda, and Richard N. Passero. 1975. "Sexism in the Language of Elementary School Textbooks." *Science and Children*, 12, no. 4, 22-25.

Haslett, Betty J. 1983. "Communicative Functions and Strategies in Children's Conversations." *Human Communication Research*, 9, no. 2, 114-129.

Helgesen, Sally. 1990. *The Female Advantage: Women's Ways of Leadership*. New York: Doubleday.

Henley, Nancy M. 1975. "Power, Sex, and Nonverbal Communication." In *Language and Sex: Difference and Dominance*, edited by Barrie Thorne and Nancy Henley, pp. 184-203. Series in Sociolinguistics. Rowley, MA: Newbury House.

————. 1989. "Molehill or Mountain? What We Know and Don't Know about Sex Bias in Language." In *Gender and Thought: Psychological Perspectives*, edited by Mary Crawford and Margaret Gentry, pp. 59-78. New York: Springer-Verlag.

Hentoff, Nat. 1992. "Who's on First? Hurt Feelings and Free Speech." *The Progressive*, 56, no. 2, 16-17.

Hill, William Fawcett. 1962. *Learning Thru Discussion*. Introduction by Herbert A. Thelen. Beverly Hills, CA: Sage Publications.

Hitchcock, David. 1983. *Critical Thinking: A Guide to Evaluating Information*. Toronto: Methuen.

Hirst, Paul H. 1974. *Knowledge and the Curriculum*. London: Routledge and Kegan Paul.

Hoffman, Eva. 1989. *Lost in Translation: A Life in a New Language*. New York: E.P. Dutton.

Hoffman, Lois Wladis. 1988. "Changes in Family Roles, Socialization, and Sex Differences." In *Childhood Socialization*, edited by Gerald Handel, pp. 299-324. New York: Aldine de Gruyter.

Hottes, Joseph H., and Arnold Kahn. 1974. "Sex Differences in a Mixed-motive Conflict Situation." *Journal of Personality*, 42, no. 2, 260-275.

Houston, Barbara. 1985. "Gender Freedom and the Subtleties of Sexist Education." *Educational Theory*, 35, no. 4, 359-369.

Howard, John A. 1991. "Lifting Education's Iron Curtain: To Rebuild the Civic and Moral Capitol." *Vital Speeches of the Day*, 57, no. 24, 756-761.

Howe, Florence. 1984. "Feminist Scholarship: The Extent of the Revolution (1981-1982)." In *Myths of Coeducation: Selected Essays, 1964-1983*, edited by Florence Howe, pp. 270-284. Bloomington: Indiana University Press.

Huxley, Elspeth. 1938. *Murder on Safari*. New York: Penguin Books.

Hyde, Janet Shibley. 1984. "Children's Understanding of Sexist Language." *Developmental Psychology*, 20, no. 4, 697-706.

Ihle, Elizabeth L. 1990. "Black Women's Education in the South: The Dual Burden of Sex and Race." In *Changing Education: Women as Radicals and Conservators*, edited by Joyce Antler and Sari Knopp Biklen, pp. 69-80. Albany, NY: State University of New York Press.

Jespersen, Otto. 1922. *Language: Its Nature, Development and Origin*. London: George Allen and Unwin.

Johnson, Ralph H., and J. Anthony Blair. 1977. *Logical Self-Defence*. Toronto: McGraw-Hill Ryerson.

Johnstone, Barbara. 1993. "Community and Contest: Midwestern Men and Women Creating Their Worlds in Conversational Storytelling." In *Gender and Conversational Interaction*, edited by Deborah Tannen, pp. 62-80. Oxford Series in Sociolinguistics, general editor Edward Finegan. Oxford: Oxford University Press. Presented (1989) at Women in America: Legacies of Race and Ethnicity Conference, Georgetown University, Washington, DC.

Jordan, June. 1992. "Just Inside the Door: Toward a Manifest New Destiny." *The Progressive*, 56, no. 2, 18-23.

Jose, P.E., F. Crosby, and W.J. Wong-McCarthy. 1980. "Androgyny, Dyadic Compatability and Conversational Behaviour." In *Language: Social Psychological Perspectives: Selected Papers from the First International Conference on Social Psychology and Language Held at the University of Bristol, England, July 1979*, edited by Howard Giles, W. Peter Robinson, and Philip M. Smith, pp. 115-119. Oxford: Pergamon.

Joyce, Susannah. 1991. *Facilitator's Manual: The Chilly Climate for Women in Colleges and Universities—Warming the Environment*. Associate Editor, Melanie Stafford. London, ON: The Ontario Ministry of Colleges and Universities and the Ontario Women's Directorate.

Jupp, T.C., Celia Roberts, and Jenny Cook-Gumperz. 1982. "Language and Disadvantage: The Hidden Process." In *Language and Social Identity*, edited by John J. Gumperz, pp. 232-256. Studies in Interactional Sociolinguistics, 2. Cambridge: Cambridge University Press.

Kagan, Jerome, Howard Moss, and Irving E. Sigel. 1963. "Psychological Significance of Styles of Conceptualization." In *Basic Cognitive Processes in Children: Report of the Second Conference Sponsored by the Committee on Intellectual Process Research of the Social Science Research Council*, 28, no. 2, 73-112.

Kahn, Arnold. 1984. "The Power War: Male Response to Power Loss Under Equality." *Psychology of Women Quarterly*, 8, no. 3, 234-247.

Kahn, Lynn Sandra. 1984. "Group Process and Sex Differences." *Psychology of Women Quarterly*, 8, no. 3, 261-281.

Kaplowitz, Henry L. 1976. "Machiavellianism and Forming Impressions of Others." In *Contemporary Social Psychology: Representative Readings*, edited by Thomas Blass, pp. 378-384. Itasca, IL: F.E. Peacock.

Keenan, Elinor Ochs. 1983. "Conversational Competence in Children." In *Acquiring Conversational Competence*, edited by Elinor Ochs and Bambi B. Schieffelin, pp. 3-25. London: Routledge & Kegan Paul.

_____. 1989. "Norm-Makers, Norm-Breakers: Uses of Speech by Men and Women in a Malagasy Community." In *Explorations in the Ethnography of Speaking*, edited by Richard Bauman and Joel Sherzer, pp. 125-143. 2d ed. New York: Cambridge University Press.

Keller, Evelyn Fox. 1983. "Gender and Science." In *Discovering Reality: Feminist Perspectives on Epistemology, Metaphysics, Methodology, and Philosophy of Science*, edited by Sandra Harding and Merrill B. Hintikka, pp. 187-205. Dordrecht, Holland: D. Reidel Publishing.

Key, Mary Ritchie. 1975. *Male/Female Language: With a Comprehensive Bibliography*. Metuchen, NJ: Scarecrow Press.

Khosroshahi, Fatemeh. 1989. "Penguins Don't Care, but Women Do: A Social Identity Analysis of a Whorfian Problem." *Language in Society*, 18, no. 4, 505-525.

Kincaid, Pat J. 1982. *The Omitted Reality: Husband-Wife Violence in Ontario and Policy Implications for Education*. Maple, ON: Publishing and Printing Services.

Kolenda, Konstantin. 1991. "Philosopher's Column: E Pluribus Unum." *The Humanist*, 51, no. 5, 40-44.

Kramarae, Cheris. 1980. "Perceptions and Politics in Language and Sex Research." In *Language: Social Psychological Perspectives: Selected Papers from the First International Conference on Social Psychology and Language Held at the University of Bristol, England, July 1979*, edited by Howard Giles, W. Peter Robinson, and Philip M. Smith, pp. 83-88. Oxford: Pergamon Press.

_____. 1981. *Women and Men Speaking: Frameworks for Analysis*. Rowley, MA: Newbury House.

Kramer, Cheris. 1975. "Women's Speech: Separate but Unequal." In *Language and Sex: Difference and Dominance*, edited by Barrie Thorne and Nancy Henley, pp. 43-56. Series in Sociolinguistics. Rowley, MA: Newbury House.

Kuralt, Charles. 1985. *On the Road with Charles Kuralt*. New York: Fawcett Gold Medal.

LaFrance, Marianne, and Barbara Carmen. 1980. "The Nonverbal Display of Psychological Androgyny." *Journal of Personality and Social Psychology*, 38, no. 1, 36-49.

Lakoff, George and Mark Johnson. 1980. *Metaphors We Live By*. Chicago: University of Chicago Press.

Lakoff, Robin. 1975. *Language and Woman's Place*. New York: Octagon Books. Reprinted in 1976 by special arrangement with Harper & Row.

_____. 1990. *Talking Power: The Politics of Language in Our Lives*. USA: Basic Books.

Lee, Ginny V. 1993. "New Images of School Leadership: Implications for Professional Development." *Journal of Staff Development*, 14, no. 1, 2-5.

Leet-Pellegrini, Helena M. 1980. "Conversational Dominance as a Function of Gender and Expertise." In *Language: Social Psychological Perspec-*

tives: Selected Papers from the First International Conference on Social Psychology and Language Held at the University of Bristol, England, July, 1979, edited by Howard Giles, W. Peter Robinson, and Philip Smith, pp. 97-104. Oxford: Pergamon Press.

LeGuin, Ursula. 1969. *The Left Hand of Darkness*. London: Macdonald Futura.

Leventhal, Gerald S., and Douglas W. Lane. 1970. "Sex, Age, and Equity Behavior." *Journal of Personality and Social Psychology*, 15, no. 4, 312-316.

Levin, Michael. 1977. "Vs. Ms." In *Sex Equality*, edited by Jane English, pp. 216-219. Englewood Cliffs, NJ: Prentice-Hall.

Levine, Joan B. 1976. "The Feminine Routine." *Journal of Communication*, 26, no. 3, 173-175.

Lightfoot, Sara Lawrence. 1980. "Socialization and Education of Young Black Girls in Schools." In *Women and Educational Leadership*, edited by Sari Knopp Biklen and Marilyn B. Brannigan, pp. 139-164. Lexington, MA: Lexington, D.C. Heath.

Lloyd, Genevieve. 1984. *The Man of Reason: "Male" and "Female" in Western Philosophy*. Minneapolis: University of Minnesota Press.

Macaulay, Ronald K.S. 1978. "The Myth of Female Superiority in Language." *Journal of Child Language*, 5, no. 2, 353-363.

Maccoby, Eleanor Emmons, and Carol Nagy Jacklin. 1974a (December). "Myth, Reality and Shades of Gray: What We Know and Don't Know about Sex Differences." *Psychology Today*, pp. 109-112.

_____. 1974b. *The Psychology of Sex Differences*. Stanford, CA: Stanford University Press.

MacKay, Donald G. 1980a. "Language, Thought and Social Attitudes." In *Language: Social Psychological Perspectives: Selected Papers from the First International Conference on Social Psychology and Language Held at the University of Bristol, England*, edited by Howard Giles, W. Peter Robinson, and Philip M. Smith, pp. 89-96. Oxford: Pergamon Press.

_____. 1980b. "Psychology, Prescriptive Grammar and the Pronoun Problem." *American Psychologist*, 35, no. 5, 444-449.

_____. 1983. "Prescriptive Grammar and the Pronoun Problem." In *Language, Gender and Society*, edited by Barrie Thorne, Cheris Kramarae, and Nancy Henley, pp. 38-53. Rowley, MA: Newbury House.

MacKay, Donald G., and David C. Fulkerson. 1979. "On the Comprehension and Production of Pronouns." *Journal of Verbal Learning and Verbal Behavior*, 18, no. 6, 661-673.

MacKinnon, Catharine A. 1993. *Only Words*. Cambridge: Harvard University Press.

Malone, Mary. 1991 (March 9). "You Do Have to Worry about Your Partner's Sexual Past." *Encounter: The London Free Press*, p. 18.

Maltz, Daniel N., and Ruth A. Borker. 1982. "A Cultural Approach to Male-Female Miscommunication." In *Language and Social Identity*, edited by

John J. Gumperz, pp. 196-216. Cambridge: Cambridge University Press.

Markowitz, Judith. 1984. "The Impact of the Sexist-language Controversy and Regulation on Language in University Documents." *Psychology of Women Quarterly*, 8, no. 4, 337-347.

Martin, Emily. 1991. "The Egg and the Sperm: How Science Has Constructed a Romance Based on Stereotypical Male-Female Roles." *Signs: A Journal of Women in Culture and Society*, 16, no. 3, 485-501.

Martin, Jane Roland. 1981. "The Ideal of the Educated Person." *Educational Theory*, 31, no. 2, 97-109.

Martyna, Wendy. 1978. "Using and Understanding the Generic Masculine: A Social-Psychological Approach to Language and the Sexes." *Dissertation Absrtacts International*, 39, 3050B.

————. 1983. "Beyond the He/Man Approach: The Case for Nonsexist Language." In *Language, Gender and Society*, edited by Barrie Thorne, Cheris Kramarae, and Nancy Henley, pp. 25-37. Rowley, MA: Newbury House.

Matsuda, Mari J. 1993. "Public Response to Racist Speech: Considering the Victim's Story." In *Words That Wound: Critical Race Theory, Assaultive Speech, and the First Amendment*, edited by Mari J. Matsuda, Charles R. Lawrence III, Richard Delgado, and Kimberlè Williams Crenshaw, pp. 17-51. Boulder, CO: Westview.

McConnell, Rick. 1992 (April 10). "The Black-belt Kids of Alberta Math." *The Edmonton Journal*, p. A1.

McKellar, Barbara. 1989. "Only the Fittest of the Fittest Will Survive: Black Women and Education." In *Teachers, Gender and Careers*, edited by Sandra Acker, pp. 69-85. New York: The Falmer Press.

McKenna, Michael C., Richard D. Robinson, and John W. Miller. 1990a. "Whole Language: A Research Agenda for the Nineties." *Educational Researcher*, 19, no. 8, 3-6.

————. 1990b. "Whole Language and the Need for Open Inquiry: A Rejoinder to Edelsky." *Educational Researcher*, 19, no. 8, 12-13.

McMillan, Julie R., A. Kay Clifton, Diane McGrath, and Wanda S. Gale. 1977. "Women's Language: Uncertainty or Interpersonal Sensitivity and Emotionality." *Sex Roles: A Journal of Research*, 3, no. 6, 545-559.

Meehan, Johanna, ed. 1995. *Feminists Read Habermas: Gendering the Subject of Discourse*. New York and London: Routledge.

Merchant, Carolyn. 1980. *The Death of Nature: Women, Ecology, and the Scientific Revolution*. San Francisco: Harper & Row.

Milburn, G. 1977. "Forms of Curriculum: Theory and Practice." In *Precepts, Policy and Process: Perspectives on Contemporary Canadian Education*, edited by H.A. Stevenson and J.D. Wilson, pp. 191-212. London, ON: Alexander, Blake.

Mill, John Stuart. 1970. "The Subjection of Women." In *Essays on Sex Equality*, by John Stuart Mill and Harriet Taylor Mill, edited with an introduction by Alice S. Rossi, pp. 123-242. Chicago: University of Chicago Press.

_____. 1972. *Utilitarianism, On Liberty, and Considerations on Representative Government. Selections from Auguste Comte and Positivism*, edited by H.B. Acton. London: J.M. Dent and Sons.

Miller, Casey, and Kate Swift. 1976. *Words and Women: New Language in New Times*. Garden City, NY: Anchor Books.

Mitchell, Carol. 1985. "Some Differences in Male and Female Joke-Telling." In *Women's Folklore, Women's Culture*, edited by Rosan A. Jordan and Susan J. Kalcik, pp. 163-186. Publications of the American Folklore Society; New Series, 8, general editor, Martha Weigle. Philadelphia: University of Pennsylvania Press.

Moely, Barbara E., and Kimberley Kreicker. 1984. "Ladies and Gentlemen, Women and Men: A Study of the Connotations of Words Indicating Gender." *Psychology of Women Quarterly*, 8, no. 4, 348-353.

Money, John, and Anke A. Ehrhardt. 1972. *Man and Woman, Boy and Girl: The Differentiation and Dimorphism of Gender Identity from Conception to Maturity*. Baltimore and London: The Johns Hopkins University Press.

Money, John, and Patricia Tucker. 1975. *Sexual Signatures: On Being a Man or a Woman*. Toronto: Little, Brown.

Morgan, Kathryn Pauly. 1982. "Androgyny: A Conceptual Critique." *Social Theory and Practice: An Interdisciplinary Journal of Social Philosophy*, 8, no. 3, 245-283.

Morgan, Kathryn Pauly, and Maryann Ayim. 1984. "Comment on Bem's 'Gender Schema Theory and Its Implications for Child Development: Raising Gender-aschematic Children in a Gender-schematic Society.'" *Signs: A Journal of Women in Culture and Society*, 10, no. 1, 188-196.

Morrison, Toni. 1988. *Beloved*. New York: Penguin Books.

Moulton, Janice. 1980. "Duelism in Philosophy." *Teaching Philosophy*, 3, no. 4, 419-433.

_____. 1983. "A Paradigm of Philosophy: The Adversary Method." In *Discovering Reality: Feminist Perspectives on Epistemology, Metaphysics, Methodology, and Philosophy of Science*, edited by Sandra Harding and Merrill B. Hintikka, pp. 149-164. Dordrecht, Holland: D. Reidel Publishing.

Moulton, Janice, George M. Robinson, and Cherin Elias. 1978. "Psychology in Action: Sex Bias in Language Use: 'Neutral' Pronouns That Aren't." *American Psychologist*, 33, no. 11, 1032-1036.

Murch, Kem. 1991. *The Chilly Climate for Women in Colleges and Universities* (Videotape). London, ON: Western's Caucus on Women's Issues and the President's Standing Committee for Employment Equity.

Newcombe, Nora, and Diane B. Arnkoff. 1979. "Effects of Speech Style and Sex of Speaker on Person Perception." *Journal of Personality and Social Psychology*, 37, no. 8, 1293-1303.

Nilsen, Alleen Pace. 1977. "Sexism as Shown through the English Vocabulary." In *Sexism and Language*, edited by Alleen Pace Nilsen, Haig Bosmajian, H. Lee Geershuny, and Julia P. Stanley, pp. 27-41. Urbana, IL: National Council of Teachers of English.

Noddings, Nel. 1984. *Caring: A Feminine Approach to Ethics and Moral Education*. Berkeley: University of California Press.

Ochs, Elinor. 1983. "Cultural Dimensions of Language Acquisition." In *Acquiring conversational competence*, edited by Elinor Ochs and Bambi B. Schieffelin, pp. 185-191. London: Routledge & Kegan Paul.

O'Connor, Aleda. 1992. "Any Woman Can Tell You: Special Report." *The Reporter: The Magazine of the Ontario English Catholic Teachers' Association*, 18, no. 2, 16-22.

Ong, Walter J. 1981. *Fighting for Life: Contest, Sexuality, and Consciousness*. Ithaca and London: Cornell University Press.

Ontario Ministry of Education. 1975. *The Formative Years: Circular P1J1, Provincial Policy for the Primary and Junior Divisions of the Public and Separate Schools of Ontario*. Toronto, ON: Ontario Ministry of Education.

_____. 1984. *Ontario Schools, Intermediate and Senior Divisions (Grades 7-12/OACs): Program and Diploma Requirements*. Toronto, ON: Ontario Ministry of Education.

Pearson, Judy Cornelia. 1985. *Gender and Communication*. Dubuque, IA: Wm. C. Brown Publishers.

Pearson, Sheryl S. 1981. "Rhetoric and Organizational Change: New Applications of Feminine Style." In *Outsiders on the Inside: Women and Organizations*, edited by Barbara L. Forisha and Barbara H. Goldman, pp. 55-74. Englewood Cliffs, NJ: Prentice-Hall.

Pedersen, Tove Beate. 1980. "Sex and Communication: A Brief Presentation of an Experimental Approach." In *Language: Social Psychological Perspectives: Selected Papers from the First International Conference on Social Psychology and Language Held at the University of Bristol, England, July, 1979*, edited by Howard Giles, W. Peter Robinson, and Philip Smith, pp. 105-114. Oxford: Pergamon Press.

Peirce, Charles Sanders. 1931-1958. *Collected Papers of Charles Sanders Peirce*, edited by Charles Hartshorne, Paul Weiss, and Arthur Burks. 8 volumes. Cambridge, MA: Harvard University Press.

Pellegrini, Anthony D. 1982. "A Speech Analysis of Preschoolers' Dyadic Interaction." *Child Study Journal*, 12, no. 3, 205-217.

Peters, R.S. 1965. "Education as Initiation." In *Philosophical Analysis and Education*, edited by Reginald D. Archambault, pp. 87-111. London: Routledge & Kegan Paul.

Peterson, Susan R. 1980. "Are You Teaching Philosophy, or Playing the Dozens?" *Teaching Philosophy*, 3, no. 4, 435-442.

Petty, Walter T., Dorothy C. Petty, and Marjorie F. Becking. 1976. *Experiences in Language: Tools and Techniques for Language Arts Methods*. 2d ed.; 1st ed., 1973. Boston: Allyn and Bacon.

Petty, Walter T., Dorothy C. Petty, and Richard T. Salzer. 1989. *Experiences in Language: Tools and Techniques for Language Arts Methods*. Marjorie F. Becking, contributor to previous editions. 5th ed.; 1st ed., 1973. Boston: Allyn and Bacon.

Philips, Susan U. 1987. "Introduction to Part I: 'Women's and Men's Speech in Cross-cultural Perspective.'" In *Language, Gender and Sex in Comparative Perspective*, edited by Susan U. Philips, Susan Steele, and Christine Tanz, pp. 15-25. Cambridge: Cambridge University Press.

Phillips, James L., and Steven G. Cole. 1970. "Sex Differences in Triadic Coalition Formation Strategies." In *Studies of Conflict, Conflict Reduction, and Alliance Formation*, edited by James L. Phillips and Thomas L. Connor, pp. 154-180. Report 70-1 Cooperation/Conflict Research Group, Computer Center for Social Science Research, Michigan State University.

Phoenix, Ann. 1987. "Theories of Gender and Black Families." In *Gender under Scrutiny: New Inquiries in Education*, edited by Gaby Weiner and Madeleine Arnot, pp. 50-63. London: The Open University.

Pollard, Diane S. 1990. "Black Women, Interpersonal Support, and Institutional Change." In *Changing Education: Women as Radicals and Conservators*, edited by Joyce Antler and Sari Knopp Biklen, pp. 257-276. Albany, NY: State University of New York Press.

Preston, Kathleen, and Kimberley Stanley. 1987. "What's the Worst Thing . . . ? Gender-Directed Insults." *Sex Roles: A Journal of Research*, 17, nos. 3-4, 209-219.

Rachkowski, Rita, and Kevin E. O'Grady. 1988. "Client Gender and Sex-Typed Nonverbal Behavior: Impact on Impression Formation." *Sex Roles: A Journal of Research*, 19, nos. 11-12, 771-783.

Rasmussen, Jeffrey Lee, and Barbara E. Moely. 1986. "Impression Formation as a Function of Sex Role Appropriateness of Linguistic Behavior." *Sex Roles: A Journal of Research*, 14, nos. 3-4, 149-161.

Rees, Ruth. 1990. *Women and Men in Education: A National Survey of Gender Distribution in School Systems*. Toronto, ON: Canadian Education Association.

Richardson, Laurel Walum, and Anne Statham Macke, with Judith Cook. 1980 (April). "Sex-Typed Teaching Styles of University Professors and Student Reactions." Report to the National Institute of Education.

Roe, Anne. 1952. *The Making of a Scientist*. New York: Dodd, Mead.

———. 1956. *The Psychology of Occupations*. New York: John Wiley and Sons.

Rosener, Judy B. 1990. "Ways Women Lead." *The Harvard Business Review*, 68, no. 6, 119-125.

Rousseau, Jean Jacques. 1911. *Émile*. Translated by Barbara Foxley, introduction by André Boutet de Monvel. London: J.M. Dent and Sons.

Ruby, Lionel. 1950. *Logic: An Introduction*. Chicago: J.B. Lippincott.

Rushton, J. Philippe. 1995. *Race, Evolution, and Behavior: A Life History Perspective*. New Brunswick, NJ: Transaction Publishers.

Ruth, Sheila. 1981. "Methodocracy, Misogyny and Bad Faith: The Response of Philosophy." In *Men's Studies Modified: The Impact of Feminism on the Academic Disciplines*, edited by Dale Spender, pp. 43-53. Oxford: Pergamon Press.

Ryden, Hope. 1989. *Lily Pond: Four Years with a Family of Beavers*. New York: William Morrow.

Sachs, Jacqueline. 1987. "Preschool Boys' and Girls' Language in Pretend Play." In *Language, Gender and Sex in Comparative Perspective*, edited by Susan U. Philips, Susan Steele, and Christine Tanz, pp. 178-188. Cambridge: Cambridge University Press.

Sadker, Myra, and David Sadker. 1985. "Sexism in the Schoolroom of the '80s." *Psychology Today*, 19, no. 3, 54-57.

Sagor, Richard D. 1992. "Three Principals Who Make a Difference." *Educational Leadership*, 49, no. 5, 13-18.

Sankoff, Gillian. 1980. *The Social Life of Language*. Philadelphia: University of Pennsylvania Press.

Sartre, Jean Paul. 1957. *Being and Nothingness: An Essay on Phenomenological Ontology*, translated by Hazel E. Barnes. London: Methuen.

Sattel, Jack W. 1983. "Men, Inexpressiveness, and Power." In *Language, Gender and Society*, edited by Barrie Thorne, Cheris Kramarae, and Nancy Henley, pp. 118-124. Rowley, MA: Newbury House.

Sayers, Janet. 1987. "Psychology and Gender Divisions." In *Gender under Scrutiny: New Inquiries in Education*, edited by Gaby Weiner and Madeleine Arnot, pp. 26-36. London: The Open University.

Schatz, Marilyn, and Rochel Gelman. 1973. *The Development of Communication Skills: Modifications in the Speech of Young Children as a Function of Listener. Monographs of the Society for Research in Child Development*, Serial no. 152, 38 (no. 5).

Schau, Candace Garrett, and Kathryn P. Scott. 1984. "Impact of Gender Characteristics of Instructional Materials: An Integration of the Research Literature." *Journal of Educational Psychology*, 76, no. 2, 183-193.

Scheffler, Israel. 1979. *Beyond the Letter: A Philosophical Inquiry into Ambiguity, Vagueness, and Metaphor in Language*. London: Routledge and Kegan Paul.

Schieffelin, Bambi B. 1987. "Do Different Worlds Mean Different Words?: An Example from Papua New Guinea." In *Language, Gender and Sex in Comparative Perspective*, edited by Susan U. Philips, Susan Steele, and Christine Tanz, pp. 249-260. Cambridge: Cambridge University Press.

Schmidt, Benno C., Jr. 1991. "False Harmony: The Debate over Freedom of Expression on America's Campuses." *Vital Speeches of the Day*, 58, no. 2, 45-48.

Schneider, Joseph W., and Sally L. Hacker. 1973. "Sex Role Imagery and the Use of the Generic 'Man' in Introductory Texts: A Case in the Sociology of Sociology." *American Sociologist*, 8, 12-18.

Schön, Donald. 1979. "Generative Metaphor: A Perspective on Problem-Setting in Social Policy." In *Metaphor and Thought*, edited by Andrew Ortony, pp. 254-283. Cambridge: Cambridge University Press.

Schultz, Katherine, John Briere, and Lorna Sandler. 1984. "The Use and Development of Sex-typed Language." *Psychology of Women Quarterly*, 8, no. 4, 327-336.

Schulz, Muriel R. 1975. "The Semantic Derogation of Woman." In *Language and Sex: Difference and Dominance*, edited by Barrie Thorne and Nancy Henley, pp. 64-75. Series in Sociolinguistics. Rowley, MA: Newbury House.

Schwartz, S., and M. Pollishuke. 1990. *Creating the Child-Centred Classroom*. Concord, ON: Irwin.

Scott, Joan Wallach. 1992 (May/June). "Reply to Joseph A. Shea, Jr.: Letters to the Editor." *Change*, p. 7.

Scriven, Michael. 1976. *Reasoning*. New York: McGraw-Hill.

Sergiovanni, Thomas J. 1992. *Moral Leadership: Getting to the Heart of School Improvement*. San Francisco: Jossey-Bass Publishers.

Shakeshaft, Charol. 1987. *Women in Educational Administration*. Newbury Park, Beverly Hills: Sage Publications.

Shantz, Doreen. 1993. "Collaborative Leadership and Female Administrators: A Perfect Partnership for the Future." *The Canadian School Executive*, 13, no. 2, 3-5.

Shepelak, Norma J., Darlene Ogden, and Diane Tobin-Bennett. 1984. "The Influence of Gender Labels on the Sex Typing of Imaginary Occupations." *Sex Roles: A Journal of Research*, 11, nos. 11-12, 983-996.

Shimanoff, Susan B. 1980. *Communication Rules: Theory and Research*. With a foreword by Dell Hymes. Beverly Hills, CA: Sage Publications.

Short, Edmund C., ed. 1991. *Forms of Curriculum Inquiry*. Albany, NY: State University of New York Press.

Sirotnik, Kenneth A. 1991. "Critical Inquiry: A Paradigm for Praxis." In *Forms of Curriculum Inquiry*, edited by Edmund C. Short, pp. 243-258. Albany, NY: State University of New York Press.

Smith, Philip M. 1980. "Judging Masculine and Feminine Social Identities from Content-Controlled Speech." In *Language: Social Psychological Perspectives: Selected Papers from the First International Conference on Social Psychology and Language Held at the University of Bristol, England, July 1979*, edited by Howard Giles, W. Peter Robinson, and Philip M. Smith, pp. 121-126. Oxford: Pergamon Press.

_____. 1985. *Language, The Sexes and Society*. Oxford: Basil Blackwell.

Smitherman-Donaldson, Geneva, and Teun A. van Dijk. 1988. "Introduction: Words That Hurt." In *Discourse and Discrimination*, edited by Geneva

Smitherman-Donaldson and Teun A. van Dijk, pp. 11-22. Detroit: Wayne State University Press.

Sniezek, Janet A., and Christine H. Jazwinski. 1986. "Gender Bias in English: In Search of Fair Language." *Journal of Applied Social Psychology*, 16, no. 7, 642-662.

Sommers, Christina. 1991. "The Feminist Revelation." In *Ethics, Politics, and Human Nature*, edited by E.F. Paul, F.O. Miller, Jr., and J. Paul, pp. 141-158. London: Basil Blackwell.

Spacks, Patricia Meyer. 1985. *Gossip*. New York: Alfred A. Knopf.

Spender, Dale. 1980. *Man Made Language*. London: Routledge and Kegan Paul.

_____. 1981. "Education: The Patriarchal Paradigm and the Response to Feminism." In *Men's Studies Modified: The Impact of Feminism on the Academic Disciplines*, edited by Dale Spender, pp. 155-173. Oxford: Pergamon Press.

_____. 1982. *Invisible Women: The Schooling Scandal*. London: Writers and Readers Publishing Cooperative Society in association with Chameleon Editorial Group.

_____. 1983. "Modern Feminist Theorists: Reinventing Rebellion." In *Feminist Theorists: Three Centuries of Key Women Thinkers*, edited by Dale Spender, pp. 366-380. New York: Pantheon Books.

_____. 1984. "Sexism in Teacher Education." In *Is Higher Education Fair to Women?* edited by Sandra Acker and David Warren Piper, pp. 132-142. Guildford, UK: SRHE and NFER-Nelson.

Stein, Audrey R. 1976. "A Comparison of Mothers' and Fathers' Language to Normal and Language Deficient Children." Doctor of Education Dissertation, Boston University, School of Education.

Swacker, Marjorie. 1975. "The Sex of the Speaker as a Sociolinguistic Variable." In *Language and Sex: Difference and Dominance*, edited by Barrie Thorne and Nancy Henley, pp. 76-83. Series in Sociolinguistics. Rowley, MA: Newbury House.

Switzer, Jo Young. 1990. "The Impact of Generic Word Choices: An Empirical Investigation of Age-and Sex-Related Differences." *Sex Roles: A Journal of Research*, 22, nos. 1-2, 69-82.

Tannen, Deborah. 1982. "Ethnic Style in Male-Female Conversation." In *Language and Social Identity*, edited by John J. Gumperz, pp. 217-231. Cambridge: Cambridge University Press.

_____. 1990. *You Just Don't Understand: Women and Men in Conversation*. New York: Ballantine Books.

Tanz, Christine. 1987. "Introduction to Part II: 'Gender Differences in the Language of Children.'" In *Language, Gender and Sex in Comparative Perspective*, edited by Susan U. Philips, Susan Steele, and Christine Tanz, pp. 163-177. Cambridge: Cambridge University Press.

Thelen, Herbert A. 1962. "Introduction." In *Learning thru Discussion*, pp. 7-12. Beverly Hills, CA: Sage Publications.

Thorne, Barrie. 1986. "Girls and Boys Together . . . But Mostly Apart: Gender Arrangements in Elementary Schools." In *Relationships and Development*, edited by Willard W. Hartup and Zick Rubin, pp. 167-184. Hillsdale, NJ: Lawrence Erlbaum Associates.

Thorne, Barrie, and Nancy Henley. 1975. "Difference and Dominance: An Overview of Language, Gender, and Society." In *Language and Sex: Difference and Dominance*, edited by Barrie Thorne and Nancy Henley, pp. 5-42. Series in Sociolinguistics. Rowley, MA: Newbury House.

Thorne, Barrie, Cheris Kramarae, and Nancy Henley. 1983. "Language, Gender and Society: Opening a Second Decade of Research." In *Language, Gender and Society*, edited by Barrie Thorne, Cheris Kramarae, and Nancy Henley, pp. 7-24. Rowley, MA: Newbury House.

Tittle, Carol Kehr, Karen McCarthy, and Jane Faggen Steckler. 1974. *Women and Educational Testing: A Selective Review of the Research Literature and Testing Practices*. Princeton, NJ: Educational Testing Service in collaboration with the Association for Measurement and Evaluation in Guidance.

Tourangeau, Roger. 1982. "Metaphor and Cognitive Structure." In *Metaphor: Problems and Perspectives*, edited by David S. Miall, pp. 14-35. Sussex: The Harvester Press.

Trudgill, Peter. 1974. *Sociolinguistics: An Introduction*. Middlesex, UK: Penguin Books.

Uesugi, Thomas K., and W. Edgar Vinacke. 1963. "Strategy in a Feminine Game." *Sociometry*, 26, no. 1, 75-88.

Unger, Rhoda K. 1979. *Female and Male: Psychological Perspectives*. New York: Harper & Row.

Van de Wetering, John E. 1991. "Political Correctness: The Insult and the Injury." *Vital Speeches of the Day*, 58, no. 4, 100-103.

Walker, Alice. 1982. "One Child of One's Own: A Meaningful Digression within the Work(s)—An Excerpt." In *All the Women Are White, All the Blacks Are Men, But Some of Us Are Brave*, edited by Gloria T. Hull, Patricia Bell Scott, and Barbara Smith, pp. 37-44. Old Westbury, NY: The Feminist Press.

Wasserstrom, Richard A. 1979. "Racism and Sexism." In *Philosophy and Women*, edited by Sharon Bishop and Marjorie Weinzweig, pp. 5-20. Belmont, CA: Wadsworth Publishing.

Weaver, Constance, with Diane Stephens and Janet Vance. 1990. *Understanding Whole Language: From Principles to Practice*. Toronto, ON: Irwin.

Webb, Lynne. 1986 (Spring). "Eliminating Sexist Language in the Classroom." *Women's Studies in Communication*, 9, 21-29.

West, Candace, and Don H. Zimmerman. 1983. "Small Insults: A Study of Interruptions in Cross-Sex Conversations between Unacquainted Persons." In *Language, Gender and Society*, edited by Barrie Thorne, Cheris Kramarae, and Nancy Henley, pp. 102-117. Rowley, MA: Newbury House.

Whorf, Benjamin Lee. 1956. *Language, Thought, and Reality*, edited and with an introduction by John B. Carroll. Cambridge, MA: M.I.T. Press.

Wilson, Elizabeth, and Sik Hung Ng. 1988. "Sex Bias in Visual Images Evoked by Generics: A New Zealand Study." *Sex Roles: A Journal of Research*, 18, nos. 3-4, 159-168.

Wilson, LaVisa Cam. 1978. "Teachers' Inclusion of Males and Females in Generic Nouns." *Research in the Teaching of English: Official Bulletin of National Council of Teachers of English*, 12, no. 2, 155-161.

Winch, Peter. 1958. *The Idea of a Social Science and Its Relation to Philosophy*. London: Routledge and Kegan Paul.

Wittgenstein, Ludwig. 1961. *Tractatus Logico-Philosophicus*. Translated by D.F. Pears and B.F. McGuiness and with an introduction by Bertrand Russell. International Library of Philosophy and Scientific Method Series, edited by Ted Honderich. London: Routledge and Kegan Paul.

Work, Henry H. 1968. "Psychiatric Emergencies." In *Handbook of Pediatric Medical Emergencies*, edited by Charles Varga, pp. 140-148. 4th ed. Saint Louis: The C.V. Mosby Company.

Zeldin, R. Shepherd, Stephen A. Small, and Ritch C. Savin-Williams. 1982. "Prosocial Interaction in Two Mixed-Sex Adolescent Groups." *Child Development*, 53, 1492-1498.

Zillmann, Dolf, and S. Holly Stocking. 1976. "Putdown Humor." *Journal of Communication*, 26, no. 3, 154-163.

Zimmerman, Don H., and Candace West. 1975. "Sex Roles: Interruptions and Silences in Conversations." In *Language and Sex: Difference and Dominance*, edited by Barrie Thorne and Nancy Henley, pp. 105-129. Series in Sociolinguistics. Rowley, MA: Newbury House.

Index